Begrimed and Black

Her name, that was as fresh
As Dian's visage, is now begrimed and black
As mine own face.
(*Othello,* Act III, Scene 3)

BEGRIMED AND BLACK

Christian Traditions on Blacks and Blackness

ROBERT E. HOOD

FORTRESS PRESS   MINNEAPOLIS

BEGRIMED AND BLACK
Christian Traditions on Blacks and Blackness

Scripture quotations from the Revised Standard Version of the Bible are copyright © 1946, 1952, 1971 by the Division of Christian Education of the National Council of the Churches of Christ in the U.S.A. Used by permission.

Cover art: "The Creation" by Aaron Douglas. Photographed for reproduction by Jarvis Grant. Reprinted by permission of Howard University, Washington, D.C.
Cover design: Nancy Eato

Library of Congress Cataloging-in-Publication Data

Hood, Robert E. (Robert Earl), 1936–1994.
    Begrimed and black : Christian traditions on Blacks and blackness
  / Robert E. Hood.
        p.   cm.
    Includes bibliographical references and index.
    ISBN 0-8006-2767-9 (alk. paper) :
    1. Blacks. 2. Race relations—Religious aspects—Christianity.
3. Black—Religious aspects—Christianity.   4. Blacks—Folklore.
    I. Title.
    BT734.2.H62   1994
    261.8'345196—dc20
                                                                        93-39510
                                                                        CIP

The paper used in this publication meets the minimum requirements of American National Standard for Information Sciences—Permanence of Paper for Printed Library Materials, ANSI Z329.48-1984. ∞™

Manufactured in the U.S.A.   AF 1-2767

98   97   96   95   94   1   2   3   4   5   6   7   8   9   10

To

Barbara Hall

Esteemed colleague and grace-filled broker
of community between cultures and races

Contents

Preface

*I*n 1989 in New York City's Italian Bensonhurst section, a black teenager named Yusuf Hawkins was lynched by a mob of local whites. Hawkins was in the neighborhood looking to buy a used car he had seen advertised. The whites thought he was the boyfriend of a local white girl and had come to attend her birthday party.

In 1991 in a racially mixed Long Island community, a black teenager named Jermaine Ewell was beaten unconscious by a mob of young local whites (one of whom was a friend of his). That horde took umbrage at seeing the black youth talking to a white girl at a graduation party to which he had been invited.

In the late Robert Mapplethorpe's controversial 1988 exhibition of erotic photography, the mythical eroticism and legendary hyperpotency of black men are highlighted in photographs of blacks with large sexual organs and sensual masculine bodies. One photograph, "Man in Polyester Suit," shows a black man in a three-piece suit absent of a head but with an enormous phallus hanging from his unzipped trousers.

These contemporary incidents link three problems that have always accompanied European and American curiosity about blacks and black cultures, problems that have been the basis of much of the tension and racial prejudice in relationships between blacks and whites: (1) fascination with the color black; (2) both intrigue with and fear of the mythical sexual prowess of blacks—that is, miscegenation and what the vernacular calls "studs"; and (3) violence as a sign of resistance and disdain by whites to what Benjamin Franklin once described as a "darkening of the American people." White anxiety about the alleged erotic allure of blacks exploded in America as early as 1662, when the British colony of Virginia passed a law that forbade sexual relations between black male slaves and white women. In 1691 Virginia statutes branded marriage between a white woman and a black, mulatto, or Native American man an "abominable fixture and spurious issue." The accused woman was liable to "banishment from this dominion forever."[1]

In fact, it was not until 1967 that statutes in southern states against interracial marriage were declared unconstitutional by the U.S. Supreme Court. It is significant that the original judgment of the Virginia county judge upholding the legality of Virginia's anti-miscegenation law cited religious underpinnings: "Almighty God created the races white, black, yellow, Malay and red, and He placed them on separate continents, and but for the interference with His arrangement there would be no cause for such marriages."[2]

If language encodes experience, especially the experience of color, into a unique sound, as some linguists maintain, why then does the experience of blackness as a color and a skin hue as well as a symbol conjure up dual sensations for most people in the United States and Western Europe? On the one hand, negative effigies are linked to images of crime, ugliness, fear, poverty, mistrust, magic, voodoo, paganism, disdain, underdevelopment, inferior intellect, and primitiveness, to mention just a few. On the other hand, blackness summons pleasurable and exotic curiosities, not only the sensual impressions of jazz, flamboyant dancing, the blues, sports, body language, mystery, and raw sexual energy, but also immorality, unbridled sensuality, and erotic allure. To cite a popular cliché about the allure of blackness: Why is it that whites make love and blacks only make sex?

1. A. Leon Higginbotham, Jr., *In the Matter of Color: Race and the American Legal Process, the Colonial Period* (New York: Oxford Univ. Press, 1978), 43–44.
2. *New York Times*, 12 June 1992, p. B20. These racial categories were created by Johann Friedrich Blumenbach (1752–1840), a German physician and founder of modern anatomy, who was fascinated with classical Greek antiquity and human skulls as a sign of superior racial intelligence.

Why is blackness the most frequent metaphor that signifies something evil, sinister, fearful, and diabolic? How does it come about that malevolent actions and evil charms are described as *black* magic over against *white* magic, a *black* lie over against a *white* lie, a *black* widow over against a *white* knight, or *black*mailing someone over against *white*washing something? How was it possible that George Bush, as a presidential candidate in 1980, could malign an entire black culture, namely Haiti, by accusing Ronald Reagan of espousing "voodoo economics," without protests from liberals and academics? Might it be that they silently agreed with such a castigation, even if they did not agree with Bush's politics?

Alternatively, why does blackness suggest sexual allure in spite of the feeling that it conveys something negative? Or does its negativity and suspected naughtiness heighten its allure? How was it possible for Bush to win popular support in 1988 by exploiting blackness as something negative, sexually threatening, and violent by accusing Michael Dukakis of being soft on crime because a black convicted murderer (Willie Horton) raped a white woman while on a weekend furlough?

Admittedly, even the term *black* has several layers of meaning in the West and the United States: (1) historical/cultural, as when speaking of Africa or African descendants in the diaspora; (2) physical, as when speaking of Negroid or Africanoid physical traits, such as woolly or kinky hair, broad noses, thick lips, skin color, even sexual organs; (3) racial, as in hierarchies classifying and "declassifying" all of humankind in early anthropology, comparative anatomy, and Egyptology; (4) biological, as used to distinguish "African/black blood" codes of identity from "European/white blood" in European countries and their respective colonies; and (5) ideological, as in Pan-Africanism and Afrocentrism over against what many call Eurocentrism and in the ideology of Afrikaner South Africa.

This commingling of fear/allure, disdain/fascination in the West, especially in the United States, also has much to do with a nurturing that has its mythical roots in the Christian and Jewish faiths, supported by economic, historical, industrial, educational, and social beliefs, conditions, and movements. I think this legacy about blackness and blacks is firmly grounded in the Christian tradition and in Christendom— important cornerstones of European and American cultures and morality. Furthermore, as I hope this book will demonstrate, it is primal and buried deep within our Western psyche and culture, whether we are Christians or not—a primal legacy reinforced by (1) a mythic and cultural heritage from the ancient Greeks and the Romans, whether we are black, white, or Latino/Hispanic; (2) ancient and medieval Christian beliefs and views, but also some Jewish views of blackness; and (3) our historical and economic formation and development as a civilization and as a nation. All come together to support the subordination of blackness to whiteness and the superordination of whiteness over blackness conceptually, religiously, socially, and politically.

This study examines key and pivotal moments in the development and formation of beliefs about blackness and blacks. I intend to enlarge religious studies by moving across different disciplines and genres to examine the mythic, religious, aesthetic, and moral views of these moments within the Western Christian tradition. Furthermore, the study will show the impact of that tradition on the cultural relationship between blacks and whites in Western thought and American culture. The study reveals an interplay between blackness, evil, sex, and magic that continues throughout Christian and Western social thought. This interplay has its antecedents in the Greek and Roman progenitors of Western culture. It was sacralized by the Christian faith in its very origins as early as the second century C.E. and in pre-rabbinic Judaism. Furthermore, this interplay in Christian thought had an impact on the formation of the relationship between blacks and whites, beginning with the American colonies. It also has nurtured black Americans' views about themselves and their own religious and moral worth in American society and compared to black African forebears.

I am really asking critical questions about whether our civil ideal of racial tolerance and inclusiveness is in fact implicitly eroded by our hidden primal myths—myths that have been religiously sanctioned and subsequently secularized though historical, political, economic, pseudoscientific, and social conditions in Europe and America, and legitimized by claims of the superiority of light and whiteness juxtaposed against the inferiority of darkness and blackness. It is not a study about the linguistic or psychosocial aspects of race in the United States, although these aspects are also affected by the mythic legacy in our psyche. Such a study is beyond my competence as a teacher in religious studies.

The first chapter traces the origins of cultural attitudes and views about blackness in classical Greek and Roman society before Christ, attitudes that formed the vortex into which the Christian faith was born in the later Roman Empire. I focus here on how blackness and blacks moved into Greek and Roman vocabularies and cultures, paying particular attention to art and literature. Chapter 2 examines the historical and theological relationship between Africa and the early Christian tradition, particularly the black/dark peoples of Egypt, Ethiopia, Nubia, and North Africa, where the church moved and assimilated much of the indigenous cultures, but also tried to resist them.

Chapter 3 looks at what happened to beliefs about blackness and blacks after Christ, as the early Jewish-Christians and the early church fathers struggled to establish credibility and integrity for the claims of Christ and the Christian life in the intellectual and political circles of the Roman Empire. Again, clues will be sought in views about Ethiopia and blackness among the intellectuals of that culture, its art, and early Christian literature, especially art and Christian literature depicting the devil and darkness (blackness).

The following chapters pay attention to what was going on in the crucial formation of medieval Christendom in Europe with its piety and religion centered in the Virgin Mary and noble Christian heroes, some of whom were black. Particularly important is the inauguration of the African slave trade by a Christian nation (Portugal), followed by other European Christian states. The effect of actually seeing, touching, and dominating black Africans had a transforming effect upon religious and cultural views of blackness.

Chapter 4 looks at blackness and its link to sexual views, Christian salvation, sanctity, and magic. The cult of the black madonna in parts of Europe is examined, from the standpoint of whether a latent conception exists of the black madonna as a worker of magic and a sorceress rather than as the traditional symbol of motherhood and love associated with the white madonna. Furthermore, questions about beliefs regarding blackness in the thought of the Protestant reformers will be explored. As far as I know, this has not been done before.

Chapter 5 looks at the crucial moments in the relationship of Christendom, Christianity, and the African slave trade in Europe and how such moments affected and changed views about blacks and blackness.

The final chapters look at the effect colonialism and the new nationalisms in Europe had on beliefs about blackness in Europe and carried into the American colonies. At the same time, blacks on American soil were a part of American colonial history and culture. They were developing views of their own blackness under the impact of colonial religious thought. Their beliefs about blackness are contrasted with the beliefs of whites.

Chapter 6 scrutinizes European thought as it began colonialism in the New World and American colonial religious thought as it shaped the future United States, especially the commingling of biblical narratives and racial attitudes for stigmatizing blacks and negative forces. Blacks, considered the children of Ham, were a part of this development.

Chapter 7 examines the religious and cultural understanding of blackness by blacks themselves as a sign of their identity. This understanding was important in the effort of blacks to grasp their relationship with the divine in American society.

Finally, an epilogue summarizes the findings by returning to my hypothesis that an implicit but powerful erosion of racial attitudes has long been at work, whose mythic and primal underpinnings have seldom, if ever, been exposed. As such our civil rhetoric and social goal of racial and ethnic tolerance in the United States and Europe may well be like chaff blowing in the wind. That is, polarities and value judgments about the image and character of blackness and blacks may be so deeply embedded in Christian tradition and subsequent historical cultural myths that even modern religious doctrines as well as civil ideals about equality and inclusiveness are sabotaged and unrealizable.

What does such a legacy say about the Christian church's claim to be a flagship and moral agent for transforming our individual and communal psyches about blacks in order to induce multicultural diversity in civil society? Is such a legacy transitory and therefore bridgeable, or eternal (permanent) and unbridgeable?

Perhaps it should be observed that in the late 1970s, Eric Bernard, the noted American interior designer, pioneered the idea of all-black interiors for houses and offices. He was apparently one of the few nonblacks who regarded blackness as an organizing motif for design and something positive in society. Eric Bernard died in March 1990.

Acknowledgments

I am grateful to the following persons and institutions for their assistance in the preparation of this book: The Schomburg Center for Research in Black Culture, New York Public Library, especially Betty Gubert, Assistant Chief Librarian (retired) in the General Research and Reference Department; the New York Public Library (Fifth Avenue); Prof. Rabbi Michael K. Chernick (The Talmud), Hebrew Union College/Jewish Institute of Religion, New York; Prof. Deirdre Good (New Testament), General Theological Seminary, New York; Matthew Grande, Reference Librarian, St. Mark's Library, General Theological Seminary, New York; Prof. Dirk Obbink (Classics), Barnard College, New York; Prof. Ramsay MacMullen (History), Yale University; Prof. Sandra L. Zimdars-Swartz (Religious Studies), University of Kansas; Prof. Karen J. Torjesen (Women's Studies), Claremont Graduate School, Claremont, Calif.; Prof. James M. Washington (Church History), Union Theological Seminary, New York; the Advocacy, Justice, and Witness Ministries Unit at the Episcopal Church Center, New York, for a research grant.

Introduction

*W*idespread negative beliefs and views associated with blackness and black skin in many cultures might lead us to ask the following questions: Is blackness universally held to be a defective variant of whiteness? Can blackness be defined only by contrasting it with whiteness and therefore making its core meaning dependent on whiteness? If this comparative but contrasting aesthetic character of blackness is fundamental, how are we to interpret this aesthetic construct when *black* is used to characterize the populations and cultures of Africa, especially those in sub-Saharan Africa and in the African diaspora? The French scholar Roger Bastide observes that in the West something much more subtle and fundamental belies the ongoing tensions between whites and blacks. What is at stake, he says, is a primal conflict between God and Satan, spiritual and carnal, good and evil: "Thinking is so enslaved to language that this chain of associated ideas operates automatically when a white person finds himself in contact with a colored person."[1]

In a study of images of blackness in the West, for example, the following characteristics are associated with the color black: gloom, woe, darkness, dread, death, terror,

1. Roger Bastide, "Color, Racism, and Christianity," *Daedalus* 96 (Spring 1967): 315.

horror, wickedness, mourning, defilement, annihilation. By contrast, the color white evokes the following traits: triumph, light, innocence, joy, purity, regeneration, happiness, gaiety, peace, femininity, delicacy.[2]

The stain of black as skin color has a history exceeding the ethnocentric cultural traditions of the West. Explicitly, whiteness means something positive and superior and blackness means something negative and inferior, be it in regard to color, culture, or race. In Chinese traditional culture, for example, much attention is paid to skin color.

The most popular metaphor for pure feminine skin is white jade. Whiteness is considered the arbiter of beauty. Indeed, a famous Chinese classical poet Po Chu-i praised the white skin of a princess in the *Shijing*, thought to be the earliest collection of poems in Chinese literature: "Her fingers were like the blades of the young white grass/ Her skin as like congealed ointment."[3] At another place he rhapsodizes about whiteness: "So white her skin, so sweet her face/ None could with her compare." A traditional Chinese folk song says: "My sweetheart is like a flower/ Please do not let the sun burn her black."[4]

The Chinese elite and intellectuals in the Middle Kingdom distinguished between all foreigners as "raw barbarians" and "cooked barbarians." "Raw barbarians" (*shengfan*) meant those who ate raw food and were considered savages and uncivilized because they ate raw food. Their nature was affected by their habits of nourishment, according to Chinese belief. The "cooked barbarians" (*shufan*) were tame and submissive. Black slaves from Africa, thought to have been brought to China by Arab and Persian traders as early as the Tang Dynasty (618–907 C.E.), were described as a people "black as ink with red lips, white teeth, and curly hair who lived in the mountains beyond the seas, and ate raw meat."[5]

Under the Zhou (1027–256 B.C.E.), black-skin slaves were referred to as *renli. Li* was a large cooking pot stained by smoke and the blackness from fire.[6] As the Chinese encountered more and more of their neighbors,

2. Kenneth J. Gergen, "The Significance of Skin Color in Human Relations," *Daedalus* 96 (Spring 1967): 397.
3. Frank Dikötter, *The Discourse of Race in Modern China* (London: Hurst, 1992), 10.
4. Harold R. Issacs, "Group Identity and Political Change: The Role of Color and Physical Characteristics," *Daedalus* 96 (Spring 1967): 370.
5. Dikötter, *Discourse of Race*, 9.
6. Ibid., 10.

who were usually darker than the Chinese, and the European world with its African slaves, particularly the Portuguese, the Chinese projected their color consciousness on to the foreign world. It became a convenient way of stratification.

A twelfth-century (1178 C.E.) Chinese document speaks of Madagascar as an island where savages live: "Their bodies are black and they have frizzled hair. They are enticed by good and then captured. . . . [A]nd it is said that they have no longing for their kinsfolk."[7] This latter phrase is said by the Africanist Basil Davidson to be the Chinese equivalent of the European claim that Africans are inferior by nature.[8] When a very influential Chinese journalist, Lang Qichao, visited the United States in 1903, he explained the widespread lynching of blacks in America as follows:

> The blacks' behavior is despicable. They only die without regret if they have succeeded in touching a white woman's skin. They often lurk in the darkness of woods to rape them. Thereafter, these women are murdered so that they will not talk. Nine out of ten cases of lynching are due to this crime."[9]

After the People's Republic was created in 1949, race as a subject of public discourse was officially forbidden, although the tradition and the legacy lingered. University anthropology and sociology departments, thought to have been chiefly responsible for propagating theories of race, were restricted after 1952. Indeed, China's political posture identified itself as a leader of "the peoples of color" fighting the white imperialists. Race was reduced to a matter of class. As Mao Zedong said in a 1963 speech:

> In Africa, in Asia, in every part of the world, there is racism; in reality racial problems are class problems.[10]

In Japan, black skin historically has been viewed as something ugly and undesirable and white skin as beautiful. Black skin is the sign of

7. Basil Davidson, *The African Slave Trade*, rev. ed. (Boston: Little, Brown, 1980), 189.
8. Ibid.
9. DikÖtter, *Discourse on Race*, 81.
10. Quoted in ibid., 192.

cultural inferiority. As early as the eighth century in Japan's Nara period (710–793 C.E.), white powder was considered most desirable by ladies of the court and in the theatre as a sign of ultimate elegance and enhanced beauty. An eleventh-century Japanese romance, *The Tale of Genji*, includes an elegy to white skin praising it as the symbol of ultimate beauty.[11] A nineteenth-century Japanese ambassador to the United States had his first stopover in an African country and noted that black Africans looked like "devils depicted in pictures," whose "faces are black as if painted with ink and [whose] physiognomy reminds me of that of a monkey."[12]

Likewise, in India blackness is generally undesirable as a sign of beauty. This disdain for blackness has deep historical and cultural roots that many trace to the early battles in ancient India of the 1500s B.C.E. between the Aryas—the original light-skinned invaders and conquerors of the northwest territory (now modern Punjab)—and the Dasas or Dasyu—the original dark-skinned inhabitants. (Excavations in 1925, however, uncovered an Indus civilization dating from C. 3000–2000 B.C.E. that predates the Aryan conquest.) *Arya*, the root word of *Aryan*, which was so corrupted by the Nazis in the 1930s, means "free-born" or "noble character" in Sanskrit.[13] *Dasas* in Sanskrit eventually came to mean "slave."[14] The dark skins of the Dasas came to be identified with the Hindu word for black, *krishna*.[15] After many conquests, *dasa* came to mean enslaved black or dark-skinned people found usually in lower castes, particularly the Sudra (servant) castes. Since an early Aryan king had *dasa* as a part of his name (Divodasa), however, it is likely that some intermingling took place between the fair-skinned Aryans and the black or dark-skinned Dasas in ancient India.[16]

11. Hiroshi Wegatsuma, "The Social Perception of Skin Color in Japan," *Daedalus* 96 (Spring 1967): 407–8.

12. Ibid., 414.

13. D. D. Kosambi, *The Culture and Civilization of Ancient India in Historical Outline* (London: Routledge and Kegan Paul, 1965), 72.

14. Ainslie T. Embree, ed., *Sources of Indian Tradition*, vol. 1 (New York: Columbia Univ. Press, 1988), 7.

15. The Rig Veda, the oldest extant Sanskrit document, calls Krishna a demon and an enemy of Indra, whose name became the generic designation for the original dark-skinned inhabitants. In the Hindu pantheon Krishna as a god is blue, not black. Later Krishna became a hero and demigod for the Aryans. Kosambi, *Culture and Civilization of Ancient India*, 115.

16. Ibid., 81.

Other color distinctions are evident in classical Hindu texts that link superior biological and divine lineage and fair skin with castes such as the Brahmins at the top and inferior lineage and dark skin with castes such as the black Sudras at the bottom, although the upper castes also have a mixture of skin hues. Other castes said to be red, bronze, and yellow, such as the Kshatriyas and the Vaishyas, which are less privileged than the fair-skinned Brahmins but more advantaged than the dark-skinned Sudras, can be found in the middle.[17]

Indeed, in many Indian languages *fair* and *beautiful* are synonyms. When families are arranging marriages, which is the tradition in India, a dark-skinned daughter is a liability because a dark-skinned wife is undesirable. Men seeking wives through newspaper notices in India frequently advertise that they wish for women who are virgins and have a light skin.[18] In fact, many northern Indians dislike southern Indians because of their dark skins. Many see a correlation between caste and skin color; hence, a northern Indian proverb says: "A dark Brahmin, a fair Chuhra [a lower caste], a woman with a beard—these three are contrary to nature."[19]

Even the Arabs had some negative views. At the time of the Prophet Mohammed, the Arabs had high regard for black Ethiopia because of its hospitality toward Muslim refugees escaping the tribal wars in Mecca. Evidence suggests that blackness in pre-Islamic Arabia was simply an aesthetic description of a people's complexion, not a sign of subordination or racial inferiority. For example, in a story about the beginning of Islam's conquest of Egypt, the Arab leader of an expedition of Muslims, 'Ubada ibn al-Samit, who was black, visited the Muqawqis (possibly from the Coptic *khaukhios* = Caucasian, a reference to Cyrus), the Christian Egyptian official whom the Arabs allowed to administer the affairs of the Christian community. The Muqawqis objects to 'Ubada's presence because he is afraid of his blackness. The other Arabs in the party protest that 'Ubada is "the foremost among us in position, in precedence, in intelligence, and in wisdom, for blackness is not despised among us."[20]

17. Issacs, "Group Identity and Political Change," 372.
18. André Béteille, "Race and Descent as Social Categories in India," *Daedalus* 96, 451. Several scholars of Indian culture tell me that Islam, Christianity, and even communism appeal to many dark-skinned Indians because their doctrine of egalitarianism regardless of color provides them an outlet for some upward mobility.
19. Ibid., 452.
20. Bernard Lewis, *Race and Color in Islam* (New York: Harper & Row, 1971), 9–10.

Early ninth-century Arab travelers and tradesmen in Africa called most black Africans *Sudan* ("black") but made an exception for Ethiopians and surrounding territories. Africa south of the Sahara was called *Bilad al-Sudan*, "land of the blacks." In spite of a lack of acrimony and negative feelings about blackness in the Koran, we find the Arabs speaking of the blackness of Africa as something quite negative. Ibn Qutayba (died 889) wrote that blacks are ugly and misshapen because their proximity to the sun in their hot climate caused them to be "overcooked" in the womb and curled their hair into kinks.[21]

The eleventh-century Arabic teacher Sa'id al-Andalusi (1029–1070) called blacks rabble, savages, and scum.[22] In the fourteenth century when the Arabs engaged in the African slave trade with the Portuguese for export, Ibn Khaldun wrote:

> The only people who accept slavery are the Negroes (*Sudan*), owing to their low degree of humanity and their proximity to the animal stage. Other persons who accept the status of slave do so as a means of attaining higher rank or power, or wealth, as is the case with the Mameduke (mamluk) Turks in the East and with the Franks and Galicians who enter the service of the state (in Spain).[23]

Certainly much of Ethiopia, like Egypt with its variations of blackness among its population after the Arab incursions across the Red Sea, resisted Islam. After the Islamic conquests in its northern provinces and surrounding territories, Christian Ethiopia, believing itself under siege, colonized territories in the central and southern highlands. (Fifty percent of modern Ethiopia is Muslim. The political core of modern Ethiopia, however, with its capital relocated in Addis Ababa in the Shoa province, consists of the central, southern, and southeastern highlands Wallo, Amhara, Gojjam, Shoa, and Tigré, the home of Aksum. Unfortunately, economically and politically, as Edward Gibbon observed, "encompassed on all sides by the enemies of their religion, the Ethiopians slept near a thousand years, forgetful of the world by whom they were forgotten. They were awakened by the Portuguese, who turning the southern promontory of Africa, appeared in India and the Red Sea.")[24]

21. Ibid., 33.
22. Ibid., 36.
23. Ibid., 38.
24. Edward Gibbon, *The History of the Decline and Fall of the Roman Empire*, 8 vols., ed. Felipe Fernáandez-Arinesto (London: The Folio Society, 1988), 6:81.

The Arabs, however, after their conversion to Islam (not unlike the Christians later in the fifteenth century), held that Ham, the primal progenitor of blacks, was cursed with black skin and slavery; the Arabs exported East African slaves to Islamic countries in Asia as well. Ibn Bahr Al-Jahiz (778–868 C.E.), considered one of the greatest classical Arabic writers and thought to be of African ancestry, said that prior to Islam, the Arabs had no noticeable prejudice against black Africans:

> From your ignorance you considered us as belonging to you as you considered your women (property) in the Period of ignorance (prior to Islam). When the justice of Islam came, you saw that this was an evil attitude; yet we have no desire to desert you. We have filled the country amply through marriage, chieftainship, and lordship. . . .[25]

He and other highly regarded black and dark-skinned Arab poets in early Islam were called "the crows of the Arabs" (*aghribat al-'Arab*). Even these black or swarthy poets, however, felt their blackness as a stigma. One poet, Nusayb (died 726), wrote:

> Blackness does not diminish me, as long as I have this tongue
>   and this stout breast.
> Some are raised up by means of their lineage;
>   the verses of my poems are my lineage.
> How much better a keen-minded, clear spoken black
>   than a mute-white!
> If I am jet-black, musk too is very dark—and there is no
>   medicine for the blackness of my skin.[26]

Yet even Al-Jahiz could not resist noting: "Blackness and whiteness come from before the creation of nations, before what God imprinted on the Earth and on the water before the proximity and distance of the sun, and before the strength of its heat and its brightness. It was originally not anything dirty, not something ugly, not a punishment and not a

25. 'Uthman 'Amr Ibn Gahr Al-Jahiz, *The Book of the Glory of the Black Race*, trans. Vincent J. Cornell (Waddington, N.Y.: Phyllis Preston Collection, 1981), 40–41. Bernard Lewis translates the Arabic as: ". . . in the time of heathendom, you regarded us as good enough to marry your women, yet when the justice of Islam came, you considered this wrong." Lewis, *Race and Color in Islam*, 31.
26. Ibid., 12.

disadvantage."[27] Elsewhere (for reasons not clear) he makes fun of black African cultures: "We know that the Zanj are the least intelligent and the least discerning of mankind, and the least capable of understanding the uniqueness of actions."[28]

Sa'id al-Andalusi harshly criticized Africans and their cultures. Even the most stupid people had some kind of monarchical government and a religion, he protested, except "the inhabitants of the deserts and wildernesses, such as the rabble of Bujja, the savages of Ghana, the scum of Zanj, and the like."[29] The reasons for this harsh judgment by al-Andalusi are not clear in light of trading systems and skills in place in Africa at that time. Ethiopia, which was pre-Islamic Arabs' first introduction to Africa, itself had a highly developed religious and economic system. Nubia, which occupied and ruled Egypt in the eighth century B.C.E., was a developed culture that had much influence on Egypt's civilization.

Furthermore, East Africa had an established literary and poetic tradition in Swahili (Arabic: *kiSwahili* = coast), which the Arabs themselves first noticed in the tenth century C.E., but which in fact is most likely older.[30] Sub-Saharan Africa had developed a technology by the seventh century for such minerals as copper, iron, and gold. Excavations have unearthed copper artifacts in Central Africa, particularly in Zaire, and iron artifacts in Zambia and Zimbabwe in southern Africa, which may go back to the first millennium C.E.:

> Towards the end of the first millennium of our era there seem to have existed a number, conceivably quite a large number, of Iron Age peoples who were organized in more or less coherent groups or units. One can reasonably infer a form of lineage government with clear elements of statehood—a proto-national sense of difference from neighbors, more or less clearly defined boundaries, and a spiritually sanctioned kingship.[31]

Also, rather sophisticated artwork was being executed in ancient Benin and Ifé. The Ashante kingdom in Ghana and the Yoruba kingdom had highly developed worldviews and cosmologies.

27. *The Book of the Glory of the Black Race*, 59.
28. Quoted in Lewis, *Race and Color in Islam*, 17.
29. Ibid., 36.
30. Davidson, *The African Slave Trade*, 181–82.
31. Ibid., 185.

The change in the Arabs' view of blackness apparently occurred after the emergence of Islam and their subsequent conquest of parts of Africa. Several factors contributed to the change. (1) Islamic writings said that Ham, son of Noah and cursed to be black and a slave forever because of his sin, was the common ancestor of all blacks. (2) As they changed from traders in Africa to conquerors, the Arabs (like many other conquerors) took on an imperial view of their privileges as the sole authentic guardians of Islamic belief and civilization. (3) The Arabs' experiences as invaders in Asia, where they met fair-skinned civilizations more developed and advanced than those encountered in the black cultures of eastern and interior Africa, led them to dismiss black African cultures. The African regions initially conquered by Islam were mostly rural and agrarian. Some maintain that the oral tradition in such agrarian territories contrasted sharply with the literary tradition of Ethiopians, whose alphabet dates from the fifth century B.C.E. and whose language dates from the Aksum civilization in the seventh century B.C.E.[32]

Yet, with all its negativity, why does black skin also seem to have a primal erotic allure? A Japanese graduate student studying in the United States decided to test the waters about the reputed carnality of blacks by having sex with a black woman graduate student. After the act, he tells of his guilt and the need for an instant purification after experiencing internal conflict with his negative view and disdain for blackness:

> I was not in love with her, nor was she with me. It was a play. To say the truth, I was curious about a Negro after hearing so much about them. When it was over, however, I had to take a shower. The idea shocked me because it was ridiculous. But I was caught by an urge. *It was almost a sudden compulsion to wash my body off, and I did.* (emphasis added)[33]

Ironically, even though Americans popularly identify the Japanese as a "yellow" race, the Japanese call themselves white (*shiroi*).[34] Japanese have historically identified black skin with the dark-skinned slaves of

32. F. Anfray, "The Civilization of Aksum From the First to the Seventh Century," *General History of Africa*, vol. 2: *Ancient Civilizations of Africa*, ed. Gamal Mokhter (Berkeley, Calif.: Univ. of California Press, 1981), 375. As noted above, however, the validity of this claim is questionable in light of the literary, economic, and political development in East and West Africa, where the Arabs also traded.
33. Wegatsuma, "The Social Perception of Skin Color in Japan," 431.
34. Ibid., 407.

the Dutch and Portuguese sailors landing in Japan in the eighteenth century.[35] Hence, it is all the more interesting that in spite of Japan's low esteem of blackness as a skin color and an aesthetic, the Japanese graduate student, in spite of himself and his culture, ventured to explore the reputed erotic allure of the alien color black.

The Boundaries of Blackness in the West

Skin color, unlike any other physical characteristic, fixes boundaries, status, stigma, privileges, disadvantages, and self-esteem for a people in the human community. Its significance, which intrigued even classical Western civilization, was heightened after Europe and America created the academic disciplines of anthropology and Egyptology and universalized the biological concept of race and racial traits. These early disciplines and theories claimed scientific objectivity, thereby adding a legitimacy to the West's universal classification of all humanity and cultures.

Initially a category used to classify plants and animals, the innovative use of the term *race* to classify human beings was thought to have originated with a French physician, François Bernier (1620–88). The Swedish botanist Carolus Linnaeus (1707–78) taught that a factual scientific correlation exists between a person's outward appearance, and their intelligence and disposition. The German founder of modern comparative anatomy, Johann Friedrich Blumenbach (1752–1840), maintained that through the study of skulls it is clear that Greek faces and bodies represent a superior standard of beauty and a higher culture compared to Ethiopians and Africans. Another Frenchman, Comte Joseph Arthur de Gobineau (1816–82) wrote that Nordic races are by nature superior to Semitic and black races.

The Ambiguity and Negativity of Blackness

Even as blackness as a color and aesthetic and blacks as persons became part of Western thought through the Greeks and later the Romans, an

35. Arnold Rubin, *Black Nanban: Africans in Japan During the 16th Century* (Bloomington: African Studies Program, Indiana Univ., 1974), 8. See Japanese depictions of blacks in seventeenth-century nanban art, 12–18.

ambiguity and an impreciseness were also associated with the color. In the United States, whose cultural and historical development cannot be understood without blacks, this impreciseness persisted. In the 1890 U.S. census, for example, "black" was defined as a blood kinship and meant persons with three-fourths or more "black blood." The 1910 census referred only to "full-blooded *negroes*" and "mulattoes," the latter term used to describe "all other persons having some proportion or perceptible trace of 'negro blood.' " The census gave no other definition for these terms. Verification depended on the perception or questions of the census taker.[36]

Even during the slave trade, Europeans lacked a precise definition for a black; indeed, often such familiar terms as *negro* and *neger* could indicate any skin color from light brown to black. In the sixteenth century, for example, Jesuit missionaries in Brazil identified the indigenous Indians as black. The Jesuits complained about Portuguese men cohabitating with indigenous Brazilian mistresses because of the mixtures of blood and skin colors. The Jesuits, noting that the natives' colors ranged from light brown to black, called all of them *negras* (Lat.: *niger, negri*; Sp. and Port.: *negro*; Catalán: *negre*; It.: *nero*; Fr.: *noir, nègre*); the English simply anglicized the term as *Negro* to mean Africans and those of African descent. As there were hardly any Africans in Brazil at that time, the term *Negras* referred to the Indians. By the sixteenth century, African slaves had been imported to Brazil and differences in color began to emerge. One Brazilian Portuguese, Manuel da Nobrega, in his 1549 letters distinguished between *negros da Guine* ("blacks of Guinea"), meaning black-skinned African slaves, and *negros da terra* ("blacks of the land"), meaning the indigenous Indians of the Americas. It is interesting that both are called *negros*.[37]

Henry Marsh points out that the cultural mind-set in medieval Portugal and Spain under its Moorish occupation considered it meritorious to enslave Islamic Africans in accordance with prevailing Catholic tradition and teachings. Such sentiments were simply transferred to black non-Moors, that is, "infidel" African slaves in need of Christian conversion and baptism; hence in both Spain and Portugal, slaves were

36. Jack D. Forbes, *Black Africans and Native Americans: Color, Race and Caste in the Evolution of Red-Black Peoples* (Oxford, England: Basil Blackwell, 1988), 90.
37. Ibid., 69.

usually baptized before they were sold at a slave auction.[38] Indeed, in
early sixteenth-century England and Scotland, Africans were called
Moors. They later were known as blackamoors, Ethiopians, and Negroes.
In sixteenth-century English initially a "blackmoor" meant an Arab and
someone from Mauritania (Gk.: *mauros*; Sp.: *mauro*, *moro* = dark-
skinned).

Blackness in fifteenth-century Britain, however, long before the British
had steady contact with black Africans or had joined Portugal and Spain
in expanding the African slave trade industry, also evoked a negative
image that was socially pejorative. According to the *Oxford English
Dictionary*, blackness in the fifteenth century meant something or someone stained with sin:

> [Black is] deeply stained with dirt; soiled, dirty, foul. . . . Having dark
> or deadly purposes, malignant, pertaining to or involving death, deadly;
> baneful, disastrous, sinister. . . . Foul, iniquitous, atrocious, horrible,
> wicked. . . . Indicating disgrace, censure, liability to punishment, etc.[39]

Black in England not only was a metaphor for negativity—dirt, foulness,
deadliness, malignancy, and malevolence—but also was a pejorative term
generally used to describe the skin color of the social underclass. In
1688, for example, an advertisement in the *London Gazette* read: "A
black boy, an Indian, about thirteen years old, runaway, the 8th. Inst.
from Putney, with a collar about his neck with this inscription: 'The
Lady Bromfield's black.' "[40] In 1724, when the French governed Haiti,
they legalized color and caste in the Code Noir, adopted by the French
in 1685. Although the Code guaranteed the privileges and rights enjoyed
by Frenchmen to "all persons born free," it did not extend these privileges
to the black slaves. The institutionalized caste system in this code served
the same purpose in the French territory of Louisiana, which led to the
creation of Creole society in New Orleans. The Code Noir, intended
for the social control of blacks (*noires*) and *affranchis*, who were mulattoes
(*mulatre* from Sp. *mulato* ; Castillian: *mulo* = hybrid young mule),[41] also

38. Henry Marsh, *Slavery and Race: The Story of Slavery and its Legacy for Today*
(Newton Abbot, England: David & Charles, 1974), 86.
39. Quoted in Winthrop D. Jordan, *White over Black: American Attitudes toward
the Negro, 1550–1812* (New York: W. W. Norton, 1968), 7.
40. Forbes, *Black Africans and Native Americans*, 85.
41. Forbes says a second theory about the origin of *mulatto* dates it to the Spanish

laid the foundation for much of the political turmoil that continues to torture and divide modern Haiti.[42]

New Orleans possibly had the most sophisticated and formalized social structure based on color. Louisiana institutionalized not only the Christian primal suspicion of blackness as malevolence and eros, but also its Creole (Port. *crioulo* = a home-born slave; Fr. *créole* = a slave born in Louisiana or French Caribbean colonies) society. Creole society, which has its origins in Louisiana's "Free People of Color"—the offspring of black slave mothers and white Spanish and French fathers—included such social stratification as mulattoes, quadroons, octoroons, griffes (offspring of a black and mulatto), and half-breeds (children with an Indian mother and a white father). These color categories reinforced the social and political disadvantages of *the stain of blackness*. Frequently, to exempt their offspring from this stigma, white fathers would give their black mistresses manumission so that their Creole children would be free.[43]

The most visible expressions of Creoles themselves exempt from the stain of blackness were the Quadroon Balls in New Orleans. These balls for young Creole women—Catholic, virtuous, and known for their beauty and mixed race—were attended by "chaste free women of color" and by young white gentlemen hunting for a quadroon mistress. Blackness as a visible icon of the negative and the distasteful, on the one hand, and the erotic and mysterious allure, on the other, was well summed up by the Duke of Saxon-Weimar, who resided in New Orleans in the 1800s:

> The quadroons are almost entirely white, from their skin no one should detect their origin. Still, however, the strongest prejudice reigns against

muladi, derived from *muwallad*, meaning a Christian Spaniard who converted to Islam. In the Sudan lighter-skinned children from a mixed Egyptian-Sudanese marriage are called *muwallad*, which is often a pejorative term used by darker-skinned Sudanese Muslims. *Mulato* passed over into Arabic and means someone with an Arab father and a foreign mother. Later in Spanish it also came to mean the offspring of a slave father and a free mother. *Black Africans and Native Americans*, 140.

42. For a careful analysis of the tension between color and caste in Haitian history and culture, see David Nicholls, *From Dessalines to Duvalier: Race, Colour, and National Independence in Haiti* (Cambridge, England: Cambridge Univ. Press, 1979).

43. See Gwendolyn Midlo Hall, "The Formation of Afro-Creole Culture," in *Creole New Orleans: Race and Americanization*, ed. Arnold R. Hirsch and Joseph Logsdon (Baton Rouge: Louisiana State Univ. Press, 1992), 58–87.

them because of their black blood, and the white ladies maintain, or
affect to maintain the most violent aversion to them.[44]

This relationship continued even after a young man married; a man
often maintained a house for his Creole concubine on the edge of New
Orleans's geographical boundaries.

Blackness is also a divisive and confusing fact in African American
and especially Afro-Caribbean cultures, regardless of whether they are
English-speaking, French-speaking, or Spanish-speaking. Movements
have arisen within Anglophone cultures to overcome this divisiveness,
such as Marcus Garvey (1887–1940) and his Universal Negro Improvement Movement (UNIA), Malcolm X (1925–65), Stokley Carmichael
(1941–   ), and Stephen Biko (1946–77) and the South African Black
Consciousness movement. This conceptual assertiveness and positivism
by blacks about blackness, which continues to reemerge from time to
time, can also be found in modern black fiction. The novelist Alice
Walker in *The Color Purple* juxtaposes blackness as a conceptual tool
against the intellectual claims of whites. Walker portrays a fictional
account of how black people were created by God first and white people
thereafter. Celie asks her sister Nettie, a missionary in Africa, to tell her
whether oral tradition about how white people were created is true, since
Nettie is in the land where humankind first began. "They say everybody
before Adam was black," Celie writes Nettie.

Then one day some woman they just right away kill, come out with this
colorless baby. They thought at first it was something she ate. But then
another one had one and also the women start to have twins. So the
people start to put the white babies and the twins to death. So really
Adam wasn't even the first white man. He was just the first one the
people didn't kill.[45]

Celie explains how Africans made fun of the first white missionaries,
who reprimanded them for not wearing clothes and insisted that Adam
and Eve wore clothes.

44. Lyla Hay Owen and Owen Murphy, *Créoles of New Orleans: Gens de Couleur
(People of Color)* (New Orleans: First Quarter Publishing Co., 1987), 2–3.
45. Alice Walker, *The Color Purple* (New York: Washington Square Press, 1982), 239.

They tried to explain to the missionaries that it was *they* who put Adam and Eve out of the village because they *was* naked. Their word for naked is white. But since they were covered by color they are not naked. They said anybody looking at a white person can tell they naked, but black people cannot be naked because they can not be white.[46]

The oral tradition cited by Celie finds some collaboration in creation myths of African traditional religion and in the studies of some Africanists.[47]

Furthermore, in an intriguing study, the Afrocentric scholar Charles Finch tries to give a scientific legitimacy to Afrocentric theories about the origins of humankind. He asks how modern humankind (Homo sapiens) got from its African origins and color to Europe as whites. Finch claims that modern man (c. 150,000 years ago) originally resembled the Twa (pygmy) of Central Africa and the San (bushmen) of southern Africa. The first appearance of modern man in Europe coincided with what he calls the late Riss glacial period. According to Finch, this period ended in 120,000 B.C.E. (c. 50,000 years ago) at the beginning of the Russ-Wurm interglacial or warm period.

To account for whites' Caucasoid color as contrasted with their probable original black or Africanoid color, Finch offers a theory of vitamin D deficiency and the loss of the "melanin cover" (protective black skin pigment; from Gk.: *melas* = dark or black) by the Homo sapiens. Vitamin D, produced primarily in the skin by sunlight, would have been affected by the more frigid climate of Europe with its fewer sunny days per year. Melanin acts as a protective against sun damage, and together with oiliness gives black skin the advantage of developing fewer wrinkles as it ages, compared with white skin. Under these circumstances, the melanin cover (that is, black skin), was a liability because it was screening

46. Ibid., 240. See also S. G. P. Brandon, *Creation Legends of the Ancient Near East* (London: Hodder & Stoughton, 1963); Charles H. Long, *Alpha: The Myths of Creation* (New York: G. Braziller, 1963); Barbara Sproul, *Primal Myths: Creating the World* (San Francisco: Harper & Row, 1979); Modupe Oduyoye, *The Sons of the Gods and the Daughters of Men: An Afro-Asiatic Interpretation of Genesis 1-11* (Maryknoll, N.Y.: Orbis Books, 1984).

47. For example, see Harold Courlander, *Tales of Yoruba Gods and Heroes* (New York: Crown Publishers, 1973), 15–20; M. A. Fabunmi, *A Traditional History of the Ilé-Ifè* (Ilé-Ifè, Nigeria: Kings Press, n.d.); Chief M. A. Fabunmi, Ifè, interview with author, Nigeria, October 1983; Robert E. Hood, "Creation Myths in Nigeria: A Theological Commentary," *Journal of Religious Thought* 45 (Winter–Spring 1989): 70–84.

out sunlight, whose availability was already drastically reduced, thereby reducing the amount of vitamin D produced. Those who survived this migration and natural selection developed a white albino skin. This theory is also supported by some archaeological findings:

> Simply put, black skin in an ice-age type of northern environment would become a liability, rather than an asset, from an evolutionary perspective. . . . White skin, without the melanin barrier, can more efficiently utilize the limited sunlight than can black skin, thus it will be able to more efficiently produce Vitamin D.[48]

The Africanist Cheikh Anta Diop cites archaeological evidence supporting the idea that European whites descended from what he calls Aurignacians (named after the cave in Aurignac, France, where artifacts from a highly developed culture of the Upper Paleolithic age have been found). Mostly likely, Diop claims, they entered what we now call Europe through the Pyrenees mountains between Spain and France.[49]

> Certain authors suppose, that in general, a time gap must elapse between corresponding European and African archeological periods. It is difficult to square this with the almost certain fact that the Aurignacians came from Africa and were 'Negroids.' Aurignacian culture was brought into Western Europe from North Africa by a new type of men, and these and all subsequent races and their cultures have been termed Neanthropic. . . . We know that the Aurignacians were superior in every way to the old Neanderthal group of men whom they conquered and probably exterminated.[50]

Uncertain knowledge about the advantages and disadvantages of blackness as a skin color that defines social status and caste has divided and confused black Americans themselves. Dark skin color among blacks has aroused disdain and allure with subsequent monumental social and economic consequences. A folk saying about the color stratification and

48. Charles S. Finch, "The Evolution of the Caucasoid," in *African Presence in Early Europe*, ed. Ivan Van Sertima (New Brunswick, N.J.: Transaction Books, 1985), 19.

49. Cheikh Anta Diop, *The African Origin of Civilization: Myth or Reality*, trans. Mercer Cook (Westport, Conn.: Lawrence Hill, 1974), pp. 65–66.

50. Ibid., 266. Some European Africanist scholars, however, seriously contest Diop's claims and definitions of *black* with regard to the ancient Egyptians. See Roland Oliver, "The African Rediscovery of Africa," *Times Literary Supplement*, 20 March, 1981, 29.

erotic allure of blackness that was once popular in black culture said: "The blacker the berry/ The sweeter the juice." Yet the second part of this saying, which was seldom recited, continued: "But if the berry's too black/ It can't be of much use." As a consequence of viewing blackness as a part of a caste system within black cultures, many blacks themselves have internalized this ambiguity and negativity about dark complexion.

At the same time, the allure and the fear of the primal myth about blackness as eros drove Europeans and American whites to justify violence against black men.[51] Gunnar Myrdal in *An American Dilemma* notes that the fear of miscegenation, which became an obsession in the American South, was acted out in irrational mob violence against blacks.[52] It interfered with the European's concept of blackness as something ontologically subordinate to whiteness in the Western Christian tradition. It was also a primary factor that corrupted the original objectives of the Portuguese in Africa in their search for gold and new commercial markets.

Hence blackness retains its ambiguity as well as arousing curiosity and disdain. Blackness has been a stigma with mythic, religious, social, and economic consequences for blacks, Western culture, and the Christian religion. Hence Shakespeare's Othello speaks of the besmirching of Desdemona's integrity as "begrimed and black/ As mine own face."

The Church's Unfinished Symphony with Blackness

The negativity of blackness is not a tradition peculiar to the West, as we have seen, although in Western Christian thought it has been used in particular pernicious ways that have reinforced and justified both

51. Feminist historians have uncovered cases where black women were lynched in the early twentieth century in Oklahoma and Mississippi. In 1911 in Okemah, Oklahoma, a black woman, whose brother was accused by whites of murdering a deputy sheriff, was first raped by the mob and then lynched by hanging. In 1918 in Mississippi, a black woman, impregnated by a local white dentist, who was subsequently killed by her brother, was hanged from a bridge over the Chickasawha River. Gerda Lerner, ed., *Black Women in White America* (New York: Pantheon Books, 1972), 161–63; also Estelle B. Freedman, "The Manipulation of History at the Clarence Thomas Hearings," *The Chronicle of Higher Education* 38 (January 8, 1992), B2–B3.
52. Gunnar Myrdal, *An American Dilemma: The Negro Problem and Modern Democracy* (New York: Harper & Row, 1962), 562.

slavery and nineteenth-century ethnocentric racial theories in Europe and the United States. Most of the negativity about blackness in the Christian tradition in fact has its origins in early patristic interpretations of biblical texts dealing with darkness, blackness, and Satan. Hence, the conceptual notion of blackness took on a moral dimension as it was linked with images and concepts related to evil, sin, and corruption in Christian thought, which also prevailed in the larger culture.

Theologically, in the Christian tradition, blackness has been characterized as something fascinating, mysterious, and even in some cases a witness to God's salvation, as in Origen. But it also has been conceptualized to interpret biblical texts dealing with evil, the demonic, and the chaotic: "And God saw that the light was good; and God separated the light from the darkness. God called the light Day, and the darkness he called Night" (Gen. 1:4-5). It also symbolized primal fears of the unknown: "The earth was without form and void, and darkness moved upon the face of the deep" (Gen. 1:2).

The social scientist St. Clair Drake considers the tendency to support moral issues and constructs, such as evil, on the basis of blackness as a metaphor to be derivative of the early Christian heresy called Manichaeism (founded by Mani [216–277]):

> Therefore, the argument continues, people will associate night and darkness with sin, evil, and impurity. Furthermore, these attributes will become associated with the dark skin of human beings, that is, "they will carry over to people." I have called scholars who make this kind of analysis of prejudice against blackness and black people the "modern Manichaeans" because their thought style resembles, in some respects, that of the ancient religious cult of Mani, in which the eternal struggle between Light and Darkness is the focal point of both the cosmic and the human drama.[53]

Nevertheless, Christian thought historically, philosophically, and aesthetically has reinforced a subordination of blackness to whiteness as a metaphor and as a later racial characterization for people of African descent, and a superordination of whiteness to blackness.

53. St. Clair Drake, *Black Folk Here and There: An Essay in History and Anthropology*, vol. 1 (Los Angeles: Center for Afro-American Studies, Univ. of California, Los Angeles, 1987), 63.

The attachment of a moral category to blackness assumed a particular deleterious and malevolent character with the inauguration of the African slave trade. Pope Nicholas V (1447–1455) no doubt reflected both Western cultural and religious views of blackness of his day in his special 1454 papal bull that ceded all of Africa to Portugal, which was the pioneer Western country creating the market of slave trading as a commercial venture. The bull ensured indulgences in heaven for enslaving and baptizing the black Africans, who were to be liberated from paganism and superstition and brought to the light of the Christian faith. The first auction of black slaves took place in a Christian country: in Lisbon, Portugal, in 1441.

The question is whether this Euro-American inversion of and negativity toward blacks and black cultures is something inherited from their parent European culture and Christian religion or something that emerged from the establishment of what Robert Handy calls "a Christian America"[54] and what Martin Marty calls a "righteous empire."[55] This inversion of blackness in American culture and religious life has resulted in some peculiar sociological, psychological, neurotic, and theological phenomena both within American dominant culture and its African American population. Innovative studies by the noted psychologist Kenneth Clark of the significance of the color black and self-hatred seen even in preschool children reveal the destructive character of this legacy in the United States:

> Just as the white of threatened status may trace his lineage to the "Mayflower" and seek refuge in the Daughters or Sons of the American Revolution, so the Negro may boast that his family were freed Negroes earlier than others were, or that his parents "had money." . . . A common fantasy is to deny one's own identification with the racial dilemmas.[56]

In black American culture, blackness over against whiteness has been a vehicle for perpetuating a traditional negative self-perception. In many ways, this is an internalizing of deeply held beliefs in Western culture

54. Robert T. Handy, *A Christian America: Protestant Hopes and Historical Realities* (New York: Oxford Univ. Press, 1971).
55. Martin E. Marty, *Righteous Empire: The Protestant Experience in America* (New York: Dial Press, 1970).
56. Kenneth B. Clark, *Dark Ghetto: Dilemmas of Social Power* (New York: Harper & Row, 1965), 225–26.

and the Christian church. Ideologically this has been countered somewhat
by such movements as the early twentieth-century Pan-African movement, the Black Power and "black is beautiful" movement of the 1960s,
and greater representation of blacks in the media, not to mention increased scholarship about black culture and issues. This in turn has
unleashed revived or new conceptual notions about blackness within
black thought and culture, such as Afrocentrism and separatist black
nationalism.

The black theologian James Cone used the peculiar American black
experience embellished by the 1960s Black Power movement as the
context for his innovative "black theology." "There is a desperate need
for a *black theology*, a theology whose sole purpose is to apply the freeing
power of the gospel to black people under white oppression."[57] William
Jones, a black philosopher, in turn criticized Cone's conceptual approach
for lacking a critical apparatus in order to examine the nature of the
black experience and racial oppression itself; otherwise Cone is in danger
of establishing an uncritical black positivism: "[T]he unique character
of black suffering forces the question of divine racism. . . . The black
theologian is obliged to reconcile the inordinate amount of black suffering, which is implied in his claim that the black situation is oppressive,
with his affirmations about the nature of God and God's sovereignty
over human history."[58]

Social scientists often link a negative view of blackness as a color and
as an organizing principle to racial prejudice. Its sources, they tell us,
are historical and result from nonblacks having regular intimate contact
with blacks. A consequence is that blacks arouse suspicious images and
emotional reactions based on mythical stories and social stratification,
thereby reinforcing existing social systems of caste (and class), power
struggles based on color superiority as an ideological device for coalescing
economic and political power and trade-offs in the larger society.[59] I
hope this study will demonstrate that deeply rooted primal myths—

57. James H. Cone, *Black Theology and Black Power* (New York: Seabury Press,
1969), 31.
58. William R. Jones, *Is God a White Racist? A Preamble to Black Theology*, C. Eric
Lincoln Series on Black Religion (New York: Doubleday, 1973), xx. See also an excellent
appraisal and critique of black theology in Klauspeter Blaser, *Wenn Gott schwarz
wäre. . .* (Zürich: Theologischer Verlag, 1972), 181–200, 284–92.
59. Drake, *Black Folk Here and There*, 1:93.

and therefore emotional feelings—and beliefs about the negative character of blackness precede sociological and economic factors. These beliefs, relying on ancient myths and ethnocentric claims, are a legacy that has been nourished by Christian ideas about blackness and its attributes. In Western philosophical and religious thought, blacks and blackness have been viewed as a distinctly secondary, inferior category that always will be begrimed and on the underside of Western (and possibly of world) civilizations in contrast to the primary, superior, and positive topside of European civilization. To test these suspicions, we must investigate the mythic and historical origins of blackness as a color and concept in Western thought, its origins as a metaphor employed in early Christian thought, its role and meaning in Christianity and Christendom of the Middle Ages, when Christian popular piety was at its height, and the entwining of European colonialism in the New World and in the American colonies, whose formation and development have been jointly shaped by whites and blacks alike, either as slave or free. For these reasons, as we shall see, there is an unfinished symphony between the church and blackness.

1 | Shades of Blackness in Greek and Roman Cultures

Before Christ

*T*he saga between Western thought and blacks began with Ethiopia and Africa. To the Greeks, *Africa* generally meant the homeland of dark-skinned people called Ethiopians, Egyptians, or Nubians, even if its location and boundaries were vague. Although *black* has biological, economic, political, historical, and ideological significance, it also became part of a color code for what anthropologists and art historians identify as Negroid physical traits, particularly since Europeans began the African slave trade in the fifteenth century. Furthermore, Africa is the ethnic homeland for what American political and academic circles identify as Afro-Americans or African Americans.

But in the context of Greek and Roman culture, *African* cannot so easily be assumed to mean Negroid or always black in the modern usage of that word. At the same time, we must not assume that the Egyptians, identified at various times in traditional Eurocentric scholarship as Caucasian and Mediterranean—a category created no doubt because of Europe's intrigue with the superior culture and intellectual claims of ancient Egyptian civilization, especially that of Alexandria on the Mediterranean—are less than African, albeit not necessarily Negroid.

The continued controversy (which has taken on an ideological thrust with the advent of Afrocentrism in the United States) about whether there is a core identity and culture that can be called African covering the entire continent and the African diaspora is complicated by the fact that it has taken almost twenty-five hundred years just to come up with an accurate map of Africa and its peoples. *African* therefore covers a host of colors and cultures. As one scholar reminds us about the color complex of peoples living along the Nile Valley:

> On an average, between the Delta in northern Egypt and the Sudd on the Upper Nile, skin color tends to darken from light brown to what appears to the eye as bluish black, hair changes from wavy-straight to curly or kinky, noses become flatter and broader, lips become thicker and more averted, teeth enlarge in size from small to medium, height and linearity of body build increase. . . . All these people are Africans. To proceed further and divide them into Caucasoid and Negroid stocks is to perform an act that is arbitrary and wholly devoid of historical or biological significance.[1]

Furthermore, we should remember that other black and dark-skinned— though not necessarily Negroid—peoples are native to such places as Australia, India, Sri Lanka, Indonesia, and Pakistan.

Tradition has it that Africans and their geography became known to the Greeks and Romans mostly through four sources: (1) the poetry of Homer (c. eighth century B.C.E.); (2) early reports of the Phoenicians and Carthaginians; (3) the writings of Herodotus (fifth century B.C.E.); and (4) the *Periplus of the Erythraean Sea* (c. second or fourth century B.C.E.), a Carthaginian chronicle about Carthage's colonization of West African coastal areas.[2] This, however, does not mean that Africa or Africans had no history or developed culture before the advent of the Greeks and Romans. Certainly Ethiopians appeared early in Greek myths.[3]

1. Bruce G. Trigger, "Nubian, Negro, Black, Nilotic?" in *Africa in Antiquity: The Arts of Ancient Nubia and the Sudan*, ed. Fritz Hintze, vol. 1 (New York: The Brooklyn Museum, 1978), 27.

2. P. Salama, "The Sahara in Classical Antiquity," in *General History of Africa*, vol. 2: *Ancient Civilizations of Africa*, ed. Gamal Mokhter (Berkeley: Univ. of California Press, 1981), 516; Grace Hadley Beardsley, *The Negro in Greek and Roman Civilization: A Study of the Ethiopian Type* (Baltimore: Johns Hopkins Press, 1929), xii.

3. Frank Snowden says that the African Ethiopians referred to most often in classical

The origins of Africa's name are as uncertain as its ancient boundaries. Some think the name was originally Berber (Gk.: *barbaros*; Lat.: *barbari* = barbarian) or Phoenician (Aourigha [pronounced Afarika], an ancient Berber tribe in Carthage and the ancestor of the modern Aouraghens, who now live in the Sahara). After the Romans conquered the land of the Afarik, meaning mostly modern North Africa, some scholars say that the word was simply absorbed into their Latin vocabulary. Roman Africa included territory west of Egypt: (1) Numidia, whose capital was Cirta (Constantine), with the indigenous Berbers and Numidians; (2) the ancient Carthage empire (formerly called Libya by the Greeks; now modern Tunisia and eastern Algeria), renamed Africa Proconsularis; (3) Mauretania Caesariensis (west of modern Algeria); (4) Mauretania Tingitana (modern Fez near the Sahara); and (5) Cyrenaica, whose capital was Cyrene. Reference to Africa first appeared in the Latin literary world in the works of Ennius (239–169 B.C.E.), written between the First and Second Punic Wars, after the Roman defeat of Carthage in the Punic Wars (264–146 B.C.E.).

Still others claim the word derives from the Latin *friqi* or *farikia*, meaning "land of the fruit," which may be related to the Arabic *Ifriqiya*. Some also trace its origins to the Greek *Aphrike* ("without cold"), while others say the word is from the Latin *Aprica* ("sunny").[4]

The Arabic name Ifriqiya (or Iffrikiya) and a Latin derivative (*friqi*, *farikia*) in classical Arabic applied only to Egypt and North Africa (mostly modern Tunisia, but also Morocco, Algeria, and modern Libya). After 642 C.E., when the Arabs moved westward from Egypt and occupied North African territories, they named their newly occupied area the Maghrib ("the West"). Territory south of the Sahara from the Nile to the Atlantic and modern Sudan was called Bilad al-Sudan ("the land of the blacks").[5] The result: an ambiguity and uncertainty in European and Arabic cultures about the origins and identity of black cultures and the geographical boundaries of Africa, particularly south of the Sahara.

---

texts mean dark- and black-skinned inhabitants in the Nile Valley south of Egypt. *Ethiopian* in Greek and Roman thought also included peoples along the southern edges of northwest Africa and even living on the shores of the Mediterranean. I am grateful to Prof. Dirk Obbink of Barnard College at Columbia University for this reference. Frank M. Snowden, Jr., "Asclepiades' Didyme," *Greek, Roman, and Byzantine Studies* 32 (Autumn 1991): 240.

4. Ali A. Mazrui, *The Africans: A Triple Heritage* (Boston: Little, Brown, 1986), 25.
5. Bernard Lewis, *Race and Color in Islam* (New York: Harper & Row, 1971), 30–31.

Roman Africa did not initially include Egypt and Ethiopia geographically or conceptually, however. Egypt was appended to the empire in
30 B.C.E. after the death of Cleopatra, the last Greek ruler in the Ptolemaic
dynasty; the Romans occupied Egypt until the fourth century C.E. Furthermore, Romans distinguished between Egypt, Carthage, and Numidia
in the west, and Ethiopia in the east. In fact, early on they dug a ditch,
the *fossia regia*, in the east to mark the demarcation between their Africa
and the territory of the Numidians. For the ancient Romans, Africa
meant mostly "northern Africa, the ancient homeland of the Iberians,
of the Carthaginians, a semitic race, of the Jews themselves, and of the
Moors, composed of many Arabic-speaking groups."[6] In the first century
B.C.E. the empire expanded the boundaries of its Africa; in the second
century C.E. Emperor Septimius Severus, a North African, expanded
the boundaries of Roman Africa even farther; in the third century C.E.
Diocletian formed two new provinces, Byzacena and Tripolitania (modern Tunisia and eastern Algeria), in the eastern and southern parts.

Hence, Africa in Greco-Roman times was a geographically and intellectually imprecise construct as the ancestral home of blackness, although shades of blackness or darkness were defined with reference to
Egypt, Ethiopia, and Nubia. Many were cultures with dark-skinned or
black peoples, such as the Garamantes in North Africa, said by some
ancients to have been black with Negroid features (woolly hair, broad
noses, thick lips) like the Ethiopians and the Nubians, and by others to
have been a lighter hue of blackness than the Nubians.[7]

Beginnings of a Greek Black Aesthetic

Whether blackness in ancient Greek and Roman society had any moral,
neutral, poetic, or racial significance in describing Egyptians and Africans

6. Emil Schultheiss, *Africa* (New York: Simon and Schuster, 1958), 22–23.

7. Many ancients identified the Moors and the Garamantes as black, inasmuch as
mauros in Greek also means "black skin." Their base was Phazania (modern Fez in
Libya) in the heart of the Sahara and their capital was Gamama (modern Germa). The
nomadic Kura'an with clearly Negroid and Berber features are thought to be modern
descendants of the Garamantes. See Jehan Desanges, "The Iconography of the Black
in Ancient North Africa," in Jean Vercoutter, Jean Leclant, Frank M. Snowden, Jr., and
Jehan Desanges, *The Image of the Black in Western Art*, vol. 1: *From the Pharaohs to
the Fall of the Roman Empire* (New York: William Morrow, 1976), 312, n. 148; E. W.
Bovill, *The Golden Trade of the Moors* (London: Oxford Univ. Press, 1958), 34.

continues to be disputed by Eurocentric- and Afrocentric-oriented scholars. Blackness as the color of Ethiopians intrigued both the Greeks and the Romans. Figures with Negroid (Africanoid) features appeared in Greek art as early as the thirteenth century B.C.E. Regular contacts between Greeks and Africans certainly occurred after the sixth century B.C.E. at Naukratis on the Mediterranean. Casts of heads with definite Negroid features from sixth century B.C.E. Naukratis can be seen at Oxford University's Ashmolean Museum. Naukratis and Daphnae in the delta were important Greek settlements earlier in the seventh century B.C.E. when Greek mercenaries were in Egypt. Herodotus claims that the Greek soldiers in Daphnae were later transferred to Naukratis, which was the only port in the delta of Egypt. It was also an international commercial gateway for many foreigners and a regional market for Africans from other parts of Africa.[8]

Early on in Greek mythology, satyrs—muscular half-man, half-beast figures with torsos joined at the waist to powerful horselike legs and long tails—inhabited forests and were known for their erotic lust, fertility, and bacchanalian fondness for wine and revelry. They first appeared in Greek literature around the sixth century B.C.E. as hedonists who made love to and seduced nymphs. Euripides included them in his play *Cyclops*. Extant sculptures emphasize their Negroid features and large genitals. One author has described them as representations of the basic primate urges: sex, hunger, and self-preservation.[9] In the sixth-century B.C.E. frieze *Return of Hephaistos*, satyrs are depicted with erect phalluses, discreetly called "ithyphallic" by art historians. One vase depicts Hephaistos, followed by a muscular black ithyphallic satyr.[10] Greek art from the fifth century B.C.E. depicts them with Africanoid features, such as thick lips, broad noses, and woolly hair, engaged in all sorts of indiscreet sexual conduct with their large phalluses.[11]

Furthermore, in the King James Version of the Bible the word *satyr* is used to translate the Hebrew word *se'irim*, which was a hairy kind of

8. *Herodotus* 2.178. The first study of blacks in ancient Greece and Rome was J. Loewenherz, *Die Aethiopen der Altklassischen Kunst* (1861).
9. Eva C. Keuls, *The Reign of the Phallus: Sexual Politics in Ancient Athens* (Berkeley: Univ. of California Press, 1985), 362.
10. See Thomas H. Carpenter, *Dionysian Imagery in Archaic Greek Art: Its Development in Black-Figure Vase Painting* (Oxford, England: Clarendon Press, 1986).
11. Jean Vercoutter, "The Iconography of the Black in Ancient Egypt," in *Image of the Black in Western Art*, 1:157, 161.

demon in Hebrew folklore thought to occupy wastelands (Lev. 17:7; 2
Chron. 11:15; Isa. 13:21; 34:14). Some Greek writers even thought satyrs
originated in interior Africa.[12] Likewise, the erotic theme of blackness
was perpetuated in Greco-Roman culture through ithyphallic black stat-
uettes and black-figure Attic vases with sexually explicit organs as symbols of fertility and charms against evil spirits.[13]

During the same period, coinage with distinctly Negroid figures was
minted in Athens and Delphi. Some scholars think this unusual representation of blackness in the culture of the important Greek city of
Delphi is made even more intriguing by Delphos's mother's names, all
of which (except the name Thyia) stem from *melas* ("black")—Melatho,
Melaena, Melanis, Malaeno. Furthermore, some believed that Delphos
originally came from Crete, where blacks had been known entities on
the island since the fifth century B.C.E.. Frank M. Snowden, Jr., contends
that scholars have overlooked such evidence in Greek mythology and
thereby failed to investigate the far-reaching idea that the Greeks indeed
understood Delphos to be black and therefore Ethiopian (African):

> It is quite possible, therefore, that the Greeks, influenced by increased
> acquaintance with the African Negro in the late sixth and early fifth
> centuries, conceived of Delphos, whom they honored on their coinage,
> as a black. Recalling that his mother was named "Black" and that he
> had come from Crete, the Greeks of the fifth century perhaps concluded
> that "Mother Black" was a Negro and that Delphos resembled some of
> the familiar Negroid types from Naukratis or those seen on the streets
> of Athens.[14]

Greek vases with Negroid figures indicate that Ethiopians lived in
Greece itself by the fifth century B.C.E. and therefore were not strangers
in daily Greek life. Even earlier pottery from Cyprus dating from the
late seventh or early sixth century B.C.E. shows the head of a black with
Negroid features—thick lips, a flat nose, and woolly hair—conjoined
back to back to a white face with a beard.[15] The Boston Museum of

12. Ibid., 1:300, n. 83.
13. Ibid. 1:281; Carpenter, *Dionysian Imagery*, 19.
14. Frank M. Snowden, Jr., "Iconographical Evidence on the Black Populations in
Greco-Roman Antiquity," in *Image of the Black in Western Art*, 1:164.
15. See excellent reproductions of these in *Image of the Black in Western Art*, 1:138–
39.

Fine Arts has an excellent sixth-century B.C.E. terra-cotta vase in the shape of the head of an elderly black with wrinkles, indicating enough contact with blacks to allow the Greeks some familiarity with their Negroid features.

Some scholars claim that any lack of enthusiasm for blackness and black skin among the Greeks was indicative of the Greeks' view of all foreigners, whom they called *barbarian* (Gk.: *barbaros* = originally a person who spoke an unintelligible language—what we might call "gibberish"). *Barbarian*, however, was not a derisive term. Homer himself, when speaking of the Ethiopians, did not reveal a fixed contemptuous attitude toward them as foreigners, thereby suggesting that during his time there was no firm concept of the Greeks as a superior race.[16]

Concepts or ideas that we might identify as ethnic, ethnocentric or racial came into Greek thought after the Greeks defeated the Persians, the most powerful military force at the time, in the fifth century B.C.E. Such a momentous victory, not unlike the experience of the United States and European states after the defeat of the Axis powers in World War II, moved the Greeks to begin to think of themselves as morally and ethnically superior to other peoples. By the fourth century B.C.E. *barbarian* meant not only foreigners who spoke an unintelligible tongue, but also inferior peoples.[17] Euripides (c. 485–c. 406 B.C.E.), one of the first Greeks to articulate a new racial superiority of the Greeks in literature, wrote: "It accords with the fitness of things that barbarians should be subject to Greeks, for Greeks are free men and barbarians are slaves by nature."[18]

Hence, the concept of a dark-complexioned people introduced earlier in the West in the eighth century B.C.E. by Homer had little pejorative or racial meaning. The most common word for black in classical (and New Testament *koine*) Greek was *melas*, although *mairos* was also used (Lat.: *maurus*). In Latin *niger* and *nigra* (Sp. and Port.: *negro*; Catalán: *negre*; It.: *nero*; Fr.: *noir* [black] and *nègre* [black-skinned or dark-skinned person]) were the most common, with *negri* apparently favored by most ancient Latin writers.

16. Simon Davis, *Race Relations in Ancient Egypt: Greek, Egyptian, Hebrew, Roman* (New York: Philosophical Library, 1952), 1–2.

17. Ibid., 2.

18. Euripides, *Iph. in Aulide*, 1400-1. Quoted in Davis, *Race Relations in Ancient Egypt*, 2.

Many mainstream classicists say that Greek at the time of Homer did not have a fixed developed aesthetic for abstract words like color. Homeric Greeks did not inquire, "What is color?" and they would not have known how to answer such a query.[19] Moreover, white (*leukos*) and black (*melas*) were visualized and imagined as contrasts and extremes in the experience of day and night rather than as hues. As fluid paradigms for light and darkness, these terms shaped an emerging aesthetic about whiteness and blackness in the West. Yet while *leukos* also represented light and brightness, and *melas* meant dark and blackness, these categories also distinguished gender, emotions, and life/death motifs in classical Greek literature.[20]

In a study of a color aesthetic in different language groups, it was discovered that all languages have two basic color terms for black and white. If a language has only three color terms, the additional one is a word for red; if it has only four terms, the fourth stands either for yellow or green, but not both. Homeric Greek had four basic colors: white (*leukos*), black (*glaukon* rather than *melas*), red (*eruthron*), and yellow (*chloron*).[21] Hence, Homer's embryonic aesthetic was simply conforming to a traditional impreciseness of these terms of his day. This is evidenced in his use of *leukos* also to characterize milk, teeth, and wool; *melas* to describe black lambs and sheep; and *eruthros* to portray bronze, nectar, and wine in his poetry. For example, in his *Iliad* Rhesus's horses are "brighter than snow" rather than "whiter than snow" (*leukoteroi chionos*); in the same text Nestor describes them with the same vocabulary to identify them as "like the rays of the sun."[22]

Before the fifth century, the Greeks had a number of words for white (or light) and black (or dark). Subsequent intellectuals like Plato (c. 429–

19. Eleanor Irwin, *Colour Terms in Greek Poetry* (Toronto: Hakkert, 1974), 22.

20. This observation by Christopher Rowe agrees with the pioneering work of Rudolf Bultmann ("Zur Geschichte der Lichtsymbolik im Altertum," *Philologus* 97, Heft 1/2 1948) and Gerhard Radke ("Die Bedeutung der weissen und schwarzen Farbe in Kult und Brauch der Griechen und Römer," Ph.D. inaugural diss., Friedrich-Wilhelm-University, Berlin: Jena, 1936), who argue that whiteness was associated with the brightness of light and meant well-being and happiness. Blackness was linked to darkness, which meant something harmful and evil. Hence, the contrast between the opposites of light and darkness is amoral rather than moral in our modern sense. See Christopher Rowe, "Concepts of Color and Color Symbolism in Ancient Greece," in *Color Symbolism: Six Excerpts from the Eranos Yearbook 1972*, ed. Adolf Portmann et al. (Dallas: Spring Publications, 1977), 27–28, 44; also Irwin, *Colour Terms in Greek Poetry*, 22.

21. Brent Berlin and Paul Kay, *Basic Color Terms: Their Universality and Evolution* (Berkeley: Univ. of California Press, 1969), 2.

22. *Iliad* 10.437, 547.

347 B.C.E.), Aristotle (384–322 B.C.E.), and Theophrastus (c. 370–285 B.C.E.) developed the Greek color aesthetic further, with additional color terms considered as hues between white and black. Whiteness in classical Greece, among other things, was a symbol of triumph and happiness, which implicitly imputes the experience or myths of superiority contrasted with the experience or myths of inferiority associated with blackness. The light of the sun, according to the classicist and New Testament scholar Rudolf Bultmann, in ancient Greece meant whiteness and was a gift from heaven, not a natural phenomenon taken for granted. Only in Olympia, the residence of the gods, for example, were sunlight *and* brightness eternally present.[23]

Light signaled well-being and good luck; well-being and good luck signaled light; darkness of night meant the opposite. Neither the light of the sun in the day nor the light of the moon at night, however, were endowed with divinity as a part of the pantheon of the gods. Nor were light and darkness viewed as moral combatants in some kind of cosmic morality play between good and evil as became an operative motif in later Christian theology.[24] It is within this cultural belief that we must understand the ritual at criminal trials in ancient Greece, whereby a white vote meant acquittal and a black vote meant a death sentence.[25]

Additionally, the contrast between whiteness and blackness in Greek thought also distinguished genders and defined their respective social functions. Because men worked outdoors, they were rough and hardy, and thus dark or black skin was a sign of manhood and virility. Conversely, because whiteness was associated with femininity and because women who worked in the home were soft and vulnerable, whiteness was also used as a sign of effeminate men. In Homer's *Odyssey* Penelope wraps her white arms (*pechee leuko*) tightly around the neck of Odysseus (*Odyssey* 23.239–40), who is black or dark with woolly hair (*Odyssey* 16.174–76).

Blackness also defined certain attributes and emotions. Among the Greeks, the most memorable traits of the dark-skinned Ethiopians, Egyptians, and Colchians were their courage and skills as warriors.[26]

23. Bultmann, "Zur Geschichte der Lichtsymbolik," 1–4.
24. Ibid., 10–12.
25. Geoffrey Lloyd, in "Right and Left in Greek Philosophy," in *Right and Left: Essays on Dual Symbolic Classification*, ed. Rodney Needham (Chicago: Univ. of Chicago Press, 1973), 181.
26. Irwin, *Colour Terms in Greek Poetry*, 111–12, 129.

Hence, a dark complexion was a sign of courage and a warrior. Women on Corinthian vases (sixth century B.C.E.) and the Attic black-figure vases were painted white or light-colored, whereas men were usually painted reddish-brown or black.[27]

At the same time, the Greeks associated blackness with the emotions of the inner person, such as blackness (or darkness) of heart and happiness. *Blackness of heart* is understood to be a metaphor for warmth as contrasted with *white-heartedness*, which meant lack of feeling or sensitivity, cold-heartedness. A "white-livered" person in ancient Greece was cowardly, comparable to what we mean by "lily-livered." "Darkness was the normal state of the internal organs. Whiteness of the internal organs was a sign of abnormality."[28] If this sounds contradictory to our aesthetic, which associates blackness with ugliness and dread, it is because of the influence of Christendom in the formation of Western culture.

Thus, *leukos* symbolized for the Greeks: (1) the light of the sun associated with the gods; (2) the color white, which identified the gods and their achievements—the Roman god Jupiter, the god of the shining sky, was transported across the heavens in a chariot pulled by white horses; Zeus kidnapped Europa disguised as a white bull; (3) purity—hence the significance of white clothing for priests and many believers in religious cults—joy, and honor; (4) triumph and success.[29] *Melas* meant: (1) the mysterious and warriorlike Ethiopians; (2) black or dark; (3) masculinity; (4) certain emotions and internal organs.

Yet Homer did link the origins of the Ethiopians to the power of the sun's rays to scorch the skin. He identified Ethiopia as a shadowy, mysterious place near the streams of Oceanus where the sun rose and set, which was visited by the Greek gods—including Zeus—regularly at the time of large public sacrifices.[30] Hence, peoples we today euphemistically call "black" as a shorthand description for kinship between

27. For examples, see Carpenter, *Dionysian Imagery in Archaic Greek Art.*
28. Irwin, *Colour Terms in Greek Poetry,* 147, 156.
29. Radke, "Die Bedeutung der weissen and schwarzen Farbe," 8–9, 57–69 *passim.* For a corresponding scale of colors in an African ethnic tradition, see Victor Turner, "Color Classification in Ndembu Ritual: A Problem in Primitive Classification," in his *The Forest of Symbols: Aspects of Ndembu Ritual* (Ithaca, N.Y.: Cornell Univ. Press, 1967), 59–92. Turner notes that in the Ndembu tradition "white" stands for twenty-four different visual and emotional sensations. They vary from goodness (*ku-waha*) to making strong or healthy (*ku-koleka/ku-kolisha*) to chieftainship/authority (*wanta*) to sweeping clean or getting rid of impurities (*ku-komba*) to the time when contact is made with ancestor spirits (*adibomba niakishi*).
30. "I must not sit, for I must go back unto the streams of Oceanus unto the land

peoples of African descent, came into Western consciousness and its vocabulary already identified by a particular skin color; their origins, however, were surrounded by mystery, ambiguity, and ambivalence.

When we focus more on the Greeks' understanding of blackness or darkness, the New Testament scholar Gerhard Kittel maintains that *melas* in classical Greek culture did in fact have moral implications, if not moral preciseness. It meant or at least implied negative qualities in the sense of sinister, dreadful, terrible, unlucky; although, as we have seen, it also was associated with manly virtues and the inner life.[31] Even Homer, for example, associated blackness with the transition from life to death, albeit without the negative moral judgment that the New Testament and Christianity render about death. In the *Odyssey* he says the souls of Penelope's dead lovers move past the *white* rock, past the gates of the setting sun, through the shadowy world of dreams until "before long they reached the meadow of asphodal, which is the dwelling place of souls, the disembodied wraiths of men."[32]

In Latin *negri* also signified something sinister and deadly, although it also meant "dark" as a description of the complexions of North African Berbers and Moors, Indians, and Ethiopians. Black bile, for example, was both a sign of death and anger and a sign of melancholy, one of the four cardinal humors (Lat.: *humor* = moisture), which, according to ancient physiology, shape a person's temperament, complexion, and physical appearance.[33]

Furthermore, the negativity of black (*melas*) as descriptive of the darkness of night is evoked when we consider the implicit terror, uncertainty, and dangers of night. *Melas* was also linked to evil spirits and described the water system of the underworld, but we must be cautious

of the Ethiopians, where they are sacrificing hecatombs [a public offering of a hundred oxen] to the immortals . . ." (*Iliad* 23.205–7). "Howbeit Poseidon had gone among the far-off Ethiopians, who dwell sundered in twain, the farthermost of men, somewhere Hyperion [father of the sun or the sun itself: *Odyssey* 12.122] sets and somewhere he rises, there to receive a hecatomb of bulls and rams . . ." (*Odyssey* 1.22–24).

31. Gerhard Kittel, ed., *Theological Dictionary of the New Testament*, trans. and ed. Geoffrey W. Bromiley, 10 vols. (Grand Rapids, Mich.: Eerdmans, 1967), 4:549.

32. Rowe, "Concepts of Color and Color Symbolism," 43.

33. The four humors in the body were blood, phlegm, choler, and melancholy. Ideally they should be balanced; an overbalance of one meant that a person was either sanguine, phlegmatic, choleric, or melancholic. Belief in this scheme can still be found in parts of the former Soviet Union.

in assuming that the Greek underworld, Hades (*hadēs*), itself was something negative as a moral equivalent of the Christian doctrine of hell.
Life after death was not a major concern in mainstream classical Greek
thought, although a few movements of the time did pay some attention
to this matter, such as Orphism. Hades was also the place where the
Eleusinian Mysteries lived,[34] the "murky darkness" at the edge of Oceanus
beneath the earth where lived the god of the underworld, whose wife,
Persephone, was also black.[35]

Blackness also characterized a level below Hades, namely Tartaros,
the place of punishment for disobedient deities, lacking in wind, and a
pit where Zeus threw the Titans and his own father Kronos. Its blackness,
according to Hesiod, was so thick that "night is poured around it in
three rows like a collar round the neck, while above it grow the roots
of the earth and of the unharvested sea."[36]

Some European and American scholars defend this stark contrast
between white and black as simply reflecting a universal order of opposites, such as up/down, right/left, light/darkness, which can be found
in all cultures.[37] The classicist Frank M. Snowden, who provides a good
summary of the white/black aesthetic, says the Greco-Roman preference
of whiteness over blackness simply reflects this "natural" scale of opposites found in other cultures:

> Among the Greeks and Romans, white was generally associated with
> light, the day, with Olympus and victims sacrificed to the higher gods,
> with good character and good omens; black with night and darkness,
> with the Underworld, death and chthonian deities, with bad character
> and ill omens. In this the Greeks and Romans resembled people in
> general who, according to research on color symbolism, have a basic
> tendency to equate blackness with evil and white with goodness. . . . It
> was obviously because of a deeply rooted tradition linking blackness with
> death and the Underworld that some writers of the early Roman Empire
> put dark-skinned peoples—Ethiopian, Egyptian, Garamantian—into all
> ill-omened contexts.[38]

34. For a full discussion of the afterlife in classical Greek mythology, see Robert
Garland, *The Greek Way of Death* (Ithaca, N.Y.: Cornell Univ. Press, 1985), 48–76.

35. Radke, "Die Bedeutung der weissen and schwarzen Farbe," 14–20.

36. *Theogony* 726ff. Quoted in Garland, *The Greek Way of Death*, 51.

37. Rodney Needham, ed., *Right and Left: Essays on Dual Symbolic Classification*
(Chicago: Univ. of Chicago Press, 1973).

38. Frank M. Snowden, Jr., *Before Color Prejudice: The Ancient View of Blacks*
(Cambridge, Mass.: Harvard Univ. Press, 1983), 82.

The danger of defending such a framework of dualities as "natural" is that it can become (and indeed has become) an intellectual grid and hierarchy for viewing racial and ethnic groups as savage/civilized, high/ low, superior/inferior, or a psychological/philosophical grid for determining subject/object among peoples and cultures. The ideological and historical evils of such a grid are familiar.

A fluidity about blackness is seen among some black African tribes. A study of color in some African traditions found that the meaning of black as a basic color differs sharply from that of classical Greek, particularly when speaking of the divine. Some African traditions associate blackness with sacrifices and offerings made to the supreme god, such as black dogs or black goats.[39] Other tribes associate whiteness with these functions; still others connect whiteness with the supreme god to indicate purity and power. The Maasai of East Africa say four gods originally existed: a black god who was very good, a white god who was good, a blue god who was neither good nor bad, and a red god who was bad. The only god now remaining is the black god, according to the Maasai. Here we see less of the sharp extremes between black and white, but rather distinction between black and blue, a basic color in the previously mentioned study that comes further down on the list of abstract color terms found in languages. Likewise, the Galla tribe identifies dark storm clouds as a sign that God is black.[40]

In spite of the impreciseness of blackness as an aesthetic category and its absence as a modern moral and political category in Greece, the Greeks did make careful distinctions between different hues of black

---

39. It is interesting to note that among the Ndembu (Zambia) the many meanings of black also include badness or evil, bad luck, disease, witchcraft/sorcery, and death. Turner says, however, that the negative attributes of black as a color can be misleading if we try to apply our Greco-Roman derived color aesthetic as a universal norm. The context in which blackness is expressed and experienced in the Ndembu tradition cannot be abstracted from their understanding of death and certain rites of passage, such as circumcision, female maturation, and marital practices.

Death for the Ndembu, as in most of African traditional religion, is not a finality or an enemy as in New Testament theology and Christian belief. Death is the occasion for passage to the larger world of the spirits, particularly ancestor spirits. Turner, *The Forest of Symbols*, 71–74. See also my comments on darkness, death, and ancestor spirits in African and "New World" Afro as theological motifs in Robert E. Hood, *Must God Remain Greek?: Afro Cultures and God-Talk* (Minneapolis: Fortress Press, 1990), 157– 64, 217–44.

40. John S. Mbiti, *Concepts of God in Africa* (New York: Praeger, 1970), 154–55.

skin, varying from dark (*fusci*) to very black (*nigerrima*).[41] Ptolemy, for example, identified the people in the region of Meroë, the second capital of the Kush Empire from the fifth century B.C.E. to the fourth century C.E., as deeply black and pure Ethiopian, whereas the population around the Egyptian-Nubian border, while not as black as Ethiopians, were called blacker than the Egyptians.

In North Africa, the Greeks created a special vocabulary for the spectrum of blackness: *Melanogaetuli* (black Gaetuli) and *Leukaethiopes* (white Ethiopians) of inner Libya, *Libyoaethiopes* (Libyan Ethiopians), and the *Mauri* (whose skin color varied from "black" [*nigri*] to "scorched" [*adusti*] to "sunburned" [*perusti*] to "swarthy" [*furvi*]).[42] Martin Bernal in his innovative work *Black Athena* claims that Greeks also considered another African populace, the Egyptians, to be primarily black, albeit of a different hue than the people of Nubia.[43] Many Egyptologists dispute this claim, however.

Parallel changes in the perception of black skin also took place in Spain after the Moors with their many dark-skinned compatriots occupied that country. As late as the thirteenth century, Spanish Christians created several terms for the different hues of black skin found in their midst. Each term conferred a descending or ascending social recognition by Spaniards in their social order: *moro lorum* (a Muslim of an "intermediate color"), *sarraceno blanco* (a white Saracen), *sarracenum nigrium* (a black Saracen), *sarracenum lauram* (a Saracen of intermediate color), *sarracenum albam* (a white Saracen).[44]

By the time of Xenophanes (C. 570–480 B.C.E.), the Ethiopians were identified a bit more precisely as black with Negroid flat noses and woolly hair. Fifth-century B.C.E. Greek literature thought Ethiopia to be

41. Some Greeks distinguished between the colors of dark-skinned people. Ethiopians were considered the blackest, Indians as less sunburned, Egyptians as mildly dark, and the Moors as somewhere in between. Snowden, "Asclepiades' Didyme," 242.

42. Snowden, *Before Color Prejudice*, 8–9.

43. Martin Bernal, *Black Athena: The Afroasiatic Roots of Classical Civilization*, vol. 1: *The Fabrication of Ancient Greece 1785–1985* (New Brunswick, N.J.: Rutgers Univ. Press, 1987), 52.

44. Jack D. Forbes, *Black Africans and Native Americans: Color, Race and Caste in the Evolution of Red-Black Peoples* (Oxford, England: Basil Blackwell, 1988), 26. Late medieval Italians also made distinctions and conferred various social privileges on the basis of different skin hues: *albo, alvi, blanco, branco* (white); *nero, nigri, negri, negro, preto* (black); *lauro, loro, llor, berretini, rufo, pardo, olivastre* (dark or lighter black). Ibid., 66.

located in the vague hinterland called Africa somewhere south of Egypt.[45] Aeschylus apparently was the first Greek to locate Ethiopia in Africa.[46] While the Greek poets such as Homer, Hesiod (c. 700 B.C.E.), Aeschylus, Euripides, and Apollonius (born c. 295 B.C.E.) wrote about the Ethiopians in mythical terms, the Greek prose writers, such as Herodotus, Strabo (c. 64 B.C.E.–21 C.E.), Pliny the Elder (c. 23–79 C.E.), and Heliodorus (fl. 220–250 C.E.), viewed them in more realistic terms, because they apparently had actual contact with Ethiopians in Greece or elsewhere.[47]

Herodotus, for example, highly commended the military skills of Ethiopians who were members of Xerxes' invading armies that attacked Greece in 480 B.C.E. He said that those from the east had straight hair and those from the west had woolly hair, thick lips, and a different type of speech.[48] He also described the population of Colchians as being of Egyptian origin because they resembled the Egyptians, who were "black-skinned," had woolly hair, and were circumcised.[49] Herodotus had visited Africa, stopping at a number of cities, including possibly Ilé-Ifè, the primordial site where creation took place according to the Yoruba, who now occupy southern Nigeria.[50]

45. Snowden, *Before Color Prejudice*, 46.
46. Aeschylus, *Supp.* 284–86. See also Frank M. Snowden, Jr., *Blacks in Antiquity: Ethiopians in the Greco-Roman Experience* (Cambridge, Mass.: Belknap Press at Harvard Univ. Press, 1971), 103; Beardsley, *The Negro in Greek and Roman Civilization*, 12.
47. Beardsley, *The Negro in Greek and Roman Civilization*, 4, 10.
48. *Herodotus* 7.70.
49. Ibid. Colchis, the mythical home of Medea and the goal of Jason's travels, was the region immediately south of the Caucasus Mountains in the west of modern Georgia bordered by the Black Sea on one side. The ancient Greeks regarded Colchis as a place of great sorcery and wealth. The complexion of its people is in dispute. Whereas some ancients said they were dark, woolly-haired, and related to the Egyptians, others described them as yellow, fat, and lazy because of their life-style. Some Africanists, who dispute whether Herodotus's commentary means "black," claim that a more accurate rendering is "dark-skinned and curly haired." At a United Nations symposium on Africa in 1974, few of the participants except Cheikh Anta Diop (Senegal) and Theophile Obenga (the Congo) claimed that the ancient Egyptians were primarily black. See *General History of Africa*, 8 vols.; vol. 2: *Ancient Civilizations of Africa*, ed. Gamal Mokhtar (Berkeley: Univ. of California Press, 1981).
50. According to a Yoruba view of history, five ancient cities in Africa existed between 3000 and 1000 B.C.E., one of which was Ifé. The inhabitants were said to be amphibides, half-man and half-ape. Cited in M. A. Fabunmi, *A Traditional History of Ilé-Ifè* (Ilé-Ifè, Nigeria: Kings Press, 1975), 11. See also David Adamo's rather provocative proposal that the Garden of Eden (Gen. 2:10-14) is indeed located in Africa as the Yoruba claim. David Tuesday Adamo, "The Place of Africa and Africans in the Old Testament and its Environment," Ph.D. diss., Baylor University, 1986, 85–94.

Beginnings of a Roman
Black Aesthetic

Rome's fascination with black as skin color took on a more practical, hands-on interest, often lacking a Latin conceptual framework. This was especially evident in the custom of the privileged social classes that imported black pygmies as entertainers and servants. Pygmies (Gk.: *pygme* = a Greek measurement corresponding to the distance between the elbow and knuckles) first appeared in Roman art in the first century B.C.E. Homer had described their mythical origins as a race of tiny people in a far-off southern land battling the cranes, who had flown there to escape the European winters (*Iliad* 3.6). Pygmies for Rome's upper classes were most likely imported from interior Africa via Egypt.[51] At the same time, the Egyptian deity Bos, popular along the Mediterranean communities, was sculpted as a black pygmy known for his powers as the protector of fertility, pregnant women, god of dance and music, and guardian against the Evil Eye and evil spirits.[52]

The Latin aesthetic of the Romans, which lagged behind Greek in its conceptual development, also had a similar lag in its color scale. By the first century B.C.E., however, educated Romans at least had abstract concepts in Latin for the four basic visual colors already established in Greek three centuries earlier: white (*candida; albus*), black (*nigri*), red (*ruber; rubens*), yellow (*flavus*), green (*viridis*), and blue (*caeruleus*). For many Latin poets, white was a sign of divinity and luck while black was a sign of dread and bad luck. For example, the Fates are described both as *candidae sorores* (the white sisters) when they bring luck and *sorores nigrae* (the black sisters) when they bring misery.[53] Other Latin words are *ater* ("dark" or "blue black"), *aquilus* ("swarthy color"), and *nocticolor* ("night color" from *noctu*, meaning "by night" or "at nighttime").[54] New Testament Greek retained the Latin to describe a dark or black Christian: "Now in the church at Antioch there were prophets and teachers, Barnabas, Simeon who was called *Niger*, Lucius of Cyrene. . .'" (Acts 13:1).

51. Herodotus wrote that while the Nasamonians were gathering fruit in the African desert in Central Africa, they were attacked by dwarfs speaking a strange tongue, who then took them to a river town (possibly along the Niger River) where other tiny people lived. *Herodotus* 2.32.

52. Jean Leclant, "Egypt, Land of Africa," in *Image of the Black in Western Art*, 1:273–78.

53. Rowe, "Concepts of Color and Color Symbolism in the Ancient World," 44.

54. Bernal, *Black Athena*, 1:2–5.

Even more significant, the Roman elite—Hellenists devoted to Greece, its customs and its language, and not Latin—assimilated Greek ethnocentric beliefs about the rest of the world. At one end of the flat world was the frozen north, home of the savage Irish, Hyperborean, and the British. Egypt lay somewhere in the middle. The south at the other end with its hot climate was the home of blacks—Egyptians, Ethiopians, and Numidians. The southerners were black because they had been burnt by the sun, had shrill voices, were bow-legged, had a blood deficiency, and made poor soldiers. Egyptians (called *Eruditi* by Apuleius) were in a class by themselves, even though the Romans disliked them because they regarded the local Egyptians as treacherous and cowards. Some Egyptians, however, were prominent in Roman society, and some Egyptians had acquired Roman citizenship, no mean feat, but a great source of pride as it was for St. Paul.[55]

The Romans also were clear about the erotic prowess of black Africans. An Ethiopian peasant woman in the *Appendix Virgiliana* (c. first century C.E.) is described as "African, every part of her body bearing witness to her origin, woolly-haired, thick-lipped, black, with great pendant breasts, pinched belly, thin legs, and huge feet."[56] Livy (c. 59 B.C.E.–17 C.E.) claimed that African men were oversexed and seducers of Roman women.[57] He compared them to wild animals in their provenance in Numidia, and reported that they produced mixed colored mongrels and originated a Greek idiom that was also transmitted into Latin as a proverb: *Ex Africa semper aliquid novi* (Out of Africa always something new).[58] African women were said to be very fertile because of their ability to produce many sets of twins, just as Egyptians were thought to be able to produce triplets because they drank the waters of the Nile, which had special powers. Precisely what endowed the African women with such a capacity was not clear.[59]

55. J. P. V. D. Balsdon, *Romans and Aliens* (London: Duckworth, 1979), 58, 68.
56. Ibid., 217.
57. The warrior Masinissa lost his heart to Sophonisba, an African woman. Livy comments about the natural carnal skills of the black Numidians: ". . . ut est genus Numidarum in Venerem praeceps, amore captivae victor captus" (". . . but with the amorous susceptibility of the Numidian race, the victor [Masinissa] was captivated by the love of the captive," 30, 12.18, *Livy*, trans. Frank Gardner Moore, Loeb Classical Library (Cambridge, Mass.: Harvard Univ. Press, 1949), 409.
58. Balsdon, *Romans and Aliens*, 69.
59. Ibid., 90, 218.

Some claim that after the Romans conquered North Africa and Egypt, their fascination with the erotic intensified as they imported dark-skinned slaves and became acquainted with Egyptian art and culture, particularly the attention Egyptian culture paid to the cult of the phallus. This cult is thought to have been established by Isis at Thebes. Black women were imported to Rome or bought from Mediterranean traders to be mistresses for the wealthy. Muscular black men said to be sexually well-endowed were also brought into the Roman Empire for wealthy women.[60]

The first Roman to write about blacks was Titus Maccius Plautus (c. 254–184 B.C.E.), a comic poet who wrote what American television jargon would call situation comedies based on lower- and middle-class life. In one play, *Poenulus*, the title character, who carries pails in the circus, is described as Ethiopian. Romans also would have met up with Africans possibly as elephant drivers during the First (264–241 B.C.E.) and Second (218–201 B.C.E.) Punic Wars between Carthage and Rome. Roman troops had captured Carthaginian elephants, which they paraded through the streets of Italy along with the drivers after defeating the Carthaginians at Panormus in 250 B.C.E.). Finally, with the coming of the Augustan era (63 B.C.E.–14 C.E.), references to blacks in Roman literature and in the visual arts increased noticeably, indicating that blacks would have been known to first-century Christians in the Roman Empire, particularly those Christians in Rome and large trading areas.[61]

Grace Hadley Beardsley traces the earliest negative attack on blacks in Roman literature to Cicero (106–43 C.E.), who calls Ethiopians stupid.[62] Juvenal expresses contempt for Ethiopians in an obvious reference to their color: "Let the straight-legged man laugh at the club-footed, the white man at the Ethiopian" (. . . *derideat Aethiopem albus*).[63]

60. Although he does not give evidence from texts or artifacts, these claims of Bernard Braxton corroborate the stereotypes of African eroticism in ancient Roman society discussed above. See Bernard Braxton, *Women, Sex and Race* (Washington, D.C.: Verta Press, 1973), 61–62.

61. Frank M. Snowden, Jr., "Iconographical Evidence on the Black Populations in Greco-Roman Antiquity," in *Image of the Black in Western Art*, 1:212–45.

62. ". . . cum hoc homine an cum stipite Aethiope." Cicero, *De Senectute*, 6. Cited in Beardsley, *The Negro in Greek and Roman Civilization*, 119.

63. Satire 2.23., *Juvenal and Persius*, trans. G. G. Ramsey, Loeb Classical Library (Cambridge, Mass.: Harvard Univ. Press, 1965), 18–19. Beardsley notes that *Aethiope* is usually translated "blackhead" (or "blackamoor") and is synonymous with "stupid" in many Latin texts, such as Cicero. Beardsley, *The Negro in Greek and Roman Civilization*, 119.

The earliest Latin text to speak of Ethiopians apparently was the play *Eunuchus* (161 B.C.E.) by Terence (c. 190 B.C.E.–c. 159 B.C.E.). Terence was a North African slave brought to Rome, who served in the household of a senator, Tarentius Lucanus, until he was given his freedom. He took his slavemaster's first name and wrote plays and other works.[64]

The classicist J. P. Balsdon makes a telling critical comment about the social order and the moral value attached to skin color in Greco-Roman culture. While little direct evidence of color prejudice may exist, at the same time we find no evidence of mixed marriages between whites and blacks in Greek or Roman upper classes. Did such resistance occur for aesthetic reasons or for moral reasons? Juvenal, disgruntled about Africans because he had been exiled to Syene in Egypt by Domitian, did allow that a married Roman man could find pragmatic reasons for having sexual satisfaction with black women and even producing illegitimate offspring from a woman of "a colored hue, whom [the Roman] would rather not meet by daylight."[65]

Archaeological data show that at least in the Greek Egyptian cities of Alexandria, Naukratis, and Ptolemais, marriage across ethnic lines was also taboo during the Greeks' occupation. The Greeks in Egypt considered themselves culturally superior to the Egyptians, although they also had great respect for Egyptian learning and religion, as did the early Jewish Christians later in the first century C.E.[66] Citizenship was refused to the sons of a mixed marriage. The charter of Naukratis even denied legitimacy to marriages between Greeks and the indigenous population, although this legal taboo did not apply to other places in Greek Egypt.[67]

Similarly in Roman culture, archaeology has uncovered sculptures of Negroid heads from the early sixth century and late fifth century B.C.E. and fourth-century B.C.E. masks in Sicily. Likewise, we know that Roman theatre had roles for Africans during this period and that black Africans

64. Beardsley, *The Negro in Greek and Roman Civilization*, 116.

65. Balsdon, *Romans and Aliens*, 218–19. For an intriguing discussion of the ethnocentric prejudices against other cultures and peoples and the subtle and not so subtle distinctions made by the ancient Greeks and Romans, see A. N. Sherwin-White, *Racial Prejudice in Imperial Rome* (Cambridge, England: Cambridge Univ. Press, 1970).

66. *Herodotus* 1.60.

67. Davis, *Race Relations in Ancient Egypt*, 54. In Greek papyri, whose origins range from the first century B.C.E. to the seventh century C.E., after 150 B.C.E. Greeks are found with both Greek and Egyptian names. This suggests either offspring from mixed marriages or Egyptians taking Greek names for cultural and political upward mobility.

accompanied Carthaginians to Sicily in their fifth-century war against
Dionysius I (c. 430–367 B.C.E.). Fashionable vases of this period often
were carved in the form of heads with obvious black features, including
curly woolly hair. In one magnificent gold phiale (a flat bowl) dating
from the fourth century B.C.E. found in southern Bulgaria, three con-
centric rows of twenty-four African heads surround a row of acorns and
a row of palmettos.[68] Furthermore, after Petronius defeated an Ethiopian
militia, many captured Ethiopians were taken to Rome as slaves. Ethiopians were also employed in Rome in brothels, in the theatre as actors
and dancers, as boxers, acrobats, bath attendants, hunters, cooks, and
other domestic servants.[69]

Virgil summarized the aesthetic and the exotic view of blacks in his
world when he described a black woman: "African in race, her whole
figure proof of her country—her hair tightly curled, lips thick, color
dark, chest broad, breasts pendulous, belly somewhat pinched, legs thin,
and feet broad and simple."[70]

Many scholars looking at this same period dissent from classicists
like Frank Snowden and Christopher Rowe about whether black skin
color had a moral and social value in ancient Greco-Roman culture. For
example, William Leo Hansberry,[71] Cheikh Diop,[72] and J. A. Rogers[73]
maintain that the Greeks viewed the color black with negative moral
imputation. Hansberry, for example, says that shortly after Greeks settled
in Naukratis in the sixth century B.C.E., uncomplimentary views of the
black Ethiopians emerged. Herodotus, "the father of history" in the
West, for example, spoke of their speech as the "shrieking of a Bat rather
than the Language of Men." Pliny the Elder said the Ethiopians "have
no heads but mouth and eyes in their breasts."[74]

68. Ibid., 180–82. This piece, at the National Archaeological Museum in Plovdiv,
Bulgaria, has been beautifully reproduced in *Image of the Black in Western Art*.
    69. Balsdon, *Romans and Aliens*, 219.
    70. Virgil, *Moretum* 31–35. Quoted in Snowden, *Before Color Prejudice*, 10.
    71. Joseph E. Harris, ed., *Africa and Africans as Seen by Classical Writers: The
William Leo Hansberry African History Notebook*, 2 vols. (Washington, D.C.: Howard
Univ. Press, 1977).
    72. Cheikh Anta Diop, *The African Origin of Civilization: Myth or Reality*, trans.
Mercer Cook (Westport, Conn.: Lawrence Hill, 1974).
    73. J. A. Rogers, *Nature Knows No Color Line: Research into the Negro Ancestry in
the White Race* (New York: Helga M. Rogers [1270 Fifth Avenue, New York, N.Y.,
10029], 1952).
    74. Harris, *Africa and Africans as Seen by Classical Writers*, xx. Also see Pliny's
"Macrobius": "Aethiopes . . . guos vicinia solis usque ad speciem nigri coloris exurit";
Cicero, *Somn. Scip.* 2, 10, 11. In Beardsley, *The Negro in Greek and Roman Art*, 120.

In summary, we see the emergence of an aesthetic and color code in Western thought in which many of the carnal forces associated with blackness in modern times and evident in such events as the lynching of the black teenagers Yusuf Hawkins and Jermaine Ewell were alive in the imagination and consciousness of both the Greeks and the Romans: curiosity, carnality, and negativity or at least social and intellectual disdain. Curiosity and beliefs about blacks began with a mythic structure. This mythic structure was reinforced by sensuality as the Greeks and particularly the Romans had contact with black-skinned peoples, such as the Ethiopians and the Nubians. This mythic structure appeared in their art and literature. As a color scheme developed and new political and military circumstances came into play, blackness became a way of identifying dark-skinned Ethiopians, Egyptians, Nubians, and other Africans. Hence, the roots of cultural beliefs about blacks were implanted early on in Western thought based on ethnocentric interpretations, even though initially the color black was fluid and imprecise. This fluidity, as we shall see, has continued throughout Western history, but it also took on fixed negative attributes, especially after Europeans began to link intelligence with color and culture.

Egypt and Ethiopia assumed different roles as black-skinned countries in Christian thought. Blackness was given a moral category by Christians as they tried to make sense of biblical notions of sin and evil in an environment dominated by Greek and Neoplatonic philosophical thought. Furthermore, sex and evil began to figure prominently as ontological attributes of blackness, in turn shaping Christian beliefs about blacks.

2 | Africa and the Christian Tradition

*A*frica, as the traditional ancestral seat of blackness and black peoples, and the Christian tradition have had a tangential relationship at best. In biblical studies, while much attention is given to Egypt, scant attention is devoted to Ethiopia. In theological studies, possibly with the exception of the use of Egypt as a metaphor for black liberation in black theology, which emerged in the 1960s, little attention has been paid either to Egypt or Ethiopia. Only in more recent years has religious studies, which is embroidered with the study and methodology of world religions, found that Africa and its traditional religions merit any attention.

What lies behind this relationship between the ancestral seat of blackness and blacks—something recognized even in classical Greco-Roman culture—and the Christian tradition, which has been so basic in the formation of Western cultural values, beliefs, and attitudes? In the 1950s, a friend from West Africa came to the United States to do graduate studies in the Old Testament at Harvard University. He wished to research some critical aspect of the question of Africa and the Bible with an eminent Old Testament scholar teaching there at the time. The scholar informed him that not only did few sources exist for doing such research, but the question itself was a not a matter worthy of serious biblical research; hence he discouraged him from enrolling at Harvard to pursue the matter. The prospective doctoral student, discouraged but relying on the authority and knowledge of this eminent Old Testament scholar, discontinued his pursuit of a doctorate.

This anecdote reminds us that until recently Africa as a cultural phenomenon or as a collection of cultures with its own integrity got scant attention in mainstream biblical or theological studies by Christian or Jewish scholars. What we popularly call "Africa" with its many nations is largely a modern creation of nineteenth-century European imperialism and colonialism with arbitrary political and geographical boundaries cutting off traditional ethnic and tribal cultures based on decisions and trade-offs at the 1884–85 Berlin Conference among European nations. Moreover, our knowledge of Africa and its cultures until the past thirty years has been largely shaped by European colonial and religious perceptions and scholarship. The Old Testament scholar Randall Bailey even extends this ethnocentric and politically influenced perception into what he calls a strategy of geographical de-Africanization among mainline biblical scholars, who insist on focusing on Mesopotamia (modern Iraq), the Syria-Palestine region, the Arabian Peninsula, and Egypt, which they separate from Africa.[1]

It is not that Africans or African countries are unfamiliar to Christians. The Bible refers to Egypt, Cush (Kush), Ethiopia, and Put (Punt), which was located in Libya, the ancient generic name for Africa.[2] Ethiopia and Cush were also generic terms for Africa in the ancient world and the Old Testament.[3] The New Testament, in addition to references to

1. Randall C. Bailey, "Beyond Identification: The Use of Africans in Old Testament Poetry and Narratives," in *Stony the Road We Trod: African American Biblical Interpretation*, ed. Cain Hope Felder (Minneapolis: Fortress Press, 1991), 165–68.

2. See the writings of such ancient geographers as Hecataeus of Miletus (c. 500 B.C.E.), Herodotus (c. 480–425 B.C.E.), and Diodorus (c. 59 B.C.E.).

3. Old Testament references to African countries and Africans have been documented in an excellent study by David Adamo: (1) the exodus and the wilderness—Num. 12:1-2; (2) the United Monarchy (1020–922 B.C.E.)—2 Sam. 18:21, 22, 31-32; 1 Kings 10:1-13; 2 Chron. 9:1-12; (3) the divided monarchy and the fall of Jerusalem (922–587 B.C.E.)—1 Kings 14:25-28; 2 Chron. 12:2-3, 14:9; Amos 9:7-8; Isa. 11:11, 20:1-6; Jer. 13:23, 36:14, 21, 23; (4) the exilic period—Ezek. 29:10, 30:4-5; Isa. 43:3, 45:14; and (5) the writings—Psalm 68:31, 87:4; Esther 1:1, 8:9; Dan. 11:43. David Tuesday Adamo, "The Place of Africa and Africans in the Old Testament and its Environment," Ph.D. diss., Baylor Univ., 1986. See also Robert A. Bennett, Jr., "Africa and the Biblical World," *Harvard Theological Review* 64 (1971): 501–24; Charles B. Copher, "The Bible and the African Experience," *The Journal of the Interdenominational Theological Center* 16 (Fall 1988/Spring 1989): 32–50; Charles B. Copher, "The Black Presence in the Old Testament," in *Stony the Road We Trod*, 146–64.

Ethiopia, contains more oblique references to "Africa" and blacks. The Acts of the Apostles speaks of natives from "Egypt and the parts of Libya belonging to Cyrene" (2:10) assembled together with other foreigners in Jerusalem on Pentecost, and of a "Simeon who was called Niger [Lat.: black], and Lucius of Cyrene [capital (?) of Cyrenaica, which is modern Libya]" (13:1). It must also be said, however, that our modern concept of Africa per se as the ancestral land of predominantly black cultures with their indigenous religions, ethnic groups, and historical integrity does not play a prominent role in either the Old Testament or the New Testament.

Although intellectual interest in Africa has existed since the advent of Egyptology and the social sciences in the eighteenth century, it has largely been the twentieth century that has seen an explosion of widespread interest in and curiosity about Africa and its peoples, particularly the cultures of sub-Saharan Africa. Prior to that time, with the exception of Egypt, Africa was dealt with generally as an oversized footnote to the colonial histories and imperialism of the various European empires. Egypt was exempted as an African country by being classified as a Mediterranean (meaning Caucasian) culture. Indeed up to time of the European scramble for land at the Berlin Conference (1884–85), maps showed an Africa with large parcels of land inaccurately labeled, indicating a prevailing ignorance in the West about Africa's geography, religions, and cultures.

Moreover, black Africa's traditions, whether conceptual or historical, were overlooked or scoffed at as unworthy of serious academic interest, with the possible exception of anthropological interest. As late as the 1960s, for example, the Regius Professor of Modern History at Oxford University mocked critical studies of sub-Saharan Africa as "unrewarding gyrations of barbarous tribes in picturesque but irrelevant corners of the globe."[4] Another British intellectual, Arnold Toynbee, wrote in his monumental *A Study of History* that "the Black Race has not helped to create any civilization."[5]

4. Quoted in Roland Oliver, "The African Rediscovery of Africa," *Times Literary Supplement*, 20 March 1981, 299.

5. Arnold J. Toynbee, *A Study of History*, 6 vols. (London: Oxford Univ. Press, 1939), 1:238. By "Black Race" Toynbee means not only sub-Saharan Africans, but also "Blackfellows" in Australia, the people of Papua, Melanesia, Ceylon (Sri Lanka), and the Todas of southern India (1:233).

With the disintegration of the French and British empires after World War II and the rise of former colonies as the Third World, however, not only political but also intellectual attention focused more on Africa. In the 1970s, two milestones contributed greatly to pushing the history and culture of black Africa into the vortex of mainstream scholarship: the UNESCO conference on Africa that produced the eight-volume *General History of Africa* and the outstanding (still to be completed), five-volume work *The Image of the Black in Western Art*. Both of these events provided a conceptual framework for dealing with the many facets of African cultures and histories and the nature of the long, torturous relationship between Africa and the West. They also reveal the development of how prevailing beliefs and superstitions in the West shaped and influenced visual and conceptual presentations of Africa in Greco-Roman society and in its offspring, Europe.

Moments of Africa in the New Testament

The story of Apollos in Acts 18:24f. ("a Jew named Apollos, a native of Alexandria, came to Ephesus. He was an eloquent man, well versed in the Scriptures. He had been instructed in the way of the Lord; . . . he spoke and taught accurately the things concerning Jesus. . . .") indicates that the Christian faith was in Egypt at least by the middle of the first century C.E.[6]

The Acts of the Apostles in the New Testament Apocrypha says Matthew baptized the King of Ethiopia, Aeglippus. This text is still cited in modern Ethiopia as ancient proof of its claim as the first Christian country. Ethiopia was the place where these divine promises assured the conversion of pagan Ethiopia. Many church fathers wrote commentaries about the baptism of the Ethiopian eunuch in Acts 8.[7]

The unique account in Matt. 2:15 of the birth narrative of Jesus Christ, which reveals a God-initiated partnership with the African nation of Egypt, is not accidental. Egypt is a land with deep historical and

6. C. Wilfred Griggs, *Early Egyptian Christianity: From its Origins to 451 C.E.* (Leiden, Netherlands: E. J. Brill, 1991), 16.
7. See William Frank Lawrence, Jr., "The History of the Interpretation of Acts 8:26-40 by the Church Fathers Prior to the Fall of Rome," Ph.D. diss., Union Theological Seminary, 1984.

theological connections in the Jewish tradition and in the ancient world of the sacred. Matthew does the unusual to establish Jesus' special authority by detailing his genealogy. This would have captured the attention of the Jewish reader as portraying Jesus as somebody special.[8] If the primary purpose of Matthew's Gospel is to proclaim the event of Jesus Christ as the universal salvation-bearing event for all of human history (1:1, 16; 3:17), as some New Testament scholars maintain, then 2:15 must be one of the earliest historical (but also theological) references linking Egypt to Jesus Christ the expected Messiah.[9]

Mainstream biblical scholars tell us that Matthew simply lifted this phrase from Hos. 11:1 and Exod. 4:22, and that it is not about historical events, seldom pointing out that Egypt lies in Africa, even though the concept "Africa" did not represent the same geographical entity in the ancient world that it does today. But why is Jesus identified with this territory? Alternative interpretations of this reference to Egypt suggested are: (1) It is a deliberate attempt to link God's deliverance of the Jews from bondage under Moses and God's promised restoration under the Messiah; (2) it is an allegorical reference used similarly in Rev. 11:8, where Egypt is the place where the dead are buried, thereby linking it to the crucifixion ("Out of death have I called my son"); (3) it is a metaphor for hope and future deliverance from the Romans, because Egypt was traditionally known as a place of refuge for people escaping despots and tyrants.[10]

The question is whether the New Testament's coupling of Egypt and Christ is simply a cross-reference to the Old Testament, or might have deeper theological significance. We dare not forget that Israel's exodus from Egypt was not only a chronological and historical event; it was also a salvation event in Israel's self-determination and self-esteem as a people, whereby God established a covenant with Israel and, through it, with all of humanity as a partner:

8. Ulrich Luz, *Matthew 1–7: A Commentary*, Wilhelm C. Linss, trans. (Minneapolis: Fortress Press, 1989), 45. See my argument for departing from the usual exegesis of this text in Robert E. Hood, *Must God Remain Greek?: Afro Cultures and God-talk* (Minneapolis: Fortress Press, 1990), 145–46.

9. Ibid., 43.

10. Raymond Brown maintains that this more likely ancient understanding of Egypt as a place of refuge for those escaping despotism rules against those saying that the Holy Family actually went to Egypt via the Gaza Strip, which lay within the boundaries of the Roman Empire. *The Birth of the Messiah: A Commentary on the Infancy Narrative in Matthew and Luke* (Garden City, N.Y.: Doubleday, 1977), 203.

You have seen what I did to the Egyptians, and how I bore you on
eagles' wings and brought you to myself. Now therefore, if you will obey
my voice and keep my covenant, you shall be my own possession among
all peoples; for all the earth is mine. . . . (Exod. 19:4-5)

Ancient Israel understood its slavery in and deliverance from Egypt
both as the historical event establishing its nationhood—albeit without
exact geographical boundaries—and as the theological event instituting
its special relationship to God via the first covenant.

But Matthew may have intended this nexus to signify an even more
profound apologetic within the contemporary historical setting of early
first-century Christians. If the community that remembered these narratives was Jewish-Christian, as some scholars think, and if the author
of Matthew was himself a Jewish-Christian,[11] then the divine reference
to Egypt—remember that God identifies Jesus here as God's Son and
previously as Emmanuel (1:23)—would make worshipers' ears perk.
Not only is the God of Israel claiming Jesus Christ as God's son—the
only christological reference in the whole of this chapter—but also
Matthew links this important title to a concrete geographical place called
Egypt. For Matthew and his audience, Egypt, as we know, was no mere
theological abstraction or historical reference in first-century Judaism;
it was a known entity geographically and culturally in the Roman Empire.

Jews had lived in Alexandria since the time of Psammetichus II (c.
590 B.C.E.).[12] Jews also remembered Egypt as the country where a
retreating Ptolemy I Soter (323–283 B.C.E.) reportedly took a hundred
thousand Jewish prisoners of war from Palestine and thereafter forced
many of them to settle as mercenaries to keep the indigenous Egyptians
in check. At the same time many Palestinian Jews fled with him in
search of greater religious tolerance and freedom than was available in
Palestine. It was the place where Ptolemy's son, Ptolemy II Philadelphus
(283–244 B.C.E.), liberated Jews captured by his father and gave them
land for settlements. The Jewish temple at Leontopolis, Egypt, built in
the second century, was recognized by Ptolemy III (d. 222?) as a legal
place of political refuge.

Egypt was also known in Jewish Palestine as the place where Jews
lived freely in its major city of Alexandria, traditionally regarded by the

11. See Luz, *Matthew*, 79–90.
12. F. F. Bruce, *The Acts of the Apostles* (Grand Rapids, Mich.: Eerdmans, 1968), 85.

ancients as the intellectual capital of the Mediterranean, and where the
first Greek translation of the Hebrew Scriptures, the Septuagint, took
place. Synagogues had existed in Alexandria, Schedia, and elsewhere in
Egypt since 400 B.C.E. A literary corpus, the *Acts of the Martyrs of
Alexandria*, which documented the tribulations of Alexandrian Jews,
existed, though there is little evidence that this work was known in
oriental Palestinian Jewish circles in the empire. According to Lucian
(c. 125–190 C.E.), Egypt was revered and highly regarded in such strong-
holds with Christian populations as Palestine, Syria, and non-Christian
parts of the empire as the place of origin of religious concepts about
gods and spirits with their respective established places of worship and
annual feast days.[13] Later Clement of Alexandria (c. 150–c. 215 C.E.),
speaking of divisions between the Jewish Christians and the Gentile
Christians, said there were two gospels in the Christian church of his
day: an "Egyptian Gospel" and a "Hebrew Gospel."[14] So Egypt was
more than a rhetorical euphemism in the spirituality and consciousness
of the first-century Jews and the Jewish-Christians in Palestine and
elsewhere. Therefore, all in all, Egypt was regarded as a friendly place
for Jews, which may be an additional reason why Matthew links it to
Jesus.

Furthermore, we know that both the Greek and Roman color scale
and aesthetic considered most Egyptians to be dark-skinned people,
albeit a lighter hue than the Ethiopians and the Nubians. So it is clear
that Matthew knew the Egyptians as including dark-skinned/black peoples when he linked Jesus to that territory. Color alone does not determine
Africans or their descendants, since peoples with dark and black skins
exist outside the African continent, but it has always been that which
other peoples have cited as the peculiar feature of Africa. If Martin
Bernal's arresting argument is correct about the African and Asian roots
of classical Greek civilization, then dark-skinned Egypt had an even
more profound impact on Jewish Christians of the early Christian church.
Popular belief in Egyptian astrological systems was widespread throughout the Roman Empire after 50 B.C.E. and as late as 150 C.E. This was
also the time of Matthew's Gospel (c. 98–110 C.E.). According to Bernal,

13. Harold W. Attridge and Robert A. Oden, eds., *The Syrian Goddess (De Dea
Syria) Attributed to Lucian* (Missoula, Mont.: Scholars Press for the Society of Biblical
Literature, 1976), 11.
14. Clement of Alexandria, *Stromata* 3.63; 2.45, 5.

it was believed during this time that the spring equinox had moved from Aries to Pisces, a momentous occasion that caused great public anxiety. Virgil (c. 70–19 B.C.E.), author of the *Aeneid*, and other Roman authors said the forthcoming age of Pisces would witness the advent of a new divinity, although some classicists deny that Virgil meant a literal new divinity. Instead, they say, the poet was speaking metaphorically and had several levels of thought in mind, such as the birth of a friend's child, the beginning of a peaceful age, or the coming of a young divinity.[15]

Bernal argues, nevertheless, that anxiety and foreboding throughout the empire, including Palestine, about the changing equinox shaped the context in which literature dealing with the expected divinities is to be interpreted, such as the *Lament* in the *Hermetic Texts*:

> There will come a time when it will be seen that in vain have the Egyptians honored the divinity with pious mind and with assiduous service. All their holy worship will become inefficacious. The gods leaving the earth will go back to heaven; they will abandon Egypt; this land, once the home of religion, will be widowed of its gods and left destitute. . . . The Scythian or the Indian, or some other such barbarous neighbor, will establish himself in Egypt.[16]

15. Martin Bernal, *Black Athena: The Afroasiatic Roots of Classical Civilization*, vol. 1: *The Fabrication of Ancient Greece*, 1785–1985 (New Brunswick, N.J.: Rutgers Univ. Press, 1987), 126.

16. Ibid., 129. This idea may not be that farfetched, albeit unconventional. Some New Testament scholars see evidence of Luke using the Zodiac in Acts 2:9-11 (c. 60–100 C.E.) for theological purposes. F. Cumont compared the list of the twelve signs of the Zodiac, the list of countries in Acts 2:9-11, and a list of countries ranked under these signs in a work on astrology by Paul of Alexandria in 378 C.E.: (1) Aries = Persia; (2) Tarsus = Babylon; (3) Gemini = Cappadocia; (4) Cancer = Armenia; (5) Leo = Asia; (6) Virgo = Hellas and Ionia; (7) Libra = Libya and Cyrene; (8) Scorpio = Italy; (9) Sagittarius = Cilicia and Crete; (10) Capricorn = Syria; (11) Aquarius = Egypt; (12) Pisces = Red Sea and Indian lands. Cumont determined that Paul's source was the work of an Egyptian of the Persian epoch, whose source in turn was a second-century C.E. work on the Zodiac by Vettius Valens. (F. Cumont, "La plus ancienne géographie astrologique," *Klio* 9 (1909): 263–73. Cited in Ernst Haenchen, *The Acts of the Apostles: A Commentary*, trans. Bernard Novu, Gerard Shinn, and R. McL. Wilson (Philadelphia: Westminster, 1971), 169–70 n. 5. Based on this research, apparently other New Testament scholars suggest that this earlier list was used around 50 C.E. in Antioch for deciding its central missionary areas. This theory has not found consensus within New Testament scholarship; however, it does pose the question of where the list of countries in Acts 2:9-11 came from. The list moves east to west geographically with northern and southern territories in the middle. Furthermore, an apologetic function is suggested by the inclusion of this list: "These names convey to the reader the

It is therefore entirely possible that Matthew identified Jesus Christ as the one "called out of Egypt" by the Hebrew God to be God's son and Messiah to announce in the midst of the general malaise and anxiety among Christian and non-Christian alike that Christ from birth is the anointed one from the superior Christian God who is the victor and the victory even over the new age of the equinox, even though it was a legacy from the revered culture of Egypt.

Egypt and Ethiopia and the Christian Tradition

The two African countries most familiar historically and biblically in the Christian tradition are, of course, Egypt (Gk.: *Aigyptos* in Homer; Lat.: *Aegyptus*; Egyptian: *Hiku-Ptah* = house of the spirit of [the god] Ptah in Memphis)[17] and Ethiopia (Gk.: *Aithiops*, [sun]burnt face, from *aithos* = sunburnt and *ops* = face); Arabic *Habash* (from *Habashat* = an Arab tribe that occupied Ethiopia's northern highlands), still the Arabic name for the country. The Arabs used *Habash* to distinguish the blacks of Ethiopia and its contiguous neighbors from blacks in the rest of Africa, which they called the Bilad al-Sudan ("the land of the blacks"). (It is interesting that the Arabs excluded Egyptians, North Africans, and other inhabitants north of the Sahara from the name Sudan. This exception may have had something to do with their low opinion of most Africans south of the Sahara. The old European name Abyssinia [Ger.: *Abessinien*] comes also from Arabic.)[18]

Ethiopia (Kush) meant roughly the territories south of Egypt, which eventually included much of modern Sudan. Ethiopia and later what confusingly was also called the Kingdom of Kush (a Nubian kingdom

---

impression that the Christian mission was already reaching out 'to the ends of the earth.' " Haenchen, *Acts of the Apostles*, 169. The British scholar F. F. Bruce also observes that the marginal notes found in an offprint of Cumont's article intimate that Luke "however strange his list is, meant in fact to say 'the whole world' . . . all nations who [sic] live under the twelve signs of the Zodiac received the gift to understand their preaching immediately." F. F. Bruce, *The Book of the Acts*, rev. ed. (Grand Rapids, Mich.: Eerdmans, 1988), 55; cf. Stefan Weinstock, "The Geographical Catalogue in Acts 2:9-11," *Journal of Roman Studies* 38 (1948): 43–46; Griggs, *Early Egyptian Christianity*, 14, 35 n. 7.

17. *The Interpreter's Dictionary of the Bible*, 4 vols. (New York: Abingdon, 1962), 2:39.
18. Bernard Lewis, *Race and Color in Islam* (New York: Harper & Row, 1971), 30.

dating from c. 760 B.C.E.) had regular contacts with Egypt very early in African history—Ethiopia certainly since the First Dynasty (c. 3100–2890 B.C.E.).[19] The name Ethiopia in the ancient world was usually applied to all dark-skinned (black) peoples other than Egyptians. The Old Testament name Cush (Kush) is of Egyptian origin, first recorded in the Twelfth Dynasty of Sesostris I (c. 1971–1930 B.C.E.) to designate the inhabitants of Upper Nubia between the Second and Third Cataracts. From the Eighteenth Dynasty onward (1551–1314 B.C.E.) Kush designated all of Nubia and the Sudan, stretching from Aswan to the territory beyond the Fourth Cataract. In turn, the Egyptian word was adapted by the Assyrian conquerors (Kusu, Kusi) and the Hebrews (Cush), meaning all of the territory south of Egypt separated by the land of Wawat.[20]

Egypt, known in the classical and biblical worlds as an enormous landmass and for its ancient and respected religious and theological weightiness, means several things. The Egyptians themselves called their land Kemit (*kmt* = "blackness" in hieroglyphics), meaning "the black land."[21] (*Kam* in Hebrew means "black," "burned," "heat," and may well be derived from the Egyptians, among whom the Hebrews lived some four hundred years as slaves.)[22]

19. Frank M. Snowden, Jr., *Before Color Prejudice: The Ancient View of Blacks* (Cambridge, Mass.: Harvard Univ. Press, 1983), 21. See also the early references to Kush in Egyptian inscriptions in James H. Breasted, *Ancient Records of Egypt*, vol. 1 (Chicago: Univ. of Chicago Press, 1906), 251.

20. *Interpreter's Dictionary of the Bible*, 2:176.

21. Cheikh Anta Diop, "Origin of the Ancient Egyptians," in *General History of Africa*, vol. 2: *Ancient Civilizations of Africa*, ed. Gamal Mokhter (Berkeley: Univ. of California Press, 1981), 2:41; Maurice Assad, "The African Coptic Church," *The Journal of the Interdenominational Theological Center* 16 (Fall 1988/Spring 1989): 98. For a dissenting view of *kmt* see Abdelgadir M. Abdalla (Sudan), "Annex to Chapter 1: Report of the Symposium on 'The Peopling of Ancient Egypt and the Deciphering of the Meoritic Script,'" in *General History of Africa*, 2:63–64, 75–76.

22. The Senegalese Africanist Cheikh Diop translates *kam* as "Negroid." Many black American anthropologists, however, disagree that the Egyptians were Negroid. See Cheikh Anta Diop, "Ancient Egypt Revisited," *Black Issues in Higher Education* (28 February 1991), 12–16; Cheikh Anta Diop, "Origin of the Ancient Egyptians," in *General History of Africa*, 2:41; Cheikh Anta Diop, *The African Origin of Civilization: Myth or Reality*, trans. Mercer Cook (Westport, Conn: Lawrence Hill, 1974). At a 1974 UNESCO symposium on "The Peopling of Ancient Egypt and the Deciphering of the Meoritic Script," a number of Africanists also disagreed with Diop's interpretation. See a summary report of these sessions in *General History of Africa*, 2:58–66. See especially the opposing interpretation of *kmt* by Prof. Abdalla (Sudan), who maintains that *km* (*kem*) does not mean black, but is of "proto-Semitic" origins. *General History of Africa*, 2:63–64, 75–

The essayist Lucian confirmed these reports in his writings. He describes a young Egyptian: "This boy is not merely black; he has thick lips and his legs are too thin . . . his hair worn in a plait behind shows that he is not a freeman." A character in the essay replies, "But that is a sign of really distinguished birth in Egypt. All freeborn children plait their hair until they reach manhood."[23]

Still another name was Tway ("the two lands"), which referred to Upper Egypt and Lower Egypt because of its topography: its dark rich soil and its vast desert sands. The ancient Hebrews called it Misraim.

The ongoing dispute about whether *black* as a skin color in antiquity meant the same as what we mean by black or Negroid, and whether it is the correct designation for the complexions of all inhabitants of Africa, was also a factor in identifying Africans in ancient Greco-Roman culture. In a fresco from the royal tomb in the Valley of the Kings (Nineteenth Dynasty: 1320–1200 B.C.E.), "the four branches of mankind" are depicted as red, dark brown, lighter brown, and black for the skin color of Egyptians, Asiatics, Nubians, and Libyans.[24]

Geographically, Egypt extended its borders several times. Prior to 2000 B.C.E., Egypt meant the territory in the Nile Valley that extended from the mouth of the Nile to the First Cataract (waterfall) near the modern town of Aswan to the Second Cataract to the coasts of the Red Sea and most of the Sinai Peninsula. (The Nile as a natural barrier has been sardonically described in the *Encyclopaedia Britannica* [11th edition] as the feature that prevents Egypt from looking like the rest of the Sahara.) But Egypt's civilizations, which began more than five thousand years ago, and the expansion of its boundaries also included ancient Nubia. Nubians lived in Egypt as early as the Fourth Kingdom of the Old Kingdom (2500 B.C.E.). The Nubian influence on Egyptian civilization has been more evident in recent archaeological finds, such as the institution of kingship in Egypt, which was established there in 3100 B.C.E. This important foundation of Egyptian religion and civilization

---

76. Still, it is interesting that in Egypt, unlike the West and other cultures, red rather than black is associated with evil. Black symbolizes fertility and life-sustaining forces. See Jeffrey Burton Russell, *The Devil: Perceptions of Evil from Antiquity to Primitive Christianity*, (Ithaca, N.Y.: Cornell Univ. Press, 1977), 78.

23. Lucian, *Navigations*, par. 2–3. Quoted in Cheikh Anta Diop, "Origin of the Ancient Egyptians," in *General History of Africa*, 2:37–38.

24. See Richard Fazzini, *Tutankhamen and the African Heritage: A View of Society in the Time of the Boy King* (New York: Metropolitan Museum of Art, 1978), 13.

had been already established in Nubia at the same time and possibly two centuries earlier.[25]

The Nubians under King Piankhy occupied the original Egyptian capital of Memphis in 747 B.C.E. and united Egypt and Nubia. The first Nubian pharaoh of Egypt was Kashta (760–747 B.C.E.); the pharaohs of the Twenty-fifth Dynasty (716–656 B.C.E.), established by Shabaqo (716–702 B.C.E.) and his successors, were Nubian/Kushite. After the Kushite dynasty, Egypt tried to remove all memory of the Kushites by erasing the names of the pharaohs of the Twenty-fifth Dynasty from all public monuments fifty years later.[26] Today one-third of modern Nubia (Lower Nubia in antiquity, located between the First and Second Cataracts) lies in modern Egypt and the rest in the present Republic of Sudan (which achieved independence in 1956).[27]

Egypt—that forever engrossing land whose ancient civilization and religion subsequently were overcrusted with the younger gods of Greece, Christianity, and Islam—provided the most direct contact with Africa and Africans for the ancient Greeks and Romans. Its Mediterranean location commanded the gateway to the Nile Valley, which ran down the Nubian corridor with the Sahara on the west and the Arabian (Nubian) desert on the east, and excited foreign military interest as well. In 332 B.C.E., Alexander the Great invaded Egypt with an army of Greeks and Macedonians. Meeting little resistance from the occupying Persians, the Greeks remained in this part of Africa until they were defeated by the Romans, who in turn incorporated it into the Roman Empire after 30 B.C.E.

Most African exports, such as ivory, gold, ostrich eggs, myrrh, spices, animal skins—and black slaves—came from Nubia and Central Africa through Egypt.[28] Egypt's occupation of Lower Nubia and Nubia's borders with Central Africa made Egypt the main entry to the rest of Africa, which also offered commercial and cultural advantages for the Egyptians,

25. *New York Times*, 11 February 1992, p. c10.

26. Karl-Heinz Priese, "The Kingdom of Kush: The Napatan Period," in *Africa in Antiquity: The Arts of Ancient Nubia and the Sudan*, vol. 1, ed. Fritz Hintze, (New York: The Brooklyn Museum, 1978), 80.

27. William Y. Adams, "Geography and Population of the Nile Valley," in *Africa in Antiquity*, 1:17.

28. Jean Leclant, "Egypt, Land of Africa, in the Greco-Roman World," in Jean Vercoutter, Jean Leclant, Frank M. Snowden, Jr., and Jehan Desanges, *The Image of the Black in Western Art*, vol. 1: *From the Pharaohs to the Fall of the Roman Empire*, (New York: William Morrow, 1976), 269–70.

sub-Saharan Africans, the Greeks, and the Romans. In Egyptian art, for example, prior to the fourteenth century B.C.E. the physical traits of the Nehesyu ("he of the Sudan," who were the "southerners" of Lower Nubia along the Nile and the Puntites on Red Sea coastal areas), whom the Egyptians considered different from themselves only in skin color, were contrasted with the Kushites.[29] Indeed, the Negroid figures in the pyramids and tombs are thought to reflect Egypt's intimate familiarity with Nilotic features found among the Nubians.[30]

Ethiopia, as we have seen, was also a generic name for all of Africa except Egypt. Jewish interpretation of why Moses had an Ethiopian wife (Num. 12:1-15) held that Moses was the commander of the Egyptian army and actually fought and lived in Ethiopia, where he married Princess Tharbia, the daughter of the Ethiopian king, after she had delivered the capital, Saba, to him and the Egyptian forces. Moses then returned to Egypt with his Ethiopian bride.[31] The prophet Isaiah distinguishes Egyptians from Ethiopians in his opposition to a proposed military alliance between Hezekiah and the Egyptian dynasty:

Ah, land of whirring wings,
which is beyond the rivers of Ethiopia;
which sends ambassadors by the Nile,
in vessels of papyrus upon the waters!
Go, you swift messengers, to a nation, *tall and smooth* [bronzed],
to a people feared near and far,
a nation mighty and conquering,
whose land the rivers divide. (Isa. 18:1-2, emphasis added)[32]

29. S. Adam, "The Importance of Nubia: A Land Between Central Africa and the Mediterranean," in *General History of Africa*, 2:231. For a discussion of the derivation of *Nehesu*, see Adamo, "The Place of Africa and the Africans in the Old Testament," 33–44. See also the way the skin color of Nubians and Egyptians was depicted in the tomb of Djehutyhotep at Debeira East (1480 B.C.E.) in Bruce G. Trigger, "Nubian, Negro, Black, Nilotic?," in *Africa in Antiquity*, 1:32.

30. Adam, "The Importance of Nubia," 242.

31. Louis Ginzberg, *The Legends of the Jews*, 7 vols., trans. Henrietta Szold (Philadelphia: Jewish Publication Society of America, 1968), 5:407-10. Josephus (born c. 37 C.E.) says that Saba was the original name of Meroë, but was renamed by Cambyses, king of Persia (530–522 B.C.E.), after his sister. Cambyses successfully defeated the Egyptians in 525 B.C.E. but failed to defeat Ethiopia. Flavius Josephus, *Jewish Antiquities. Books 1–4*, trans. H. St. J. Thackeray, Loeb Classical Library (Cambridge, Mass.: Harvard Univ. Press, 1967), 273.

32. Herodotus also described Africans as "the tallest and most beautiful people in the world." *Herodotus* 3.20.

Western antiquity's knowledge of Ethiopia and Africa, as we have
seen, began with ambiguity and confusion about its origins. The eighth-
century B.C.E. poet Homer (Gk.: *homeros* = blind man) introduced the
name Ethiopian into Western thought, although his Ethiopia is a mythical place.³³ He describes the complexion of Odysseus's favorite aide-
de-camp, Eurybates, as a "visage solemn sad, of sable hue" and his hair
as kinky and woolly. (Some classicists think these are really beauty marks
rather than racial traits, especially inasmuch as Odysseus also had the
same characteristics.)³⁴ Fresco fragments from Pylos in Western Messenia
(near the modern Bay of Navarino on the western coast of Peloponnesus
= Island of Pelops)³⁵ from the thirteenth century B.C.E., however, show
a black man girded in a loincloth. This suggests that the Greeks in fact
had contact with black Africans earlier than Homer. Likewise, clay tablets
from Pylos from this same period speak of *ai-ti-jo-qo*, which means
Aithiops. This tells us that the Greeks had a name for Ethiopia and
black Africans prior to the eighth century B.C.E.³⁶ Such ambiguity about
Ethiopia's origins certainly continued into the fourth century C.E.³⁷

Herodotus identified two kinds of dark- or black-skinned Ethiopians:
those in the west with woolly, kinky hair and those in the east with
straight hair. His description corroborates the opinions of other Greek
historians and geographers who said Ethiopia stretched between Egypt

33. *Iliad* 1.423–24; 23.205, 207; *Odyssey* 1.22–24; 4.14; 5.282, 287; 19.246–47.
English translation in Homer, *The Iliad*, 2 vols., trans. A. T. Murray, Loeb Classical
Library (Cambridge, Mass.: Harvard Univ. Press, 1971), and *The Odyssey*, 2 vols., trans.
A. T. Murray, Loeb Classical Library (Cambridge, Mass.: Harvard Univ. Press, 1953).
34. "A favorite herald in his train I knew. His visage solemn sad, of sable hue: Short
woolly curls o'erfleec'd his bending head" (*Odyssey*. 19.246–47). Odysseus is also dark-
skinned: "he became dark-skinned again, his jaws filled out, and the beard grew dark
on his chin" (*Odyssey*. 16.174–76), and he has "woolly hair" (23.157–58). Classicists
disagree whether these descriptions indicate a racial identity as African (Florence Elizabeth Wallace, *Color in Homer and in Ancient Art*, Smith College Classical Studies 9
[1927]) or whether they are marks of beauty of the time, since Eurybates came from
Ithaca, not Africa (*Iliad*. 2.183–84). See Eleanor Irwin, *Colour Terms in Greek Poetry*
(Toronto: Hakkert, 1974), 114.
35. Pelops, grandson of Zeus, had enormous fame and power among the gods, so
much so that the ancients called the entire peninsula his island (Peloponnesus). Pelops
also presided over the games at Olympia with great flair and aplomb. To honor him
at Olympia, a temple was built by Heracles, his descendant, where a *black* ram was
sacrificed by the magistrates.
36. Frank M. Snowden, Jr., "Iconographical Evidence on the Black Populations in
Greco-Roman Antiquity," in *Image of the Black in Western Art*, 1:137–38.
37. 4,4; 10,41, Heiliodorus, "An Ethiopian Story," in *Collected Greek Novels*, ed.
Bryan P. Reardon (Berkeley: Univ. of California Press, 1989).

(those with woolly hair) and India (those with straight hair).[38] Herodotus said the citizens of Colchis must have been originally Egyptian because they too had black skin (*melanochroes*), woolly hair, and were circumcised.[39] Furthermore, he and a few other Greeks had actually visited Ethiopia by 665 B.C.E., going as far as Korosko. Ptolemy II (285–246 B.C.E.), son of Ptolemy I (367–283 B.C.E.), sent the first Greek explorers to Ethiopia and to the west coast of the Red Sea.

While color designations in Greco-Roman culture may not have signified anything pejorative or prejudicial, they certainly implied some hierarchy on a descending or ascending scale. A distinction was made between those Ethiopians who were dark (*fusci*) and those who were very dark (*nigerrimi*). Those living along the border between Egypt and Nubia were said to be a lighter shade of blackness than Ethiopians but darker than Egyptians. At times even North Africans were described as Ethiopians.[40]

In modern times, Ethiopia has been on an ethnic and racial pendulum among Western anthropologists. At times, Ethiopian (Kush) rulers have been classified as Caucasoid, meaning Hamitic, when anthropologists decided to consider Ethiopia as a source of civilization for the rest of sub-Saharan Africa. At other times, these same Ethiopian rulers were classified as Negroid, meaning black, when their achievements were compared to those of ancient Egypt.[41]

It is interesting to note that at least once in the Bible Egypt and Ethiopia are yoked to each other and to Israel's God: "Princes shall come out of Egypt; Ethiopia shall soon stretch out her hands unto God" (Ps. 68:31, KJV). But in the politicized "Table of the Nations" in Genesis 10, Canaan, an offspring of Ham, one of Noah's three sons and primordial ancestor of Egypt and Ethiopia, is cursed by Noah to be the servant/slave of Ham's two brothers forever. (This biblical legend of Ham as the ancestor of blacks and transmitter of the curse had particularly strong intellectual and political appeal in medieval Christendom and during

---

38. E. A. Wallis Budge, *A History of Ethiopia, Nubia, and Abyssinia*, 2 vols. (London: Metheun, 1928), 1:vii–viii. The Kushites are thought to have occupied Mesopotamia c. 2800 B.C.E. Ancient Armenian sources say that Kush meant Persia and the entire region between the Indus and Tigris rivers. See Adamo, "The Place of Africa and Africans in the Old Testament," 63, 105.

39. *Herodotus* 2.104. Cited in Diop, *The African Origin of Civilization*, 243.

40. Snowden, *Before Color Prejudice*, 8.

41. Trigger, "Nubian, Negro, Black, Niothic?," in *Africa in Antiquity*, 1:28.

the Renaissance. It was used to support European cultural claims of superiority over non-European cultures. It also had strong religious appeal for the same reason in the antebellum American South and to anthropology and Egyptology in their infancy.) The sons of Ham are identified by the Hebrews as Cush (the Nile Valley, including Nubia and Ethiopia), Misraim (Egypt), Put or Phut (northern Libya or the northern coast of Somalia), and Canaan (Palestine and Phoenicia [Lebanon]).[42]

This biblical legacy played a crucial role both for Jews and Christians, particularly when the curse was imbued with empirical evidence to explain the lower status of dark-skinned peoples over against white-skinned peoples. One scholar reminds us how deeply ingrained biblically derived beliefs were:

> The Hebrew term *siyyim*, the Greek *Aithiops*, the Latin *Aethiops*, the Ge'ez *habasut*, and the Arabic *Habash* all designate a part of the posterity of Chus. Because this particular group was black, it was identified by some as a symbol of sin, and by others—worse yet—as the Devil's portion on earth. . . . Concomitant to the curse [of Noah] was a forced migration toward the most unwholesome regions of the earth, and there the *Aethiopes* turned black.[43]

Hence, it is likely that by the first century C.E. when Christian Scriptures and the Christian church were emerging in the Roman Empire, Egypt and Ethiopia already connoted particular social and ethnic conditions for the general populace. Furthermore, skin color had a concrete societal significance and a cultural ranking in the empire.

At the same time, these two African countries, Egypt and Ethiopia, have lasting historical and theological relevance for Jews and Christians.[44]

42. See Edward Ullendorff, *Ethiopia and the Bible* (Oxford, England: Oxford Univ. Press for the British Academy, 1968), 6; A. Hamid Zayed, "Egypt's Relations with the Rest of Africa," in *General History of Africa*, 2:144.

43. Jean Devisse, *The Image of the Black in Western Art*, vol. 2/i: *From the Demonic Threat to the Incarnation of Sainthood*, trans. William Granger Ryan (New York: William Morrow, 1979), 60.

44. Recent research suggests an even more significant role of Ethiopia as a joining of Judaism and Christianity: namely, that Ethiopia may be where the long-lost Ark of the Covenant is currently located. See Graham Hancock's innovative *The Sign and the Seal: The Quest for the Lost Ark of the Covenant* (New York: Crown Publishers, 1992). Some scholars claim that differences and distinctions based on racial characteristics were a part of early Christian life in Egypt and Ethiopia: see Chancellor Williams, *The*

As already mentioned, the Twenty-fifth Dynasty, which ruled Egypt 751–623 B.C.E., was Ethiopian or Kushite before it was driven out by the Assyrians. Both Egypt and Ethiopia are linked to founders of the two biblical faiths: Moses and Jesus. Not only did Moses lead the enslaved Hebrews to freedom from enslaving Egypt, but he also married an Ethiopian, thereby incurring the wrath and rejection of Miriam and Aaron (Num. 12:1). In the New Testament both Egypt and Ethiopia are also related to Jesus Christ and the Christian faith in two places and possibly a third: (1) the christological reference of Matt. 2:15: "Out of Egypt have I called my son"; (2) Acts 8:25-40; the conversion of the Ethiopian eunuch; and (3) a curious reference in Acts 13:1 to "Simeon who was called Niger," most likely a black native from Africa, although no specific country is named. Both Egypt and Ethiopia, which opened the African continent to the spread of the Christian faith, also play prominent roles in the subsequent history of Christianity. The role of Alexandria and the Egyptian Coptic Church, for example, in the history and formation of the Christian church is well known. Ancient Christian tradition identified Mark the Evangelist, one of Jesus' close disciples, as the founder and first bishop of the Egyptian church.[45] Indeed he continues to be commemorated in the Coptic Church on April 25 as the first bishop and Christian martyr of Alexandria.

Many Western scholars dispute the connection between Egypt and Mark.[46] Neither Clement, Origen, nor Dionysius, Bishop of Alexandria (died c. 264), mention this tradition. Papias (c. 60–130), Bishop of Hierapolis in Asia Minor, even denies that Mark was an eyewitness and close disciple of Jesus, stating that Mark was a scribe for Peter's recollections of Christ's sayings and activities.[47] (Still, as one British scholar

---

Destruction of Black Civilization: Great Issues of a Race from 4500 B.C. to 2000 A.D. (Chicago: Third World Press, 1974); Joseph E. Harris, ed., *Pillars in Ethiopian History: The William Leo Hansberry African History Notebook*, 2 vols. (Washington, D.C.: Howard Univ. Press, 1974–77). Similar claims can be found in the less rigorous work based on much research and museum visits by J. A. Rogers, *100 Amazing Facts about the Negro with Complete Proof: A Short Cut to the World History of the Negro* (1957).

45. Eusebius, *The History of the Church from Christ to Constantine*, trans. G. A. Williamson (Minneapolis: Augsburg, 1965), 89.

46. See, for example, Adolf von Harnack, *The Mission and Expansion of Christianity in the First Three Centuries*, trans. James Moffatt (London: Williams and Norgate, 1908), 158; Walter Bauer, *Orthodoxy and Heresy in Earliest Christianity*, ed. and trans. Robert A. Kraft and Gerhard Krodel, et al. (Philadelphia: Fortress Press, 1971), 45.

47. Eusebius, *History of the Church*, 152.

notes, silence from these two theologians should not be interpreted as certitude: "I do not know how often F. D. Maurice or Bishop Westcott mentioned St. Augustine of Canterbury; if they never mentioned him, it would be neither here nor there."[48]

Ethiopia's first bishop was an Egyptian, Frumentius, according to the historian Rufinus (345–410) in his *Historica Ecclesiastica*. Frumentius was consecrated Bishop of Aksum (modern Axum in northeastern Ethiopia) by Athanasius in the fourth century. Frumentius is still commemorated in the Ethiopian church year as "Abba Salama, Revealer of the Light," known for his zealousness for the Christian faith.[49] (After Haile Selassie was restored as emperor after World War II, future Albunas— heads of the church—have been Ethiopian. In 1950, the office was elevated to a patriarchy.)[50]

In the subsequent relationship between Africa and the Christian tradition, other than the ancient Christian centers in Egypt (Alexandria) and North Africa (Carthage), many modern African theologians and historians identify several phases: (1) the establishment of the Christian church in Egypt (officially under Theodosius) and Ethiopia;[51] (2) the

48. G. M. Lee, "Eusebius on St. Mark and the Beginnings of Christianity in Egypt," in *Studia Patristica*, ed. Elizabeth A. Livingstone, vol. 12, part 1 (Berlin: Akademie Verlag, 1975); 424 (for bibliography, 422–431). In support of the tradition that Mark the Evangelist was the founder-bishop of the Egyptian church, Lee cites Demetrius, Patriarch of Alexandria from 189 (died c. 231), who appointed Origen to be head of the catechetical school in Alexandria around 203. Demetrius scandalized the Egyptian Christians by being married when elected bishop of Alexandria: "no [married man until he] had sat upon the archiepiscopal throne of St. Mark the Evangelist, who was no virgin" (p. 429).

Eusebius (c. 260–c. 340) supports the tradition that the Gospel-writer Mark established the church in Egypt at Alexandria. The number of Christians was so large and significant that Philo decided he had to act as a scribe in writing about their services and manner of living. *History of the Church*, 89.

49. Edward Ullendorff, *The Ethiopians: An Introduction to Country and People* (Oxford, England: Oxford Univ. Press, 1973), 96–98; also A. H. M. Jones and Elizabeth Monroe, *A History of Ethiopia* (Oxford, England: Clarendon Press, 1955), 26–31.

50. Jones and Monroe, *A History of Ethiopia*, 35–36; Ullendorff, *The Ethiopians*, 103.

51. Christian texts from the first century C.E. have been found along the Nile Valley, suggesting indigenous Coptic Christian communities. These texts reflect an established literary tradition and theological thought more sophisticated than those in the emerging Catholic tradition. Furthermore, Coptic versions of some Old Testament books and the Book of Acts date from the third century. Coptic Christian churches were autonomous under local elders rather than a bishop. Catholic ecclesiastical structures, such as the oversight of the Bishop of Alexandria, were imposed toward the end of the second century, which also brought more structured doctrinal and legal systems. C. Wilfred Griggs, *Early Egyptian Christianity: From Its Origins to 451 C.E.* (Leiden, Netherlands: E. J. Brill, 1991), 79–81, 229.

emergence of Christianity in North Africa; (3) European Christian missionary activity in Africa during the Middle Ages, a phase generally
overlooked; and (4) the eighteenth- and nineteenth-century missionary
movement in Africa south of the Sahara (when Europeans invented the
concept "darkest Africa").[52]

On the whole, however, with the exception of Alexandria—which
the Romans called *Alexandria ad Aegyptum* ("Alexandria *near* Egypt"
rather than "*in* Egypt")[53]—and North Africa, the Christian tradition has
generally disallowed positive theological contributions from black Africa
south of the Sahara, even into modern times. Alexandria's site had been
chosen by Alexander himself, but it was founded after his death (323
B.C.E.) under the Ptolemy dynasty in Egypt. It became the political and
economic capital of Hellenistic Egypt. The decline of its famous library
and museum happened after the Romans conquered Egypt. The Gnostic
Basilides taught there during the reign of Hadrian (117–138) and by
185 C.E. through its famous catechetical school it was one of the two
significant theological centers in the early Christian church, Antioch
being the other. At its noted catechetical school Clement of Alexandria,
Origen (185–252), Athanasius (293–373), and Cyril (412–444) were
educated.[54] The continuing theological conflicts between the church in
Alexandria and the church in Antioch dominated the early ecumenical
councils as an ancient premonition of the ideological and political rivalry
between East and West in the cold-war era after World War II.

Many early Christian theologians, whose geographical knowledge
about Ethiopia and the rest of Africa reflected that of intellectual circles
in the Roman Empire, viewed Ethiopia largely in religious terms according to the prophecy in Psalm 68:31 ("Princes shall come out of
Egypt; Ethiopia shall soon stretch out her hands unto God" [KJV]), and
the story of the Ethiopian eunuch in Acts 8:26-40.

52. See Mercy Amba Oduyoye, *Hearing and Knowing: Theological Reflections on
Christianity in Africa* (Maryknoll, N.Y.: Orbis Books, 1986), 1–28; Lamin Sanneh, *West
African Christianity: The Religious Impact* (Maryknoll, N.Y.: Orbis Books, 1983), 1–13;
Hans W. Debrunner, *A History of Christianity in Ghana* (Accra, Ghana: Waterville
Publishing House, 1967), 7–38.

53. H. I. Bell, "Evidences of Christianity in Egypt During the Roman Period,"
Harvard Theological Review 37 (July 1944): 190.

54. For details about the planning and internal life of ancient Alexandria under the
Romans, see H. Riad, "Egypt in the Hellenistic Era," in *General History of Africa*, 2:189–
94.

Furthermore, eventually Egypt and Ethiopia as well as the rest of black Africa were isolated from mainstream Christianity after they were the losers in the fifth-century Monophysite (Gk.: *monos* = only one; *physis* = nature) controversy and the subsequent Islamic conquests of Egypt, North Africa, and parts of Ethiopia.[55] (Egypt was the first African country invaded by the Arabs and was quickly conquered.) The Egyptian church insisted that Christ was only of one stuff or nature, which was divine. The bishops at Chalcedon said he was of two natures, human and divine. To the Egyptians, to speak of Christ having two natures sounded like dualism and meant that Christ's humanity existed independently of the Logos or the Word.

The church historian Cyril Richardson in his book on the Trinity says the Egyptians and the other Monophysites were correct in their objection to the Chalcedonian formula because the incarnation was always under the threat of being understood as two natures. At the same time, the Monophysites were always in danger of deemphasizing the humanity of Christ. In the long run this paradox about the identity of Jesus Christ that the church has faithfully concocted by using Greco-Roman concepts to interpret the largely oriental witness and record of the Bible remains just that: a paradox that cannot be easily explained or overcome.[56] Trying to state such a paradox theologically has allowed Greek metaphysics and its descendants to maintain control over the theological legacy of the Christian tradition to the exclusion of non-Greco-Roman oriented cultures, particularly those of Africa. Another phase in the relationship between Africa and the Christian faith often overlooked or underemphasized is the period during the Middle Ages up to the fifteenth century when various Christian monastic orders journeyed to Africa to missionize. Francis of Assisi, for example, visited Egypt in 1219 with some of his religious brothers, and the Dominicans visited Egypt in 1234 and later North Africa. Nor should we forget that monks accompanied the Portuguese and Spaniards as they exploited Africa's natural and human resources in the fifteenth century. In 1482,

55. See Edward Rochie Hardy, *Christian Egypt: Church and People: Christianity and Nationalism in the Patriarchate of Alexandria* (New York: Oxford Univ. Press, 1952), 111–76; H. Idris Bell, *Egypt: From Alexander the Great to the Arab Conquest* (Oxford, England: Clarendon Press, 1948), 101–34; Bell, "Evidences of Christianity in Egypt During the Roman Period," 185–208.

56. Cyril Richardson, *The Doctrine of the Trinity* (New York: Abingdon, 1958), 151–52.

the first mass in Ghana was celebrated at the coastal town of Elmina (Port.: *El Mina*; later Edina) at the foot of a tree where a Portuguese expedition under Diogo da Azambuja had landed in their search for gold and where they later built a fortress. One of those attending this historic occasion noted that they all had the hope "that the Church which they would found there might endure until the end of the world."[57] Requiem masses commemorating the dead were offered daily, as well as votive masses to the Blessed Virgin Mary.[58] The fortress, which still stands in Ghana, was dedicated to St. George (San Jorge) and named El Mina. It was taken by the Dutch in 1637.[59]

North Africa and the Christian Tradition

The nexus between Africa and the Christian tradition would not be complete without giving some attention to North Africa, which produced some of the church's most outstanding Latin-speaking theologians: Tertullian (c. 160–c. 225), Cyprian (died 258), and Augustine (354–430). Especially noteworthy are the Moors of North Africa. The Moors greatly influenced Christendom's view of blacks and blackness. Their origins as an African people began most likely as an amalgamation of the Maurs (Gk.: *mauros* = black, dark; Lat.: *maurus*; Sp.: *moro*; It.: *moro*; Port.: *mouro*; Fr.: *maure*), who lived in present-day northern Morocco and western Algeria, and the tawny-colored Berbers (Lat.: *barbari* = barbarians), who also lived in North Africa and were the descendants of light-skinned Libyans and black Arabs. The Romans, thinking of Africa as the territory from Egypt through the Fezzan and the west of the Sahara to what was then called Mauritania (modern Morocco and Algeria), identified all dark-skinned Africans as Moors.[60]

57. Debrunner, *History of Christianity in Ghana*, 17.

58. Sanneh, *West African Christianity*, 15–52.

59. The Africanist Basil Davidson says the name originally was El Mina ("the mine") because the Portuguese thought (correctly) that this would be their main location for discovering gold on the Gold Coast. *The African Slave Trade*, rev. ed. (Boston: Little, Brown, 1980), 28.

60. Wayne B. Chandler, "The Moor: Light of Europe's Dark Age," *African Presence in Early Europe*, ed. Ivan Van Sertima (New Brunswick, N.J.: Transaction Books, 1985), 151. Many historians, however, disagree that the Moors were black; they identify their color as tawny or light brown, the so-called "white Moors." Apparently, until the

Carthage (modern Tunisia) was conquered and colonized by the Romans in 146 B.C.E. during the Punic Wars, which Rome began as aggressor. Christianity in North Africa, which was largely Latinized, although the language of the Roman church was still Greek, dates from the second century. While it is not certain how Christianity got to North Africa, no mention is made of a Christian community before 180 C.E. and no bishops of Carthage are listed before Agrippinus at the beginning of the third century C.E.[61] The church in the West began to pay attention to North Africa in 183 C.E. when reports of the martyrdom of twelve Christians beheaded by the order of the proconsul in the town of Scilli circulated in Rome. Because of this event, North African Christians, much like Shiite Muslims in Iran under the teachings and leadership of Ayatollah Ruhollah Khomeini in the late twentieth century, identified themselves as a church of martyrs.

The Christian faith grew in North Africa and produced the first pope who was able to write in Latin, Victor I (189–199). By 220, Christianity had taken such roots that a synod was called that was attended by seventy-one bishops. Twenty years later some ninety bishops attended another synod. Furthermore, the threatening indigenous Donatist movement began in North Africa.

Called Donatists because they vigorously supported and rallied around Donatus the Great as Bishop of Carthage rather than the establishment candidate and the choice of Emperor Constantine, the former archdeacon Caecilian (311–c. 345), this indigenous North African nationalist movement accused Caecilian and other bishops who cooperated with the enemy during the Diocletian persecutions of being traitors and collaborators, and therefore unholy and unworthy of being bishops. Caecilian and other bishops, who had maintained contact with other branches of the church in the Roman Empire during this time, styled themselves the "catholic" church. Furthermore, the Catholic church had a self-interest in supporting the state and the status quo because it was also a great landowner and had accumulated a great deal of wealth. Catholic

---

eighteenth century the Dutch used *Moor* and *Morian* instead of *Negro* for black Africans and *Turk* for Muslims. Jack D. Forbes, *Black Africans and Native Americans: Color, Race and Caste in the Evolution of Red-Black Peoples* (Oxford, England: Basil Blackwell, 1988), 86.

61. W. H. C. Frend, *The Donatist Church: A Movement of Protest in Roman North Africa* (Oxford, England: Clarendon Press, 1952; reprint, 1985), 87.

monasteries in North Africa, for example, were established not in the desert, as was the tradition in Egypt, but in and near populated urban areas, where the Catholics were stronger and, says William Frend, perhaps the most authoritative student of Donatism, "where orchards promised (the monastery) a good return."⁶² (It should be noted that Donatist churches in cities and towns, though few, also enjoyed affluence.)

Donatism, with its power base in Numidia, was largely a movement of Christian peasants, who came mostly from Numidia and Roman Mauretania, though a number of their leaders were educated and cultivated in the thought and manners of the Romans. They protested the imperial established church, exploitative tax collectors, and wealthy landowners, who had collaborated with the pagan civil authorities during Diocletian's reign, and they disputed the validity of the consecration of Caecilian.⁶³ Their charge against the apostate bishops had a theological reason, namely that the Holy Spirit could not be in a church whose bishops were heretical. They also were convinced that the Caecilianists had "sold out" any sense of personal poverty and social justice and therefore had betrayed ideals of the early Christian church. "The Donatist [leaders] were revolutionary leaders in spite of their outward cultivated manners and tastes. They represented the will of an oppressed and embittered people whose religious fantasy and lust for revenge [the leaders] understood and knew how to direct."⁶⁴

62. Ibid., 328.
63. The British classicist A. H. M. Jones disputes that the Donatist movement was an indigenous nationalist movement. He points out that in the beginning the Donatists only insisted that the state and emperor not interfere in church affairs after the emperor rejected their appeal against the Caecilian party, i.e., the Catholics. A large proportion of the Donatists spoke Berber (a descendant of Libyan, an indigenous African language) and Punic (a Semitic language); because Roman Africa was a predominantly rural country, where few people spoke Latin—the language of the educated and intellectuals—the Donatist clergy spoke indigenous languages to communicate effectively. All surviving Donatist literature and church inscriptions, however, are in Latin, suggesting that not all the Donatists were peasants or spoke peasant languages. Jones claims that there is no evidence that the Donatist church proclaimed revolutionary teachings, such as a communism of wealth and goods or freeing all slaves or forgiving all debts. "Modern historians are retrojecting into the past the sentiments of the present age [where nationalism and socialism are powerful forces and provoke intense feelings] when they argue that mere religious or doctrinal dissension cannot have generated such violent and enduring animosity. . . ." A. H. M. Jones, "Were Ancient Heresies National or Social Movements in Disguise?" *Journal of Theological Studies* 10 (Oxford, England: Clarendon Press, 1959): 280–98.
64. Frend, *The Donatist Church*, 331.

Conventionally, we think of this area as Latinized because of the Roman occupying powers, but historically the mother tongues were Libyan (an African language), Punic (a Semitic language), and lastly Latin (the official language of the Romans).[65]

Constantine, fearing political instability in an already frayed realm, was forced to summon first a small synod of bishops in the Lateran and then a larger council in Arles, France, in the fourth century, which roundly condemned the Donatists. But the Donatists continued to grow in North Africa, so much so that by 336 some 270 North African bishops, including all in Numidia (present-day Algeria), supported the movement. By the end of the fourth century, Donatist bishops numbered some 400.

Soon the Donatists were supporting social and economic grievances in solidarity with dissatisfied peasants who called themselves "soldiers of Christ." They dispossessed wealthy landowners and redistributed their land. They also allied with Gildo, a political official and Berber chieftain, in sabotaging grain shipments headed for Rome from North African ports. This action threatened Rome's food supply and the empire's agricultural economy. In 398, a Roman expedition went to North Africa, captured Gildo, and stymied the movement, but Rome was unable to kill off the Donatists entirely. In the seventh and eighth centuries, with the spread of Islam to North Africa and its conquest of all of North Africa, Donatism effectively ended.

Black African scholars differ appreciably from European scholars in their assessment of Donatism in the development of an indigenous African Christianity. Mercy Oduyoye (Ghana) offers a populist interpretation of the Donatists. She singles out three major contributions by the Donatists: (1) the Christian gospel was intimately linked to what she calls the people's "primal religion," which includes an active engagement with the spirits and the social and economic environment in which the gospel is heard and fueled by a vision of a better life on this earth and after this life; (2) Christianity included a populist component in that the piety and theology of a people cannot be satisfied primarily

65. Frend charges that the confusion about the indigenous languages of North Africa can be laid to Augustine, who in his letters identified the indigenous language of the rural areas as Punic. In fact, while this was the language spoken by the inhabitants of Hippo and other Roman urban areas of Carthaginian origin and a local indigenous aristocracy in pre-Roman times, Libyan and later Berber were the mother tongues of Numidia and its plains. Frend, *The Donatist Church*, 50–57 *passim*.

by a philosophical or foreign elite and hierarchy, "but one born from the people's experience of God-in-action"; (3) conversation with the traditional religion of the culture was ongoing, proven by the fact that the few Berbers left in the Christian faith after Islam's conquest of North Africa developed a Christianity based on their own cultural institutions rather than relying simply on foreign imports.[66]

Lamin Sanneh (Gambia), in contrast, represents an assimilationist viewpoint. The Donatists proved that the church in North Africa, like the church elsewhere, had its orthodox followers, its dissidents, and its heretics: "In another way Africa was representative of the Church in other lands. . . . The Churches in Africa in our own day reflect this diversity of tradition, and a similar challenge of translating the Church's teaching into the local religious and cultural idiom."[67]

The British classics scholar A. H. M. Jones assesses Donatism's significance as: (1) a struggle between the peasant classes, many of whom had indeed been martyred during the persecutions, and the wealthy privileged classes, many of whom had either lapsed from the church or collaborated with the state, and needed episcopal justification for their actions and evasion, and (2) the occasion for a power play by the emperor within the church, whereby the church admitted that he had the right of adjudication in church and theological disputes as well as the privilege of calling synods and councils of bishops. But this recognition also increased the power of the state in the person of the emperor to confiscate church property, exile bishops, and inhibit religious gatherings. "The Church had acquired a protector, but it had also acquired a master."[68]

Ernst Troeltsch underscores the sociological and theological importance of the Donatist dispute. It polarized the opposition between the "church-type" development of Christian teaching and institutions with its emphasis on the sacramental-hierarchical and the "sect-type" development with its ascetical and exclusive emphasis aimed at keeping a distance between the world and the church: "[T]he sects, with their greater independence of the world, and their continual emphasis upon the original ideals of Christianity, often represent in a very direct and characteristic way the essential fundamental ideas of Christianity."[69]

66. Oduyoye, *Hearing and Knowing*, 23–24.
67. Sanneh, *West African Christianity*, 13.
68. A. H. M. Jones, *Constantine and the Conversion of Europe* (Harmondsworth, England: Penguin Books, 1972), 124–25.
69. Ernst Troeltsch, *The Social Teaching of the Christian Churches*, 2 vols., trans. Olive Wyon (New York: Harper & Row, 1960), 1:333–34.

The yoking of Egypt, Ethiopia, and blackness (even with its different hues) has been an issue for Westerners certainly since the thirteenth century B.C.E. The mythical beginnings of Ethiopia and the religious reverence for Egypt were influences in early Christian literature. While the ancients and the New Testament writers did not mean by "Africa" what we have meant by that name since the nineteenth century, there is little doubt that this land mass with its dark-skinned populations was more than a metaphor in early Christian thought. Hence, the conclusion of New Testament scholars to pass off references to Jesus and Egypt as only harking back to the Old Testament legacy is to be seriously questioned in light of what we know about the knowledge of this African country in the first and second centuries C.E. Likewise, that the Egyptians identified themselves as black or dark (*kmt*) can no longer be overlooked, as long as we do not confuse "black" with "Negroid." It is with this dark/black country that God intimately associates God's Son, the Messiah Jesus Christ. I cannot speculate about the theological consequences of God establishing such a link. It is an astonishing claim, which may have had deliberate apologetic objectives, given the esteem and reverence for Egypt as the origin of religion among the early Christians.

In summary, I have tried to demonstrate how Ethiopia and Egypt moved into Western consciousness and knowledge as specific geographical and cultural entities. The biblical tradition inherited by the Christians, however, also had a stigma attached to blackness, as evident in the legend about Ham. This legend and others, as we shall see, reappear later in the Middle Ages as Christendom and Western culture were trying to define Africans and determine their ontological and moral status. The Ham legend has been a part of the mythic structure about blackness and the inferiority of blacks that comes up again and again in Western thought. It was also crucial during the colonial period in America.

Egypt and Ethiopia had important roles in the development of the Christian tradition, particularly the city of Alexandria and the Coptic Church, even during the christological controversies between what I call European Catholicism (which included Latinized North Africa) and African Catholicism, which was puzzled about the Greek metaphysics of Chalcedon. The Monophysite struggle was not simply theological, it was also political and cultural. Likewise, Egypt is linked traditionally with one of Jesus' disciples, Mark, as the founder of Christianity in that country. North Africa not only produced some of the most outstanding Latin thinkers; it also was the site of one of the earliest attempts of indigenous people in Africa to depart from orthodoxy in shaping the character of Christianity. This is not unlike the nineteenth- and twentieth-century dynamic emergence of the African independent churches in sub-Saharan Africa, the fastest-growing churches in modern Africa.

The mythic underpinning of blackness intensified as early Christians identified blackness and Ethiopia with sin and the devil, as we shall see. This intensified negativity was added to beliefs about the erotic character of blacks inherited from the Greeks and the Romans, particularly in the Latin-speaking theologians such as Jerome.

3 | Blackness as Evil and Sex in Early Christian Thought

*D*uring the formative years of the Christian church in the Roman Empire, blackness not only had a distinctive negative connotation, but also was personalized as the devil. The New Testament scholar and classicist Rudolf Bultmann traces this change in the concept of blackness, on the one hand, to the downfall of the Greek *polis* as the military and societal anchor for much of ancient Greek thinking and, on the other hand, to the subsequent influence of Persian astrological beliefs about the sun exported into the Roman Empire during the Hellenistic period. This Persian influence also transformed the ancient Greco-Roman understanding of light/dark and white/ black. It moved from a Greek aesthetic to a cosmic drama of good and evil, which both rabbinic Judaism and early Christianity inherited and constructed into doctrines. Light/white became synonymous with spirit, which in turn became identified with divine godly power and good, and dark/black came to represent the imprisoning evil material world.[1]

In the Old Testament, for example, Satan (Heb.: *stn*) is a member of the heavenly court with particular tasks.[2]

1. Rudolf Bultmann, "Zur Geschichte der Lichtsymbolik im Altertum," *Philologus* 97 (Heft 1/2, 1948), 12, 23–26.
2. Neil Forsyth points out that *stn* vocalized as *Satan* resembles the Greek *skandalon*—something blocking the right path—or our

Second Isaiah adds a new theological claim: that Israel was intended by God to be "a light to the nations," which extends to all of history. (Ironically, both the American colonies and Afrikaner South Africa made this biblical claim the basis of their Manifest Destiny doctrines.) God is the creator of light and darkness, good and evil (Isa. 45:4-9; cf. Job 10:8-9).[3] It is within this theological change that *Satan* appears in Job, not as a proper name, but as a title equivalent to what we might call "Attorney General" or "Public Prosecutor," a member of the heavenly establishment. "The primary function of the heavenly court was judgment, and it thus mirrored the conflicts it was called upon to judge and would eventually be unable to restore its own unity. It was in the Satan figure, himself a member of the heavenly court and in many ways parallel to the *mal'ak Yahweh* (messenger of God) that the tensions within the monotheistic faith would emerge most clearly."[4]

By the time of the Chronicles in the Old Testament, however, Satan had assumed an autonomy and acts without God's permission, though not necessarily as an evil being. In the *Book of Jubilees* (c. 104 B.C.E.) the prince of the hostile angels, Mastema (Heb.: *stm* = enmity), does the wrathful acts that God performs in the Torah (for example, in Genesis and Exodus). Since the names Mastema and Satan have a similar linguistic root, they became interchangeable in the popular mind. "Thus the role of Satan as accuser, prosecutor, and tempter is included within the more general function of an enmity to Israel." However, Jubilees also makes a distinction between Mastema and Satan.[5]

Certainly during the Hellenistic period (323–30 B.C.E.), under the influence of Persian religion and dualism, Satan's function changed from

---

English word *opponent*, meaning "to place in the way" or "to obstruct." Most uses of *stn* in the Old Testament therefore are linked to scandal (from Gk.: *skandalon*). Neil Forsyth, *The Old Enemy: Satan and the Combat Myth* (Princeton, N.J.: Princeton Univ. Press, 1987), 113.

3. Ibid., 108–9.

4. Ibid., 112. In Zech. 4:10, however, Satan is scolded by Yahweh's angel (*mal'ak Yahweh*) for going too far and needing some restraint. Forsyth claims that here the role of Satan has changed from that of the public official whose mandate is given him by God to a public official acting on his own, thereby not only exceeding his office as public prosecutor, but also trying to act independently of his creator. "Now we sense for the first time a genuine danger to the solid monotheism of II Isaiah. This public official entrusted with the duties of seeking out and accusing unjust men now threatens to exceed the limits of his office, e.g., a J. Edgar Hoover [as in the case of Martin Luther King, Jr.] or a CIA director who no longer clears his every move with the President." Ibid., 115.

5. Ibid., 182, 188.

that of a rebellious angel (1 Sam. 16:14) and servant of God allowed to roam the earth and test Job (Job 1:6) to that of a primordial force of evil and opponent of God in the cosmic battle between good and evil. If Bultmann is correct, then contrary to what such classicists as Frank Snowden and Christopher Rowe claim about blackness and whiteness not having any moral significance in classical Greek thought, certainly by the first century C.E. both in Jewish and Jewish-Christian circles light/whiteness came to be associated with good and dark/blackness with evil. By the time of the first Christian theological writings, many in the early church allied light/white with God and darkness/black with sin and evil (cf. Eph. 4:17-19), the devil or Satan and demons.

The color black particularly fascinated many early Christian patristic theologians because it was the color of the Ethiopian in the famous Old Testament text in the Song of Songs (1:5-6) and the New Testament text about the baptism of the Ethiopian eunuch ("And behold, an Ethiopian, a eunuch, a minister of Candace, queen of the Ethiopians . . . had come to Jerusalem to worship . . ." [Acts 8:27-40]). But the Old Testament attaches no particular moral significance to the color black.[6] The Greek-language Septuagint translates the Hebrew "I am black *and* beautiful"; the Latin Vulgate by Jerome resisted the theological implications of the Greek *Nigra sum et pulchra* and instead renders it in the Latin *Nigra sum sed formosa*: "I am black *but* comely" (or "beautifully formed"). (Cf. RSV: "I am very dark, but comely.")

Even when the prophet Jeremiah speaks about the skin color of Ethiopians (that is, Africans)—"Can the Ethiopian change his skin or the leopard his spots?" (13:23)—the reference is rhetorical rather than pejorative.[7] Ezekiel 30:18 speaks of the "day [which] shall be dark," and Ezek. 32:7 speaks of God blotting out the heavens and making the stars dark. In both cases, Latin manuscripts render the Hebrew for "dark" as *nigresco* (Lat.: *niger* = black). Likewise, in the New Testament only Matthew ("you cannot make one hair white or black" [5:36]) and Revelation (6:5, 12) mention the color black (*melas*).

6. See Gen. 30:35, 40; Lev. 13:31; Song of Sol. 5:11; Zech. 6:2, 6:6.

7. David Adamo also says this text is not meant to be anti-black. It is Jeremiah declaring judgment on the deep-seated evil and wickedness in Judah at the time, which has become like an unbreakable habit. See his "The African and Africans in the Old Testament and its Environment," Ph.D. diss., Baylor University, 1986, 190.

Blackness in the Christian
Apocrypha

In the *Epistle of Barnabas* (c. 70–117), however, the devil is personalized as the "Black One," an opponent of Christ who is a constant, ever-present threat to Christians: "Wherefore let us pay heed to the last days, for the whole time of our life and faith will profit us nothing, unless we resist, as becomes the sons of God in the present evil time . . . that the Black One (*ho melas*) may have no opportunity of entry" (4:9).[8] In contrast to the way of Light, overseen by "light-bringing angels of God," the way of "the Lord from eternity to eternity" (18:1-2), and the Christian life (19:1-12), the way of the Black One is the way of Darkness overseen by "angels of Satan" (18:1); Satan is the "ruler of the present time of iniquity":

> But the Way of the Black One [*melanos*] is crooked and full of cursing, for it is the way of death eternal with punishment, and in it are the things that destroy their soul: double-heartedness, adultery, murder, robbery, pride, transgression, malice, self-sufficiency, enchantments, magic, covetousness, the lack of the fear of God. (20:1-2)[9]

Jesus Christ as the lord of light will redeem Christians from the way of darkness and "prepare a holy people for himself" (14:6).

Some might claim that this view of blackness is simply derived from the classical Greek aesthetics about light and dark and natural opposites. Others think this view of blackness reflects first-century mainstream Jewish and Ebionite (a first-century Jewish Christian sect that had its own apocryphal gospel) influences. The devil is black because he has fallen from the grace and whiteness of God; he subsequently tries to subvert God's creation by moving humankind from Christ's kingdom of light to his own kingdom of evil and darkness. Because the present

8. The Greek and an English translation can be found in *The Apostolic Fathers*, ed. and trans. Kirsopp Lake, vol. 1, Loeb Classical Library (Cambridge, Mass.: Harvard Univ. Press, 1959), 14.

9. For a intriguing proposal about the significance of brownish green as the color of Lucifer and of the dead Christ in Matthias Grünewald's Isenheim altarpiece (1512–16), see Ruth Mellinkoff, *The devil at Isenheim: Reflections of Popular Belief in Grünewald's Altarpiece*, California Studies in the History of Art (Berkeley: Univ. of California Press, 1988), 19–31.

age stands under the influence of the devil, only those who have been "whitened" by God can gain spiritual purity and wholeness.[10]

Other prominent early Christian texts viewed blackness as a primordial negative force. The *Acts of Peter* (c. 180–200) says Satan is black and an enemy of Christ, "the source of wickedness and abyss of darkness," who shoots poisoned arrows at the souls of innocent Christians.[11] One narrative tells of a Christian who has a vision in which a female demon appears. She is described as "a most evil-looking woman, who resembled an Ethiopian." But the writer distinguishes quite pointedly between the complexions of Ethiopians and Egyptians, saying the Ethiopian-looking demon was "not Egyptian, but altogether black."

The *Testament of Abraham* (late first century C.E.) tells how Death in conversation with Abraham ridded himself of "all the beauty and loveliness and all the glory and sunlike form" at creation and instead assumed a new appearance: "dark and more fierce than any sort of beast, and more unclean than any uncleanness."[12] Likewise, the *Acts of Thomas* (second century) links blackness and evil in the story of a man

> hateful of countenance, entirely black, and his clothing exceedingly dirty. And he led me to a place in which there were many chasms, and much ill odor and a hateful vapor was given off thence. And he made me look down into each chasm, and I was in the (first) chasm a flaming fire. . . . But there was none to deliver. And that man said to me: "These souls are kindred to thee, and in the days of reckoning they were delivered for punishment and destruction."[13]

10. Frank M. Snowden, Jr., *Before Color Prejudice* (Cambridge, Mass.: Harvard Univ. Press, 1983), 100; see also Jeffrey Burton Russell, *The Devil: Perceptions of Evil from Antiquity to Primitive Christianity* (Ithaca, N.Y.: Cornell Univ. Press, 1977), 62–66. The theological implications of the devil as evil blackness with demons as his soldiers in the world are even more portentous when we recall the acrimonious confrontation between Jesus and other Jews in the Gospel of John. Jesus accuses the Jews: "You are of your father the devil, and your will is to do your father's desires. He was a murderer from the beginning, and has nothing to do with the truth, because there is no truth in him" (8:44). In turn, the Jews accuse Jesus of being possessed by a demon (8:48, 52).

11. Edgar Hennecke and Wilhelm Schneemelcher, eds., *New Testament Apocrypha*, vol. 2, trans. R. McL. Wilson (Philadelphia: Westminster 1976), 291; also Jeffrey Burton Russell, *Satan: The Early Christian Tradition* (Ithaca, N.Y.: Cornell Univ. Press, 1981), 62.

12. *The Testament of Abraham: The Greek Recensions*, trans. Michael E. Stone (Missoula, Mont.: Scholars Press for the Society of Biblical Literature, 1972), 47.

13. Hennecke and Schneemelcher, *New Testament Apocrypha*, 2:473.

As we have seen, the Old Testament includes no antecedents for such a depiction and interpretation of personalizing the devil or Satan as the "Black One" and evil as "black." Nor are there precedents in the Septuagint or the Mishnah. Moreover, even though both versions of the Talmud (Babylonian: c. fifth century C.E.; Palestinian: c. sixth century C.E.) include commentaries from the second century onward, their use of the Hebrew word *shachor* ("black") has no moral significance. *Shahar* describes the color of hair, ink, blood, leather, animals, textiles such as wool, and certain fruits. Where the Talmud does describe a person's complexion, a negative aesthetic tone is intended, but it is not linked to evil. A light complexion was preferred because a dark complexion was considered indicative of extreme malnutrition or even starvation.[14]

Blackness as a symbol of evil acquired a new, more malevolent attribute in second-century Christian belief through the doctrine of privation, or what we might call deprivation: God as perfect being is totally good; the devil, deficient in perfection and goodness, is evil. Privation means a deficiency of good and real being as intended by God for creation. Karl Barth says privation is similar to what the Germans call "nothingness" (*das Nichtige*): the "shadow side of creation."[15] Evil is that which God did not will at creation:

> Nothingness is that which God does not will. It lives only by the fact that it is that which God does not will. But it does live by this fact. For not only what God wills, but what He does not will, is potent, and must have a real correspondence. . . . The first and most impressive mention of nothingness in the Bible is to be found at the beginning of Gen. 1:2, in which there is a reference to the chaos which the Creator has already rejected, negated, passed over and abandoned even before He utters His first creative Word. . . .[16]

It is interesting to note that in the Old Testament red and sometimes white, not black, are the colors associated with sin and evil.[17] The French scholar Jean Devisse observes that this may account for Jerome's insistence on degrading the color black by identifying it with the devil

14. BT Bekorot 45b; Nedarim 65b–66a; Ketubot 10b; Sotah 12a; Moèd Katan 27a.
15. Karl Barth, *Church Dogmatics*, vol. 3/3: *The Doctrine of Creation*, trans. G. W. Bromiley and R. J. Ehrlich (Edinburgh: T.& T. Clark, 1960), 302–48.
16. Ibid., 352.
17. See Isa. 1:18.

(although he may also be reflecting the Greco-Roman tradition about black as the color of evil and death). Isaiah, one of the most prominent biblical figures, said that a cleansed and purified Israel would be a beacon light of salvation for all other nations, including black Ethiopia (Isa. 56; 66:19). But certain patristic scholars found this claim at odds with the great commission in Matthew's Gospel, which claimed that all nations will be called to Jesus Christ; hence they deemphasized the theological implications of universality in Isaiah by transforming blackness to mean the darkness of sin:

> For the Byzantines Africa and Egypt were not lands unknown and unimportant, and their tradition diverged sharply from the Latin. The latter, originating in its broad lines with Jerome, was encumbered with the notion that black was the color of sin and death and was troubled by the reaction against Origen's liberalism, which threw the doors of salvation wide open to all peoples. Jerome, determined to make no concession to the Old Testament or to the Jews who refused to recognize the divinity of Jesus, simply abandoned Africa, a land foreign to Judaism as well as to Christianity.[18]

I think the doctrine of privation was a matter of particular urgency for the patristics as a theological defense of Greco-Roman metaphysical claims that held together their vision of the world, namely, that absolute cosmic unity and order as the ideal is to be reflected in this material world. Evil represented chaos and nothingness as potent forces in a power struggle that goes on cosmologically and on earth. Hence, blackness as a visual reminder was both a sign of the primal inferior being of the devil fallen from the light of Christ and a sign of cosmic disorder and nonbeing. Blackness meant malevolence. Cultures and peoples stained, even allegorically, with this mark of privation were thus seen as an outward and visible reminder of the threat of nonbeing and annihilation of the good, at least in the Latin fathers. (Is it not significant, as we shall see later, that when the Portuguese began the African slave trade in the fifteenth century, they first baptized the black souls of the black heathens before selling them at auction, an action sanctioned by the Pope?)

18. Jean Devisse, *The Image of the Black in Western Art*, vol. 2/i: *From the Demonic Threat to the Incarnation of Sainthood*, trans. William Granger Ryan (New York: William Morrow, 1979), 59.

Origen: First Apostle
of Blackness

Origen (c. 185–c. 254), an Egyptian African from Alexandria, was the
first Christian to transform blackness from a negative affirmation of evil
to a positive witness to the divine good by linking blackness to Jesus
Christ himself. In his exegesis of the well-known text in the Song of
Songs ("I am black and beautiful, O ye daughters of Jerusalem, as the
tents of Kedar, as the curtains of Solomon. Do not consider me because
I am black (swarthy), because the sun has scorched me."), he writes in
his *Homilies on the Song of Songs* that the black bride represents the
Gentile church, the bride of Christ. She is black because she continues
the legacy of Moses' bride, who was Ethiopian (Num. 12:1-16). That
marriage represented a union between the law and the Gentiles outside
the traditional requirements of the law. Because she was black, the
Ethiopian was rejected by her sisters, the daughters of Abraham (that
is, the Jews), who also rejected the Gentiles.[19]

As we know, Origen and the church fathers used allegory to perform
exegesis on Scripture. Thus, it is theologically significant that the black
bride represents the Gentile church, the vehicle for continuing God's
revelation of salvation in Jesus Christ. The allegorical method (a legacy
from Greek metaphysics) said that obvious material symbols in our
world reveal less obvious eternal and profound truths about God. Allegory, which dominated Christian interpretation of the Bible up to the
end of the Middle Ages, generally meant three things: (1) the written
meaning; (2) the moral or hidden meaning progressing toward perfection
in human conduct; and (3) the mystical or spiritual meaning that reveals
the mysteries and truth of God. Joseph Trigg reminds us:

> Allegory was not just a code language, it was an awesome, powerful
> means of conveying the truth, well adapted to pique the curiosity of the
> learned and to compel the respect of the simple. . . . This tradition
> began with Jews at Alexandria who were convinced that the faith of their

---

19. The Jewish historian Josephus (first century C.E.) said that Moses actually lived
in Ethiopia for some time between his fortieth and eightieth years. Flavius Josephus,
Jewish Antiquities, vol. 4, trans. H. St. J. Thackeray, Loeb Classical Library (Cambridge,
Mass.: Harvard Univ. Press, 1978), 269–75; cf. Louis Ginzberg, *Legends of the Jews*, 7
vols. (Philadelphia: Jewish Publication Society of America, 1909), 2:286–89.

fathers was more consistent with the highest aspirations of Hellenism than the polytheistic and morally unstrenuous religion of the Greeks.[20]

For this reason, Origen thinks it theologically and morally important to remind us that blackness in this passage is accidental. It refers only to something skin deep and superficial in terms of Christian perfection and salvation. The skin of the bride is black, but her soul is white and pure.[21] Yet in spite of this, God elects blackness to reveal eternal truths, even in Moses' marriage to the Ethiopian woman. Miriam's and Aaron's resentment toward the Ethiopian woman prefigures the resentment of the Jews toward the Gentile church as the receptacle of God's new revelation in Christ. Interestingly, God's rebuke of Miriam's rejection is shown in Miriam being turned *white*—the negative sign associated with lepers.[22] The Ethiopian woman is the Gentile church that has been chosen in spite of her lowly, obscure origins and color to receive the Son of God, "who is the Image of God, the Firstborn of every creature and who is the brightness of the glory and the express Image of the substance of God. . . ."[23]

Yet at the same time Origen was ambivalent about the moral significance of blackness. Blackness means sin and privation. The bride's color is a scorching and a stain that will pass away in eternity, but it is also congenital for all Africans:

> She shows that she is not speaking of bodily blackness, because the sun is wont to tan or blacken when it looks *at*, and not when it looks down *on* anyone. And it is commonly said among the whole of the Ethiopian race, in which there is a certain natural blackness inherited by all, that in those parts the sun burns with fiercer rays, and that bodies that have once been scorched and darkened, transmit a congenital stain to their posterity.[24]

20. Joseph Wilson Trigg, *Origen: The Bible and Philosophy in the Third-Century Church* (Atlanta: John Knox Press, 1983), 123.

21. Origen, *The Song of Songs: Commentary and Homilies*, trans. R. P. Lawson (London: Green and Co., 1957), *passim*.

22. "And the anger of the LORD was kindled against them, and he departed; and when the cloud removed from over the tent, behold, Miriam was leprous, as white as snow. And Aaron turned towards Miriam, and behold, she was leprous. And Aaron said to Moses, 'Oh, my lord, do not punish us because we have done foolishly and have sinned. Let her not be as one dead' " (Num. 12:9-12). I thank Prof. Jacob Neusner, who generously called this part of Hebrew tradition to my attention.

23. Origen, *The Song of Songs*, 93.

24. Ibid., 107.

The soul as the link to the divine is only scorched or stained, not permanently black. Blackness comes from neglect and sloth, not from congenital sin. With disciplined spiritual exercises, blackness can be changed to its intended color of whiteness. In the case of the bride as the bride of Christ, her soul is really white. Athanasius (c. 296–373), a fellow African also from Alexandria and the great defender of the Catholic faith, followed Origen in believing that the devil was nothingness and therefore black. The devil was devilish in that he could transform himself into different shapes, varying from an angel of light to a giant in the air able to prevent Christians from ascending to heaven, to a black boy, a sure sign of darkness and evil character as well as inherent inferiority over against the superior power of Christ.[25]

Jerome: First Theological Critic of Blackness

Christianity poisoned eros, Friedrich Nietzsche is reputed to have said. It is not without significance that the Old Testament legend of Ham as the progenitor of blacks also includes a sexual component, namely Ham's forbidden carnal knowledge of his father's nudity. Jerome (342–420) was the first Christian theologian to link blackness with carnal knowledge and erotic action, although the monk Saint Pachomius (c. 298–346) linked the devil with sensuality.

Jerome, first translator of the Latin Bible, in his Vulgate rendering of Origen's Song of Songs, says, "I am black *but* comely [*formosa*]." He personalizes blackness as the symbol of sin and evil. Citing Moses' marriage to the Ethiopian, he says that after the Ethiopian hears the wisdom of Christ, her black skin will change to white.[26] "For what fellowship hath light with darkness? And what concord hath Christ with Belial? What has Horace to do with the Psalter, Virgil with the Gospels, Cicero with Paul?"[27]

In a homily on Psalm 7 ("A plaintive song of David which he sang to the Lord because of Chusi the son of Jemini" [RSV: "which he sang to the LORD concerning Cush a Benjaminite"]), Jerome says that *Chus*

25. Russell, *Satan*, 170.
26. *The Letters of St. Jerome*, vol. 1, trans. Charles Christopher Mierow (Westminster, Md.: Newman Press; London: Longmans, Green, 1963), Letter 22.1(5), 135.
27. Ibid., Letter 22.29(6), 165.

is Hebrew for Ethiopian—one who is "black and dark, one who has a soul as black as his body." Chusi thus is the Ethiopian devil. This claim that the Ethiopian is actually the devil went beyond the prevailing tradition at the time.[28] Even Origen believed that although the outward limbs of the Ethiopian were black, her blackness did not make her akin to the devil.

Chusi symbolizes Saul, who was David's "black and dark enemy. . . . Just as the Ethiopian cannot change his skin, Saul cannot change his character." Ethiopians were created by God as was all of humanity, but in spite of this they are black because of vice; the Ethiopian represents the devil, a roaring lion, who is the adversary that stalks Christians to devour them. "The devil is a snake . . . the very serpent who spoke to Eve." "He is called a snake because the whole of his body moves on the ground."

> Because Chusi, that is, our Ethiopian, is himself the lion. . . . Because he is pregnant with inequity and has brought forth failure . . . he has been sent into hell, and so "his mischief shall recoil upon his own head; upon the crown of his head his violence shall rebound."[29]

Jerome is also one of the first theologians to link blackness to carnal lust and sexual prowess. In a letter (c. 384) to the young noblewoman Eustochium entrusted to his care by her mother Paula during the former's stay in Rome, Jerome commends virginity and abstinence as desirous Christian virtues and warns her not to be tempted by the devil. The devil is black like the night, in which the "beasts of the woods go about, the young lions roaring after their prey and seeking their meat from God."[30] Furthermore, the devil's "strength is in his loins, and his power is in his navel" with "inordinate sexual powers."[31] Jerome gives this exegesis of this reference in the Psalms:

> For the sake of propriety, the male and female organs of generation are called by other names. Hence the promise that one from the loins of

28. *The Homilies of Saint Jerome,* vol. 1, trans. Marie Liguori Ewald (Washington, D.C.: Catholic Univ. of America Press, 1963), Homily 3, 28.

29. Ibid., 34. In letters to Oceanus in 394 (Letter 69) and his charge Eustochium in 404, (Letter 108), however, Jerome says that even though it is unnatural, through Christian baptism the Ethiopian can change his black skin to white and the leopard can change his spots.

30. *The Letters of St. Jerome,* Letter, 22.11(2), 137.

31. Ibid., 143; see also Russell, *Satan,* 190.

David is to sit upon his throne. . . . Accordingly, all the strength of the
devil against men is in the loins, all his force against women is in the
navel.[32]

This linking of the black devil with imprudent erotic lust may have
several sources: (1) a throwback to the satyrs (Lat.: *faun*) of Greek
mythology, who, as we have seen, were portrayed in Greek art with
Negroid features and in Greek mythology and drama with superior
sexual powers and fertility;[33] (2) the belief among Romans that the warm
climate of Ethiopia caused Africans to be very sensuous and oversexed;[34]
(3) the rise of Neoplatonism in the third and fourth centuries in Roman
educated circles with its sharp contrast between the One, who is Being
beyond all being and the material world; and (4) the lingering influence
of Persian religions, such as Zoroastrianism, during the formation of
rabbinic Judaism and early Christian thought in the first century, and
Manichaeism in third- and fourth-century Roman intellectual circles.
Their cosmologies emphasized the struggle between light, which was
good, and darkness, which was evil. Mani taught that this struggle went
on in the material world; we should seek purgation through asceticism
and abstinence from the world.

Jerome emphasizes the negativity of blackness in his commentary on
Ps. 68:31 ("let Ethiopia hasten to stretch out her hands to God") in his
Tractatus in Psalmos: "[Since] we were black because of our sins and
passions, we have taken the lead over the people of Israel and we believe

32. Ibid., 144.
33. When the eighteenth-century French painter Antoine Watteau depicted the
seduction of Antiope by Jupiter, he painted Jupiter as a brown-skinned muscular satyr
in the act of seducing the sleeping white beauty. Eugéne Le Poitevin painted erotic
lithographs in which a black satyr devil with an exposed and erect phallus is clearly
the culprit. In one of his pictures a woman uses the extended genitals of the black devil
to water the garden; in another, black devils are seen deflowering a young white virgin.
See Bradley Smith, *Erotic Art of the Masters: The 18th, 19th, and 20th Centuries* (Secaucus,
N.J.: L. Stuart, 1974), 68.
34. One scholar notes that after the Romans occupied Egypt, "the increasing interest
in phallic art and the myths and legends about the African's eroticism led wealthy
Romans to new adventures in sex. They began to import black mistresses. Sometimes
they bought black women at high prices from traders along the shores of the Mediterranean, or from army generals returning from the wars. . . . Big black men were
brought from Africa to provide the desired pleasures for women in private chambers
and at gaudy banquets that frequently degenerated into more licentious orgies." Bernard
Braxton, *Women, Sex and Race* (Washington, D.C.: Verta Press, 1973), 62.

in the Savior, as the woman with the issue of blood came ahead of the daughter of the ruler of the synagogue and recovered her health" (Matt. 9.20-22). Blackness signifies sin:

> *People of the Ethiopians* means those who are black, being covered with the stain of sin. In the past we were Ethiopians, being made so by our sins and vices. How? Because sin had made us black. But then we heeded Isaiah (1.16)—"Wash yourselves, be clean"—and we said, "Thou shalt wash me, and I shall be made whiter than snow" (Ps. 50[51]:9). Thus we, Ethiopians that we were, transformed ourselves and became white.[35]

The moral and social values attached to black skin emerged early in the formation of the Christian tradition. The interplay between curiosity, ambiguity and ambivalence, and the sensual were joined with the devil as the symbol of evil and sin to confirm traditional myths and establish new myths about blackness and black skin. Saint Pachomius, founder of communal (*koinos bios = coenobitic* = common life) monasticism and of the first monastic order to live a common rule of prayer and daily routine of work,[36] told of a vision in which the devil appears as a black girl to tempt and seduce him. Pachomius drives her away with a slap in the dream, but maintained that her stench stayed on his hand for two years afterward.[37]

During the patristic period, various anecdotes circulated that characterized the Ethiopian as a demon or a devil bent on sabotaging Christian spirituality and Christian liturgy. One anecdote told of Melania the Younger (c. 383–438), who together with her husband fled the Goths in Rome for North Africa, where they founded two monasteries at Tagaste in modern Algeria. She argued theology with the devil, who was disguised as a black and defended the heretic Nestorius (died c. 451). She managed to overcome the devil by evoking Christ, but for six days afterward suffered groin pains that attacked everyday at the same hour she had had her discussion with the black devil.[38]

35. Quoted in Jean Marie Courtès, "The Theme of 'Ethiopia' and 'Ethiopians' in Patristic Literature," *Image of the Black in Western Art*, 2/i:27.

36. According to Jerome, three types of monasticism existed in Egypt: (1) the cenobites, (2) the anchorites, those who lived alone in the desert, and (3) the *remnuoth*, who were autonomous communities of two or three monks in or near urban areas who pooled their earnings in a joint fund. *The Letters of St. Jerome*, 169–70.

37. Russell, *Satan*, 171.

38. This and other anecdotes are recounted in Courtès, "The Theme of 'Ethiopia' and 'Ethiopians' " 19–21.

The Later Empire

The negative mythic understanding of blackness continued throughout the Roman Empire of early Christianity. We can see this in Julian the Apostate (332–363; emperor, 361–363), nephew of the Roman emperor Constantine and declared an apostate by the established church because he favored non-Christian and pagan religions. Julian insisted that Greek philosophical thought proved the natural supremacy of Greeks and Romans over ethnic groups. Why is it, he asks, that Celts and Germans are prone to fierceness and war while Greeks and Romans are predisposed to a gentler and more civilized life, yet able to be resolute and aggressive during times of war? Why are there differences between such races as the Egyptians, who are more intelligent and proficient in technology, and the Syrians, who are unwarlike but hot-tempered and full of vanity? Julian insists that these ethnic differences are due to a natural order according to a divine-given "spirit of humanity":

> How utterly different are the bodies of Germans and Scythians from those of Libyans and Ethiopians! Surely this difference is not to be ascribed to any empty *fiat*, but climate and country operate jointly with the gods to determine even color.[39]

It is interesting to note that Ambrose (339–397), bishop of Milan, who was instrumental in the conversion of Augustine of Hippo, thought it important to explain how flesh could be both black and beautiful. Blackness accumulates from the body's struggle with sin, but the grace of Jesus Christ gives it a spiritual ointment that washes away this undesirable stain. To eradicate the blackness of sin, Ambrose sacramentalizes the struggle through baptism, which consecrates the cleansed flesh that was originally exiled from God through Eve. Baptism reconciles this sinful black flesh to God via the Blessed Virgin Mary, the new Eve.[40]

Moreover, Ambrose contrasted the negative character of blackness with the positive character of whiteness in matters of heresy in the church. Before, the church was "black in broad daylight," but after ridding itself of such heresies as Manichaeism and Arianism, the church is now

39. Quoted in Charles Norris Cochrane, *Christianity and Classical Culture: A Study of Thought and Action from Augustus to Augustine* (Oxford, England: Univ. Press, 1957), 276.
40. Courtès, " 'The Theme of Ethiopia' and 'Ethiopians,' " 17.

white. "The daughters of Jerusalem who wonder at the coming of the Bride, now whitened [*dealbata*], represent the Old Law contemplating the new sacrament."[41]

Even Augustine (354–430), himself a North African though there is little evidence that he was black (rather he was most likely of Berber descent), claims that all people are black like the Ethiopians until they find salvation in Christ:

> Those are called to the faith who were black, just they, so that it may be said to them, "Ye were sometimes darkness but now are ye light in the Lord." They were indeed called black but let them not remain black, for out of these is made the church to whom it is said: "Who is she that cometh up having been made white?"[42]

Thus, the hierarchy of color in early Christianity enlarged the Greco-Roman aesthetic of blackness and endowed it with a moral disadvantage, namely evil and sin. These associations shaped the perception of blacks by Christians. A good illustration is the story of a fourth-century Ethiopian monk, Abba Moses (c. 320–407), a black slave (although "Ethiopian" may have been a synonym for his black skin, as was the tradition at that time).[43]

According to the legend, Moses had a great physique and enormous muscular strength and was a thief, a bandit, and a sexual libertine before he joined an Egyptian monastery.[44] During his life in the monastery, Abba Moses was known as a strict holy man: "All the monks regarded

41. Ibid., 18.

42. Augustine, *Enarrationes in Psalmos* 73.16. Quoted in Snowden, *Before Color Prejudice*, 104.

43. Some scholars suggest he may have been Nubian. See Kathleen O'Brien Wicker, "Ethiopian Moses," in *Ascetic Behavior in Greco-Roman Antiquity*, ed. Vincent L. Wimbush (Minneapolis: Fortress Press, 1990), 331. Nubia itself received the first Christian missionaries in 543 at Faras, the capital of the northern Nubian kingdom of Nobatia. The missionaries had been sent and financed by Empress Theodora, wife of Justinian and partisan for the Monophysites. The rival Nubian kingdom of Makuria in turn received missionaries favoring Chalcedon in 569. Greek was the liturgical language and the Byzantine liturgy prevailed in early Nubian Christianity. See R. A. Caulk, "North-East Africa before the Rise of Islam," in *The Cambridge Encyclopedia of Africa*, ed. Roland Oliver and Michael Crowder (Cambridge, England: Cambridge Univ. Press, 1981), 111.

44. A fourteenth-century Italian manuscript depicts a nude Moses swimming across the Nile with some sheep he plundered from a shepherd. See Devisse, *Image of the Black in Western Art*, 2/i: 113; cf. Wicker, "Ethiopian Moses," 336, 344.

Moses as father, shepherd, leader, for thus had the most Holy Spirit
determined. . . . The desert, the mountains, the city, and all the surrounding areas all resounded with Moses, Moses, Moses."[45]

The other monks objected to Moses' presence in the community
because he was black. At his ordination to the priesthood, the ordaining
archbishop said to him, "Behold, you have become completely white."
Moses replied; "Indeed, the outside, O Lord Father; would that the
inside were also white."[46] The other monks, however, remained unsa-
tisfied and continued to harass him until he was driven from the monastery, chiding, "Go away, Ethiopian."

Abba Moses was thrown into severe self-doubt about his blackness:
"Rightly, have they treated you, ash skin, black one. As you are not a
man, why should you come among men?" Some pilgrims who wanted
to meet this famed holy man came to the monastery to enquire about
him; unknowingly they met Moses, who was in disguise. They asked
the disguised Moses where they might find the monk. Moses replied:
"What do you want with him? He is an imbecile."[47]

If ancient Egyptians understood their color to be black (*kmt*), then
the abuse of Moses because of his dark color may indicate several things:
(1) As the ancient Greeks and Romans made color distinction between
the Egyptians, the Ethiopians, and other Africans, so these Egyptian
monks may also be reflecting that caste system within the Egyptian
Christian community—a caste system similar to that found in black
American society and in Caribbean and Latin American countries. (2)
The Egyptian monks (and Moses) may have internalized the Christian
belief that blackness and black skin represented a stain and symbol of
evil and carnality—a belief affirmed by the archbishop, who said after
the ordination that Moses was "white." As rigorous ascetics whose spiritual ideal was holiness, the monks may have wanted to distance themselves and their community from such an aberration in God's creation.
(3) The Egyptian monks may have been exhibiting cultural ethnocentric
behavior as heirs of an ancient land and culture in which this black
Ethiopian now found himself, even though Christians inside and outside
the monastery recognized Moses as a holy man. (4) Prior to Moses'

45. Wicker, "Ethiopian Moses," 346.
46. Ibid., 340; Devisse, *Image of the Black in Western Art*, 2/i: 62.
47. Wicker, "Ethiopian Moses," 340, 341.

conversion, the tradition linked his blackness to negative behavior and to carnal lust.

Another example reflecting the traditional view of blacks at the time is the extant Greek romantic novel *Aithiopika* (sometimes rendered as *An Ethiopian Story*) by Heliodorus (c. fourth century C.E.), written around the same time as that of Moses the Ethiopian. The literati of the times read Heliodorus with the same reverence given Homer and Virgil. Charikles (Charicleia), daughter of Hydaspes and Persinna, king and queen of Ethiopia, was born white. Fearful that she will be accused of adultery, the queen leaves her baby by the roadside in hopes the infant will be found and raised by a stranger.

Charikles, raised by the priests of Apollo, later finds a letter from her mother that affirms the aberration of a mixed heritage, which she traces to the Greek idea of "maternal impression." The queen claims that her pregnancy was influenced by a painting in the royal bedchamber of Perseus and Andromeda (an Ethiopian princess, even though she was usually painted white). The image of Andromeda, "who was depicted stark naked . . . had shaped the embryo to her exact likeness."[48] Charikles becomes a priestess of Apollo in Delphi, where she meets and falls in love with Theageries, a Thessalian nobleman. They are eventually married in the presence of the king and queen.

The church officially reinforced this entanglement of aesthetics, carnality, and negativity of blackness at the fifth-century Council of Toledo. The council declared the devil a monster with cloven hooves, horns, the ears of a donkey, fiery eyes, an awful smell of sulphur, and an enormous penis. In an eighth-century manuscript, the devil is portrayed as black and naked. In some medieval Christian iconography the devil appears black with hair, horns, hooves, and a large penis.[49] This interplay between blacks and carnality continued throughout the West through the Middle Ages, then went into decline until the nineteenth century.

What was the effect of a color-conscious Greco-Roman culture and its philosophical thought on the perceptions of the early church fathers as they tried to interpret biblical references to Africa via Ethiopia? We may never know the final answer, but there can be no doubt that they

48. Heliodorus, "An Ethiopian Story," in *Collected Greek Novels*, ed. Bryan P. Reardon (Berkeley: Univ. of California Press, 1989), 433.
49. Jeffrey Burton Russell, *Lucifer: The Devil in the Middle Ages* (Ithaca, N.Y.: Cornell Univ. Press, 1984), 68–69.

read and reflected on the biblical references to Ethiopia through the medium of the Greek and Latin language and thought. Jean Courtès observes acutely that while the ancient Greeks and Romans may not have had what we would call racial views about the Ethiopians, still their metaphysical equality was more theoretical and philosophical:

> It must be said that . . . their equality was only theoretical, metaphysical, notional. The tenet that all peoples are equally called to eternal salvation led to no corollary such as the equality or inequality of their earthly cultures. . . . The symbolism of the color black, of light and darkness, was so strong an influence that the theology of the divine image and likeness in man could do no better, all things considered, than to try to play down negritude—to pretend it did not exist. . . . The Gospel was to reach the most unusual kinds of people, and this signifies the unity of mankind in the New Adam and in the totality of the Church.
>
> Once given that principle, which restores all races their original status as sons of light made in the likeness of Christ who took a white body, the triumphant post-Constantinian Church and her historians showed no interest in the progress of the faith *trans flumina Aethiopiae*, and still less in its advance among other black peoples.[50]

In summary, the vortex of the world of the Roman Empire shaped early Christian myths and beliefs about blackness and black skin. Blackness (1) revealed the threat of chaos to the divine cosmic order and the threat of nonbeing to our creaturely being; (2) was synonymous with Ethiopia; (3) allegorically represented the church of the Gentiles that was elected by God to receive Christ himself and to spread his gospel; (4) signified eros and malevolence and sin prior to its cleansing by the light of salvation, which restored its intended whiteness; (5) symbolized the demonic and the devil. Thus, blackness in early Christian thought overwhelmingly conveyed social values and a moral rank subordinate to whiteness, an attitude that became a cornerstone of Western cultural views reinforced by the slave trade, economics, Egyptology, physical and social sciences, and later Christendom. Blackness so perceived by the church fathers, however, while certainly ethnocentric, cannot be understood strictly as an ancient equivalent of modern racism or racialism.

50. Courtès, "The Theme of 'Ethiopia' and 'Ethiopians,'" 32.

4 | Blackness and Sanctity

*T*hree monumental historical events in medieval Europe ensured that Christendom and Christianity would deal with blackness and black skin as negative forces: (1) the fall of Edessa to the Muslims in the twelfth century; (2) the Black Plague in the fourteenth century; and (3) the African slave trade in the fifteenth century. In addition, medieval spirituality and piety portrayed popular and theological views of blackness in art, devotional manuals, and the escapades of the Crusades (1096–1291), whose sole mission was to rescue Christian sites in the Holy Land from the dark-skinned heathen infidels, the Muslims and the Turks.[1]

The terms *medieval* and Middle Ages represent both a metaphor and a concept; they also describe a mentality. The Italian historian Flavio Biondo (1392–1463), most likely for nationalist ethnocentric reasons, described the Middle Ages as the thousand years between the decline of the ancient world and the rise of the new world of the Renaissance. Much of medieval Christendom is also understood through its monasticism; theologians like Anselm (c. 1033–1109), Peter Abelard (1079–1142), Thomas Aquinas (c. 1225–74), and scholasticism (Lat.: *scholas-*

---

1. See Rosalind Brooke and Christopher Brooke, *Popular Religion in the Middle Ages: Western Europe 1000–1300* (London: Thames and Hudson, 1984), 46–62, 146–55.

ticus = scholars or schoolmasters);[2] church councils like Trent (1545–63); the final split between the Latin church of the West and the Byzantine church of the East in 1054; and the Protestant Reformation.

One of the defining events that influenced medieval Christians' view of blacks and blackness was the great insecurity and crisis of faith created by the Muslim occupation of Christian holy sites. This was an embarrassment, which was exacerbated after Edessa fell to the Muslims in 1144. At Edessa, Christian Crusaders were defeated by Muslim soldiers, Christian churches and shrines demolished. Jaroslav Pelikan remarks that the Islamic conquests and the advent of the Crusades forced Latin Christendom to take Islam's theological claims much more seriously than before. In 1143, for example, Peter the Venerable completed a Latin translation of the Koran.[3] Otto, bishop of Freising, Germany (c. 1114–58), a major figure in the Western church, preached that Muslims were victorious because of a lack of faith among Christians. The dreaded enemy, also called the Saracens (Gk. *sarakenos*) in the fifteenth century, certainly included many dark-skinned and swarthy, if not black, people. The West interpreted their color as living visible proof of divine damnation by God, which only compounded the great offense for European Christians.[4]

Medieval Christian beliefs about blackness were also influenced by the Moorish occupation of parts of Christian Europe, such as Spain, Sicily, southern Italy, Cyprus, and Rhodes. Islamic Moors controlled most of Spain for almost seven hundred years until they were defeated in Grenada in 1492. They threatened even the imperial city of Rome itself. Particularly distasteful to Christians was the fact that since 638 the sacred city of Jerusalem and its holy places had been also in the

2. Scholasticism emerged in the eleventh century as the approved philosophically based method for explaining the revealed truths of the Christian faith. Initially pioneered by the schools of monasteries and cathedrals to train future monks, priests, and administrators under the tutelage of schoolmasters, scholasticism took on an intellectual life of its own after such figures as Lanfranc, Anslem, and Abelard took charge of some schools. By the thirteenth century, scholasticism embedded within Greek Aristotelian logic and concept of natural truth had triumphed as the orthodox approach for interpreting Western Christian thought.

3. Jaroslav J. Pelikan, *The Christian Tradition: A History of the Development of Doctrine*, 5 vols. (Chicago: Univ. of Chicago Press, 1978), 3:243.

4. Jean Devisse, *The Image of the Black in Western Art*, vol. 2/i: *From the Demonic Threat to the Incarnation of Sainthood*, trans. William Granger Ryan (New York: William Morrow, 1979), 61.

hands of these "infidels," as popes labeled them. Yet, the "captivity in Babylon" under the infidels and their culture also benefited Spain, making it possible for Spain to become a European intellectual center for the new learning: mathematics, philosophy, astronomy, and medicine.

The disdain of Christian piety toward the Muslims/Moors is reflected in a medieval treatise, *On the Catholic Faith Against the Heretics of His Times*. The author declared that the first two books of the treatise were against Christian heretics, the third against the Jews, and the fourth against the dark-skinned Muslims. Peter the Venerable (c. 1092–1156), abbot of the important monastic community at Cluny, France, identified the "heresy of Mohammed" as "the dregs of all heresies . . . that have been aroused by the diabolical spirit in the 1,100 years since the time of Christ."[5]

Around the same time the doctrine of antichrist was revived. Muslims came to be identified as antichrist, an association that fed popular and religious disdain for blackness. While not a new doctrine—patristic fathers such as Tertullian, Irenaeus, and Jerome treat the subject— antichrist has always had a particular fascination for Christians during times of political and religious crisis. Medieval Christians felt besieged and overwhelmed by invisible forces surrounding them but beyond their control. The origins of the term itself can be traced to several references in 1 John (2:18, 22; 4:3) and 2 John 7 in the New Testament. Christians applied typological exegesis, however, which held that all biblical texts reflected historical events and forecast the same, to interpret Old Testament apocalyptic texts such as Daniel and New Testament texts such as 2 Thessalonians and Revelation as true signs of antichrist.

The medieval Antichrist was a human being under the control of the devil or Lucifer and the forces of evil and deceit, whose appearance signified the end of history. His purpose was to frustrate God's creation by tempting and persecuting God's followers (that is, Christians), as a false Christ. Although he would kill Enoch and Elias, Old Testament prophets who medieval Christians believed would return in the last days to convert Jews to Christianity and battle the Antichrist (based on Mal. 4:5 and Revelation 11), the Antichrist would eventually be destroyed by Jesus Christ.[6] Medieval Christians believed in six stages of world

---

5. Pelikan, *The Christian Tradition*, 3:242.

6. Richard Kenneth Emmerson, *Antichrist in the Middle Ages: A Study of Medieval Apocalypticism, Art, and Literature* (Seattle: Univ. of Washington Press, 1981), 7.

history, beginning with creation and the fall and ending with the incarnation and the defeat of the Antichrist by Christ at the end of history.

After the success of Muslims in overcoming traditional realms of
Christendom, particularly Edessa and the defeat of Constantinople—
the third holiest city in the Christian tradition after Jerusalem and
Rome—by the Turks in 1453, popes, devotional manuals, and theologians began to identify Islam as antichrist, the prince of evil and enemy
of Christ.[7] In medieval art and literature the antichrist is frequently
black, has Negroid features, and resembles the devil or a dragon.

This negative view toward the darkness of the Moors often appeared
in Western art, often combined with figures with distinct Negroid features. For example, in a twelfth-century Canterbury psalter (now in
Paris's Bibliothèque Nationale) Christ heals the Gadarene demoniac and
exorcises black demons who have Negroid features and wear loincloths.
Another twelfth-century painting shows John the Baptist being beheaded
by an executioner with a black face and woolly hair. In fact, throughout
the Middle Ages, executioners and torturers of Christ or John the Baptist
or Christians were usually portrayed as black or with African features
such as woolly hair and Negroid noses. One writer states the obvious:

> Lucifer, the fallen angel of light, occupies a complex position in our
> inquiry. As the Devil he is almost never represented with the physical
> traits of a Negro, and we rarely find him colored black. . . . Conversely,
> when the Evil One crossed into the created order of the natural world
> and appeared as a man in order to tempt men, artists seem to have been
> no more hesitant than writers about introducing "Negroid"
> characteristics. . . . Here color and ethnic connection are joined, and in
> many cases such personages are carefully depicted with the physical traits
> of the Negro."[8]

Hitherto, conceptions of black and blackness were based mostly within
the theological and devotional imagination, but the Muslims removed
these ideas from the abstract to the concrete. The devil, or Lucifer, and
his fallen angels especially were black in medieval paintings and iconography, and often naked as well.[9] One author aptly summed up

7. See an exhaustive study of the various forms of the Antichrist, ibid., 74–107.
8. Devisse, *Image of the Black in Western Art*, 2/i:72.
9. See medieval paintings and manuscripts showing the devil as black and naked.
Ibid., 2/i:62–71.

Christian influences on popular cultural notions of blacks and blackness in medieval Europe:

> Christian exegesis and popular prejudice put together a stable image in which blackness was a sign of evil. While this was not a matter of conscious hostility to black people, the picture impressed upon the Western European mind was added to the ancient tradition, with the result that the black and his land were thought of as abnormal elements in creation.[10]

A second defining event was the Plague. The Middle Ages was a time of ardent piety born out of economic deprivation, fear, and great anxiety about God's judgment on human society. From 970 to 1040 Europe suffered through forty-eight years of famine. Later, from 1347 to 1349 and continuing with occasional outbreaks from the fourteenth through sixteenth centuries, the Black Death epidemic (a combination of the bubonic plague and pneumonic plague) occasioned a repetition of medieval sagas of suffering. The Black Death decimated and fatigued most European Christian states. Between 1347 and 1349, 30 to 50 percent of the European population died.

Christians required a divine scapegoat to cope with such earthly misery and suffering. They also needed incentives that encouraged them to prepare for the anticipated eternal bliss of heaven. Good works, such as pilgrimages, collecting the relics of holy persons, crusades to liberate the holy places from the clutches of pagan infidels and heathen, and indulgences for the building of churches and cathedrals provided such incentives.[11] As a popular medieval version of the *Rolandslied* makes clear: "The heathen are cattle for the slaughter; war in a holy cause is good, and to destroy the infidel is to do God's work, for which he will reward you; death in such warfare is martyrdom."[12]

The third defining event, the African slave trade, began in the mid-1440s with the landing of the Portuguese on the West Africa coast. The first slave auction was held in Lisbon in 1444. The Portuguese made contact with black Africans when Antao Gonçalves and Nuño Tristo

10. Ibid., 2/i:60–61.
11. Williston Walker, *A History of the Christian Church*, ed. Cyril C. Richardson, et al. (Edinburgh: T. & T. Clark, 1959), 219.
12. Brooke and Brooke, *Popular Religion in the Middle Ages*, 58–59.

purchased ten "black Moorish" male and female Africans from Guinea
from Arab slave traders. A Portuguese chronicler in the *Chronicles of
Guinea* wrote that the slaves were so black that the Portuguese thought
they were from hell. He blamed their enslavement on their being descendants of Ham and hastily added that the Africans should be led to
the true faith, which would put them on the road to heaven:

> [The black Moors] live in the perdition of their souls and bodies—of
> their souls because they are pagans, without any clarity of light of holy
> Faith, and of their bodies because they live like animals, not behaving
> at all like rational creatures. They know neither bread nor wine; they do
> not know enough to cover themselves with clothes or to live in a house.[13]

The early Portuguese expedition to Africa initially had two objectives:
to discover gold and to find a trade route to India and Asia in search
of their silk and spice markets. From 1486 to 1493 more than 3,500
Africans were imported into Lisbon; overall it is estimated that between
1450 and 1500 some 150,000 African slaves were brought to Portugal.[14]

Blackness and Carnality

The dominant belief about blackness during much of this period and
thereafter was its association with evil and sin, chaos and disorder. Black
cultures and lands, such as Africa, were like aberrations in the divine
order of creation. Christian iconography used the color black for Satan
and demons. For example, in the sixth-century Rabulla Gospels (Syriac),
a black devil is exorcised from ailing demoniacs. In ninth-century Stutt-
gart Gospels the demons inflicting pestilence and disease are painted
black, as are Satan and the forces of evil in the ninth-century *Apocalypse*.
An eleventh-century illustration of the parable of the rich man and
Lazarus in the *Codex Aureus* depicts the rich man in hell as a black
man. Thus, color in early Christian iconography did not operate in a
value-free society or in an autonomous hermetic Christian world of ideas
unaffected by Greco-Roman social and intellectual thought. It is not,

13. Jean Devisse and Michel Mollat, *The Image of the Black in Western Art*, vol. 2/
ii: *Africans in the Christian Ordinance of the World*, trans. William Granger Ryan (New
York: William Morrow, 1979), 156.
14. Henry Marsh, *Slavery and Race: The Story of Slavery and Its Legacy for Today*
(Newton Abbot, England: David & Charles, 1974), 83.

therefore, so easy to claim (as some have done) that negative perceptions of blackness are more likely causes of, rather than caused by, ethnocentric racism.[15]

Old beliefs about blackness and carnality were also prominent. Nowhere do we see this more prominently than in the mystic and ascetic Saint Hildegard of Bingen (1098–1179). In one of her many visions, for example, Hildegard describes a rather crass image of a woman whose very womb is invaded by little black demons as symbols of evil and sin. The woman is the church, "as large as a great city with a wonderful crown on her head and arms from which a splendor hung like sleeves, shining from Heaven to earth." Her womb is "pierced like a net with many openings with a huge multitude of people running in and out":

> Then I saw black children moving in the air near the ground like fishes in water, and they entered the womb of the image [of the woman] through the openings that pierced it. But she groaned, drawing them upward to her head, and they went out by her mouth, while she remained untouched.[16]

The Christ child in the womb "blazing with a glowing fire" tears the black skin off the children, disposes of it and then clothes them in white garments that open to them the serene light of Christ. The newly clothed formerly black children are admonished to

> cast off the old injustice, and put on the new sanctity. And if you love Me rightly, I will do whatever you shall wish. But if you despise Me and turn away from Me, looking backward and not seeking to know or understand Me, Who am recalling you by pure penitence though you are filthy with sin, and if you run back to the Devil as to your father, then perdition will take you, for you will be judged according to your works, since when I gave you the good you did not choose to know Me.[17]

Blackness for Hildegard is also the color for the enemies of Christ, heretics and Jews. It is a sign of the waywardness of Synagoga (unconverted Jews who resist the Christian gospel):

15. Jeffrey Burton Russell, *The Devil: Perceptions of Evil from Antiquity to Primitive Christianity* (Ithaca, N.Y.: Cornell Univ. Press, 1977), 65.

16. *Hildegard of Bingen: Scivias*, trans. Columba Hart and Jane Bishop (New York: Paulist Press, 1990), 169.

17. Ibid., 169–70.

She is black from lap to feet. This implies that she is defiled in all her wide borders by her violation of the law and her transgression of the testament of her fathers, for she neglected the divine precepts to follow after the lusts of the flesh.[18]

A thirteenth-century Spanish cartoon shows a white woman condemned to death because she has committed adultery with a Moor. One scene shows them caught in the act of cohabitation by guards. The offending Moor is burned at the stake, but not the woman, probably because Spanish law provided that a Christian female guilty of sex with a Moor was only liable to the loss of half of her goods for a first offense and all of them for a second offense.[19]

An exception to this social taboo is the medieval epic *Parzival*, written between 1209 and 1215 by Wolfram von Eschenbach (c. 1170–c. 1217). This narrative brings together many medieval themes and myths: chivalry, romantic love, the heathenism of Muslims, blackness and the taboo of sexual allure, the superiority of Christendom over Islam.

Gahmuret, a Christian knight, on one of his journeys meets a Moorish queen, Belakane, who was quite "unlike a dewy rose; her complexion was black of hue."[20] He falls in love with her, courts her, sleeps with her, and fathers a child by her. "Yet his black wife was dearer to him than his own life. Never was there a woman more endowed with charms, and that lady's heart never failed to include in its retinue a worthy company of womanly virtues and true modesty."[21]

Nevertheless, he abandons the black queen during her pregnancy. A son, Feirefiz, is born "of two colors and in whom God had wrought a marvel, for he was both black and white" with half of his lips colored red. In joy the queen kisses the baby again and again, but only "his white spots."[22] Gahmuret, meanwhile, travels to another land, where he meets the white Queen of Walesis, who tells him to forget the black queen: "The sacrament of baptism has superior power. Therefore give

18. Quoted in Ruth Mellinkoff, *The Devil at Isenheim: Reflections of Popular Belief in Grünewald's Altarpiece* (Berkeley: Univ. of California Press, 1988), 62.
19. Ibid., 90.
20. Wolfram von Eschenbach, *Parzival, A Romance of the Middle Ages*, trans. and intro. by Helen M. Mustard and Charles E. Passage (New York: Vintage Books, 1961), 14.
21. Ibid., 31.
22. Ibid., 33; bk. 15, 395.

up your heathenry and love me by our religion's law, because I yearn for your love."[23]

He marries the Lady Herzeloyde and they have a child, whom they name Parzival. The contrast between his birth and that of the black and white spotted first child borne by the heathen Moorish mother is made clear to the listener. Herzeloyde breast-feeds the baby, noting at the same time: "The supreme Queen gave her breasts to Jesus. Who afterwards for our sake met a bitter death in human form upon the Cross and Who kept faith with us."[24]

Years later, in search of the Holy Grail like all medieval knights, Parzival encounters his half-brother Feirefiz, unknown to him, for the first time. They battle and Feirefiz the heathen defeats him. Eschenbach comments:

The heathen was gaining now. What shall I do about the baptized man? . . . Avert that, Grail of power! . . . One may say that "they" were fighting this way if one wants to speak of them as two, but they were indeed only one, for "my brother and I," that is one flesh, just as is good man and good wife.[25]

Parzival asks his name, since both claim to be the lord of Anjou. Parzival tells the stranger that he has a half-brother whom he has never met. "[His countenance] is like a parchment with writing all over it, black and white all mixed up." The heathen victor reveals that he is the half-brother, and "with kisses Feirefiz and Parzival concluded their enmity, and friendship beseemed them both better than heart's hatred against one another."[26]

In the end Feirefiz is persuaded to be baptized by an aged priest "who had dipped many a child from heathendom in [the baptismal font]." The priest says to this spotted black/white adult at the font: "You will believe—and thereby rob the Devil of your soul—in the

23. Ibid., bk. 2, 53.
24. Ibid., 63. For parallels between Eschenbach's story and the *Kebra Nagast* ("Glory of Kings"), a thirteenth-century Ethiopian manuscript originally in Ge'ez about the relationship between King Solomon and the Queen of Sheba and the birth of the half-breed son, Menelik, claimed by Ethiopia as the beginning of its dynasty, see Graham Hancock, *The Sign and the Seal: The Quest for the Lost Ark of the Covenant* (New York: Crown Publishers, 1992), 74–78.
25. Eschenbach, *Parzival*, bk. 15, 385.
26. Ibid., 390.

Highest God alone, whose Trinity is universal and everywhere of equal yield."[27] After Feirefiz's conversion and his marriage to a Christian European princess, they decide to name their first son Prester John, the mythical emperor of Christian Ethiopia who was expected to liberate medieval Christian Europe from the Muslim infidels.

Blackness and Salvation

The economic, spiritual, cultural, and health exigencies in Europe of the Middle Ages, which meant largely provincial Latin Christendom, suddenly were exposed to global perspectives as the result of the Crusades and naval expeditions undertaken by such nations as Portugal and Spain. At the same time, new views of blacks and blackness emerged that were linked to Christian salvation; namely, blackness as a channel for sanctification. When we consider that the prevailing mind-set in medieval society at large reflected the theological mind-set of the church—that God had revealed divine truths, which the church interprets—then the linking of blackness and blacks with salvation and sanctity was theologically significant. This sanctification of blackness was revealed largely in (1) the figure of the black warrior, centered in the eleventh-century revival of the cult of Saint Maurice (a third-century Christian Egyptian who was martyred during the Diocletian persecutions), and the thirteenth-century mythical black king of Ethiopia called Prester John; (2) the rise of the cult of the black madonna; (3) the blackening of one of the Three Magi in the twelfth century onward. Interestingly enough, most of these developments originated neither in Portugal nor Spain, but rather in Germany, France, and Italy. That such developments took place suggests that for a period of time, the social and religious negative perception of blackness in European Christendom underwent some positive change or at least acquired an ambivalence.

Blackness and Sanctity: The Warrior

Although prominent in the eleventh century, the Maurician cult began as early as 515 at the Abbey of Agaunum, France. Collects commemorating his feast day, 22 September, were extant in the seventh century, and a ninth-century liturgical text specifically mentions prayers to Saint

27. Ibid., bk. 16, 425–26.

Maurice.[28] He was venerated largely in France from the seventh to ninth centuries. During the eleventh century the primary center for Maurician piety shifted to Magdeburg, Germany. In fact, the vassals of that city were known as *milites mauriciani*. The army of Magdeburg invaded the homeland of Slavs marching under the banner of Saint Maurice.[29] By the twelfth century, Saint Maurice had joined the ranks of the knightly saint-patrons of the military elite, Saint George and Saint Sebastian, largely due to the influence of Frederick II of the house of Hohenstaufen.

Frederick wanted to embellish and propagate his claims of universality as the Holy Roman Emperor, so when he encountered dark-skinned Muslims living in Sicily, he moved many of them to Lucera in Apulia and included them in his court. His personal chamberlain was a black African called Johannes Maurus, whom he later appointed governor of Lucera. The physical presence of blacks strengthened Frederick's claim that his realm as emperor included "the two Ethiopias, the country of the black Moors, the country of the Parthians, Syria, Persia . . . Arabia, Chaldea, and even Egypt."[30] When the cathedral at Magdeburg was renovated in 1240–50, Frederick dedicated it to Maurice as patron saint. A statue of Maurice was sculpted with Negroid features and installed in the presence of the king and the bishop. Although Negroid Maurician sculptures became the convention throughout Germany, thereby replacing previous European-looking works, other artisans resisted Magdeburg's radical change. Matthias Grünewald (1460–1528) also sculpted Maurice at the cathedral in Halle (c. 1525).

After Charles of Bohemia (1316–78; king: 1346–78) became Holy Roman Emperor (1355–78), in order to create unity within the empire and a solid front against his enemies, he invoked all the popular saints at the time as divine protectors of his imperial rights and powers. Maurice was represented among them.

The cult spread throughout the various Germanic kingdoms, including the Prussian Hohenzollern family, which later became a Protestant stronghold after the Reformation, and France and Italy as well.[31]

Another black warrior was the mythical Ethiopian Prester John. Medieval Christendom, longing for a final victory over Islam, devised this

28. Devisse, *Image of the Black in Western Art*, 2/i:151.

29. Ibid., 154.

30. Paul H. D. Kaplan, *The Rise of the Black Magus in Western Art* (Ann Arbor, Mich.: UMI Research Press, 1985), 10.

31. Devisse, *Image of the Black in Western Art*, 2/i:164.

legendary figure, who brought together the New Testament story of the baptism of the Ethiopian eunuch (Acts 8:26-40) with expectations of a messianic deliverance from the antichrist—that is, the Muslims—as well as myths about ancient Ethiopia as a Christian kingdom. Significantly, the most authoritative guide to political and intellectual thought in Carolingian Europe at the time, the *Chronican Boemorum* (c. 1358), distinguished between Africa, whose origins it assigned to the progeny of Ham, and Ethiopia, whose origins along with Asia and India were attributed to the patrimony of Shem.[32]

Ethiopia, ruled by a mythical king called Prester John, was idealized as a Christian ally against the Muslims. Prester John was a priest-redeemer who ensured Europe salvation through Christian victory over the infidels. Ethiopia intrigued the European imagination of the twelfth-century in spite of its blackness because Ethiopia was considered the source of the Nile, one of the primary rivers in Gen. 2:10-15, and thus a link to Paradise.[33]

A fifteenth-century Catalonian map of the world (c. 1450–60) has Ethiopia represented by a black Prester John in a bishop's cope and miter on a throne, described as "lord of the Indias where the people are black by nature." Considering that the 1440 map *Nova Cosmographia* placed Prester John in islands of the ocean somewhere between Asia and Africa, it was a telling revision to locate him in Ethiopia. This map with a central focus on Prester John illustrated all routes to him from the west and the east:

> All the new place names learned in the past three or four generations receive mention; the "lord king of Melli" is present, black and wearing a turban; the rich caravans bound for the Sudan are recalled; the conquest of Nubia by the Muslims is known. Yet for all this, the legendary elements are not left out. A black cynocephalus king is placed to the south of Africa; . . . the departure of the Three Magi from "Tarsia" for Bethlehem. . . .[34]

32. Kaplan, *Rise of the Black Magus*, 83.

33. Henri Baudet, *Paradise on Earth: Some Thoughts on European Images of Non-European Man*, trans. Elizabeth Wentholt (New Haven, Conn.: Yale Univ. Press, 1965), 15.

34. See Devisse and Mollat, *The Image of the Black in Western Art*, 2/ii:124. One historian observes that even sixteenth-century cartographers had ethnocentric ideas about the portrayal of African kings in spite of their own cultural disapproval of black

Blackness and Sanctity: The Virgin Mary

Another powerful moment in beliefs about blackness was the linkage of blackness to the holy sanctity of the Blessed Virgin Mary in the form of black madonnas. The origins of black madonnas remain uncertain, although "black" is not to be understood to necessarily mean Negroid or Africanoid, as some modern African American scholars wish to maintain. More than one hundred images of black madonnas are extant in various cultures and more than thirty exist in Europe, found in southern Catholic countries, where they are objects of fastidious devotion. Mary holds a unique place in Western religious piety that distinguishes Western Christianity from Eastern Christianity. She has been singled out from all other women as mother and virgin. Her role as mother is obviously easier to understand than that of virgin, which is more complicated. She was the mother of Jesus Christ. But Mary's role as virgin refers to (1) a belief in the virgin birth without sexual relations with a male, (2) Mary's virginity *in partu*; that is, Mary's maidenhead was never ruptured even though she was a mother, and (3) Mary's perpetual virginity; that is, Mary abstained from sex after the birth of Christ.[35] Mary as virgin *in partu* and as perpetual virgin were popular beliefs in the church from early on, but they were made official doctrine in 451 at the Council of Chalcedon under the influence of Pope Leo the Great.

The concept of Mary as mediatrix between God and humankind also has an early history dating back to the eighth century, although it was not popularized in the West until the twelfth century, the same time the black madonna cult became popular. Germanus, an eighth-century patriarch of Constantinople, was one of the early advocates of this doctrine. As Mother of God, Mary diverts the awesome wrath and

---

skin and nudity. They also linked blackness to carnality, even in royalty. In portraying Mensa Musa, the legendary king of Mali (1301–32), European map makers were puzzled by his short woolly hair and his nakedness. "In their view, a beard was essential to kingship. [Angelino] Dulcert [of Majorca] cautiously gave Mensa Musa a very short scrubby beard. This was not dignified for later draftsmen, so they gave him a flowing beard." Succeeding cartographers thought he looked too European, however, so he began to be depicted seated on a throne, "crowned and robed, but with the royal robe cut down to a brief cloak, and otherwise stark naked. The cartographers did not neglect the opportunity which this afforded for emphasizing an *alleged physical attribute of the negro* [*sic*]" (emphasis added). E. W. Bovill, *The Golden Trade of the Moors* (London: Oxford Univ. Press, 1958), 92n.

35. Michael P. Carroll, *The Cult of the Virgin Mary: Psychological Origins* (Princeton, N.J.: Princeton Univ. Press, 1986), 7.

damnation then associated with God because of her love for Christians and for her son. After her ascension she became the mediatrix on humankind's behalf.[36]

The earliest feast in the West honoring Mary as Virgin is the Purification, dating from the seventh century. Marian devotional life, particularly hymnody and litanies, grew quite popular from the twelfth century onward; an example is the still popular Salve Regina, introduced into liturgical worship at Cluny in 1135. Likewise, Marian antiphons and the popular Hail Mary appear at this time, acknowledging humanity's state as pitiful sinners alienated from God in need of the assistance of the exalted Mother of God to plead our case before a wrathful God. The rosary, originally beads used to count the Our Fathers during penances, also became a popular form of Marian devotion in the twelfth century.

The most ancient image of the Blessed Virgin was found in a second-century mural in the catacombs of Priscilla in Rome. Some think this is really an image of the Egyptian goddess Isis. A comparison of Mary with the Egyptian goddess, however, reveals many dissimilarities in spite of some apparent similarities. Although Isis was one of the most popular goddesses in the Roman Empire, nevertheless Isis to the average Roman was associated with sexual promiscuity, not with virginity or chastity. Isis was the wife of Osiris and the mother of Horus, but she and Osiris were also sister and brother. Sibling incest was a taboo even in the Roman Empire. The Isiac temples were associated with promiscuous sexual activities and brothels in Greco-Roman culture. These were obviously not attributes that Christians linked to the Virgin Mary.[37]

The first known icon of the Blessed Virgin, traditionally thought to have been painted by Saint Luke, was sent in 438 by Empress Eudoxia as a gift to her sister-in-law Empress Pulcheria. Popular Marian devotion did not really emerge until late in the fifth century, probably the result of Mary being declared *Theotokos* ("God-bearer"; "Mother of God") at the Council of Ephesus in 431—a doctrine intended to settle the dispute between Nestorius of Constantinople, who insisted on *Anthropotokos* ("Mother of the Man") or *Christotokos* ("Mother of Christ"), and Cyril of Alexandria.

36. Hilda Graef, *Mary, A History of Doctrine and Devotion*, vol. 1 (New York: Sheed and Ward, 1963), 147–48.
37. Carroll, *The Cult of the Virgin Mary*, 8.

Black madonnas as objects of religious devotion date variously from the fourth century (Chartres, France), the eighth century (*La Morenata*, or The Little Black Madonna, in Montserrat, Spain, 718), and later (the Black Virgin of the Hermits in Einsiedeln, Switzerland, c. 835). In the Middle Ages they gained a special visibility and devotional power in Christian piety. Examples include Santa Maria di Siponto, Italy, and the Black Virgin of Le Puy, France (c. twelfth century), La Madonna di Constantinopoli (c. 1340), Brno (Brünn), Czechoslovakia (c. 1356), and Tenos, Greece.[38]

The origins of black madonnas are mysterious. Texts verifying their existence date from the thirteenth century, although some scholars trace their origins to Egyptian iconography of Isis breast-feeding Horus, whom she holds on her knees. Roman statues in black stone of Isis holding Horus dating from the first century are extant.[39] Other scholars trace their existence to the church's adaptation of remnants of Greek and Roman religion of the European tribes that later became Christians. Still others think they are derivatives of terra-cotta statues that represent Gallo-Roman goddess-mothers with child that have blackened over time.[40]

Some historians maintain that ethnographically the black virgins have their origins in (1) an ethnic model that incorporated archetypes of a Jewish Virgin Mary, made black by her time in Egypt before the birth of Christ; (2) Oriental cultures in Asia; (3) the Song of Songs (1:5) as an intentional image of the black woman there who was interpreted as symbolizing the church, as we saw in the patristic fathers.[41] One scholar proposes the provocative idea that black madonnas combine the erotic of the black woman in the Song of Songs and the virtues of the young Jewish virgin in the gospels:

> In Christian art and literature Shulamite [= someone at peace; Salmah = an ancient Arabian tribe: Song of Songs 1:5] is a mystical figure. In

38. Leonard W. Moss and Stephen C. Cappannari, "In Quest of the Black Virgin: She Is Black Because She Is Black," in *Mother Worship: Theme and Variations*, ed. James J. Preston (Chapel Hill: Univ. of North Carolina Press, 1982), 58.

39. Jean Leclant, "Egypt, Land of Africa, in the Greco-Roman World," in Jean Vercoutter, Jean Leclant, Frank M. Snowden, Jr., and Jehan Desanges, *The Image of the Black in Western Art*, vol. 1: *From the Pharaohs to the Fall of the Roman Empire* (New York: William Morrow, 1976), 285.

40. Ibid., 315 n. 95.

41. Marvin H. Pope, *Song of Songs: A New Translation*, The Anchor Bible (New York: Doubleday, 1977), 312–14.

early Byzantine miniatures she symbolizes the Church in a dual image. She is either the bride of Jesus or the Virgin Mary. . . . For instance, in the sixteenth-century tapestry, "Story of the Virgin" in Rheims Cathedral the identification is complete but with the roles reversed: it is Mary who is depicted as Shulamite. Medieval French and Spanish portraits of the Virgin with black complexion, the celebrated "black madonnas," are in fact representations of the Shulamite described in the Song of Songs as "black but comely." Biblical metaphors for Shulamite, the "Rose of Sharon," the "Garden-dweller," and the "Fountain of the Gardens" were also interpreted by Christian theologians as references to the Virgin Mary.[42]

Additional pagan origins of the black virgin are attributed to the myth of the earth goddess found in many ancient cultures. Remains have been uncovered of a tenth-century B.C.E. Greek temple dedicated to Demeter Melania, the goddess of fertility, in southeast Italy with its black soil, where the Isis cult was introduced after the region of Lucera allied itself with Rome as a colony in the fifth century B.C.E.[43] Likewise, a cult in Ephesus was devoted to Diana, protectress of women in childbirth, generatrix of fruits, and a virgin. Her statue was made of ebony and she was often confused with Mother Earth. As Diana/Artemis she is thought to be the predecessor of the cult of the Blessed Virgin near Ephesus, where legend says that Mary spent her final years with Saint John before his exile to Patmos and before her dormition and assumption. In the fourth century, the Dominican mother house Santa Sabina was built over the Temple of Isis at Le Puy, France. Thus, black madonnas represent a combination of Mariology, fertility goddess, and possibly sorcery or black magic (as contrasted with white magic).

Black as the color of the earth and the black madonnas provided Christianity with a way of invading cultural beliefs of non-Christians for evangelistic purposes by depicting the Blessed Virgin as the black Mother Earth, just as she was also represented as the New Eve, mother of Jesus Christ as the New Adam:

Long before there was a discipline of anthropology, these [Christian] proselytizers realized that new ideas are more readily accepted if they

42. Oliva Bitton-Jackson, *Madonna or Courtesan: The Jewish Woman in Christian Literature* (New York: Seabury Press, 1982), 11.
43. Moss and Cappannari, "In Quest of the Black Virgin," 62.

can be made more compatible with the existing culture. . . . Christianity thus became dominant over the existing faiths of the empire. It is in this light that we offer our hypothesis that the black madonnas exemplify a reinterpretation of pagan customs, that they have functioned as aids in the preservation of continuity in the transition from pagan beliefs to Roman Catholicism.[44]

A chronicle written in 1255 describes Saint Louis's return from the Crusades and says he "left in the country of Forez several images of Our Lady made and carved in wood of thick black colour which he had brought from the Levant."[45] Likewise, a document from 1619 notes that the Virgin of Myans, *La Noire*, existed in 1248, and other documents give evidence that black madonnas were known and visited by Christians in the fourteenth and fifteenth centuries.[46]

Why was the color black applied to madonnas in such nonblack cultures as those of Europe? Some think that because most of the shrines of black madonnas were built on or near former sites of Greek and later Roman goddesses of fertility, the Christian faith simply adopted their attributes and assigned them to the tradition of the Virgin Mary for conversion purposes. Nor can it be without significance that the oldest black madonnas, regarded by the faithful as especially powerful miracle workers, are generally found in areas formerly occupied by Roman imperial legions. Another explanation is that Cybele of Phrygia in Asia Minor was sent to Rome in 204 B.C.E. as a black stone at the request of the senate seeking some respite from the threatening victories of Hannibal. She was probably the first oriental cult borrowed by the Romans. Also the Roman legions no doubt brought black oriental fertility goddess with them on their return.[47] Moreover, since many extant black

44. Ibid., 71.
45. Ean Begg, *The Cult of the Black Virgin* (London and Boston: Arkana, 1985), 5. For systematic studies of the black madonna, see Marie Durand-Fefèbvre, *Etude sur l'origine des Vierges Noires* (Paris: G. Durassié, 1937), 101–82; Emile Saillens, *Nos Vierges Noires, leurs origines* (Paris: Editions Universelles, 1945).
46. Ibid.
47. Ibid., 58; Begg, *Cult of the Black Virgin*, 56. It is not coincidental that the black Virgin of Guadalupe in Mexico (1531) also appeared to an indigenous Indian on the site of a former temple to Tonantsi, the Aztec goddess of fertility and the earth: Tepayac Hill just outside Mexico City, which was located near Tenochtitlan, the ancient Aztec capital. Some think the Spanish settlers identified with the Mexican Guadalupe because she resembled the black Virgin of Guadalupe in Spain. The indigenous population identified with her because she was the Christian version of Tonantsi. Ena Campbell, "The Virgin of Guadalupe and the Female Self-Image: A Mexican Case History," in *Mother Worship*, 6–12.

madonnas are painted or sculpted from nonblack woods indigenous to Europe, such as oak and cedar, and not ebony, this suggests that the black or dark brown paint was considered by the artist to be indigenous to the effigy itself.

Thus, blackness in connection with the madonna at best has a dual or an ambivalent meaning. She signifies either (1) the fertility functions of earth goddesses known for their powers of darkness and death and transferred to the Blessed Virgin, or (2) a further development in the Christian belief that all spirits and demons as manifestations of evil and magic are black, which have been defeated by grace in the Virgin.[48] At the same time, there is an ambivalence about whether the black madonna and the white madonna as *theotokos* are considered to have the same powers. Might the black madonnas be primal mothers and sorceresses of magic under the guise of miracle? If this is so, then does not blackness even in connection with the Virgin Mary contain many of the themes associated with blackness historically in Western culture, such as exotic and magic powers? The ambiguity of the black madonnas as primal mother and worker of magic is perhaps best summed up in a commentary by the Russian Boris Pilnyak when he describes the bond found in Russian piety between Mother Earth and the peasantry:

> Mother Earth, like love and sex, is a mystery; for her own secret purposes she divided mankind into male and female; she lures men irresistibly; the peasants kiss the earth like sons, carry her with them as an amulet, talk softly to her, cast spells in her name to charm love and hatred, sun and day. The peasants swear by Mother Earth as they do by love and death. . . . It is for a woman to take the part of Mother Earth. But Mother Earth herself is fields, forests, swamps, coppices, hills, distances, years, nights, days, blizzards, storms, calm. . . .[49]

The issue is whether these black madonnas are simply pigmented representations of the traditional virtues of motherhood, purity, compassion, *theotokos*, and virginity—virtues traditionally associated with

48. A Latin American parallel is the famous dark-skinned madonna, the Virgin of Guadalupe in Mexico, who is remembered as a miracle worker reversing natural phenomena such as epidemics and floods, and bringing victory over enemies.

49. From Boris Pilnyak, *Mother Earth and Other Stories* (Garden City, N.Y.: Doubleday, 1968). Cited in Joanna Hubbs, "The Worship of Mother Earth in Russian Culture," in *Mother Worship*, 123.

the white virgin as *mater ecclesia*; or are works of art symbolizing works
of magic that have been baptized as miracles. A sixteenth-century Scot-
tish archbishop complained: "[These statues] darkened into something
not far from idolatry . . . when . . . one image of the Virgin [generally
a black or ugly one] was regarded as more powerful for the help of
supplicants."[50]

Roger Bastide has said that the black madonnas essentially connect
the negativity of blackness with Christian virtues associated with the
fair-skinned madonnas and therefore function like sorceresses. "The
symbolism of her dark color is not eliminated in the cult; it is only
repressed because it infiltrates into the prayers that are directed toward
her."[51] As one writer points out, these medieval black madonnas were
and continue to be more than objects of veneration (*dulia*) or adoration
(*hyperdulia*); rather they were vigorous objects of worship (*latria*):

> [The] black madonnas are *powerful* images; they are miracle workers
> (although not all miracle-working images are black). They are implored
> for intercession in the various problems of fertility. Pilgrimages covering
> hundreds of kilometers are made to these specific shrines. The degree
> of adorational fervor far exceeds that attached to other representations
> of the Virgin. . . . We are, thus equating the blackness of the images
> with their power. The attitude of the pilgrim approaches not reverence
> but worship.[52]

Blackness and Sanctity: The Magi and Magic

While sorcery and magic in the Middle Ages (as they still are in African
cultures) were largely related to charms and doing evil to one's enemy,
they also had a bearing on Christian piety and devotion beyond the
black madonna. Magic in Christian thought and in Western culture was
as imprecise as blackness was in ancient Greek and Roman cultures.
The general population failed to make a clear distinction between what
the educated and the clerics called magic and what the people regarded
as religion. Even the expression *magic* is an imprecise conceptual legacy
more discussed by intellectuals, clerics, and theologians than by the
general populace. The word comes from Persia, where the magi were

---

50. Moss and Cappannari, "In Quest of the Black Virgin."
51. Roger Bastide, "Color, Racism, and Christianity," *Daedalus* 96 (Spring 1967), 316.
52. Moss and Cappannari, "In Quest of the Black Virgin," 65–67.

originally most likely Zoroastrian priests, whose arts included astrology, ritual healing, and knowledge of the occult. Thus, their activities regardless of content were known as the "arts of the magi," "the magical arts," or "magic" for short.

Likewise, because the magi were foreigners and their arts regarded as something exotic, in ancient Greek culture *magic* conveyed something apprehensive and suspicious, certainly by the fifth-century B.C.E. Both the Greeks and Hellenistic Judaism regarded this rather imprecise term as threatening and sinister, associated with darkness. Jewish teachers, fearful that the dualism in popular Persian beliefs about the forces of light and the forces of darkness threatened their own claims about a superior monotheistic Hebrew God, anathematized the idea that a prince or angel of darkness and deceit could even compete with the Hebrew God. Such forces under the leadership of a Belial or Satan included spirits, which Judaism also anathematized as *evil* spirits. The meaning of the word *demon* (Gk.: *daimon*; Lat.: *daemon* = an unknown supernatural power [Homer]; a spirit intermediary, not necessarily evil, between heavenly powers and earthly forces [Plato]) changed to refer to evil spirits.[53] Demons were described as a special order of angels under the authority of Satan or Belial, the angel of darkness and perversion; and as apostate angels who rebelled against God and caused havoc in God's creation.

This meant that magic or trafficking with the spirits was demonic by definition and by its very nature. Soon the term *magic* was extended to all activities dealing with the occult, be they foreign or domestic.[54] By the time of the Septuagint, *demons* meant pagan gods and destructive spirits rather than beneficial intermediaries, as the word originally meant. The New Testament and the early Christians inherited this pre-rabbinic Jewish view. Satan and Beelzebul became the prince of darkness and evil, the "prince of demons" (Matt. 10:25; 12:24; Mark 3:22; Luke 11:15-19), who took on a cosmic nature as an enemy of God (Eph. 6:11-12)

53. Hesiod (c. eighth century B.C.E.) was the first to use *daimon* for the souls of the dead who guarded and protected humankind and distributed prosperity and wealth. They came at night in order to perform their tasks without being detected or seen. James Hastings, ed., *Encyclopedia of Religion and Ethics*, 13 vols., s.v. "Demons and Spirits (Greek)," 4:590–94; *Encyclopedia Judaica* (Jerusalem: Macmillan, 1971), 5:1525.

54. Richard Kieckhefer, *Magic in the Middle Ages* (Cambridge, England: Cambridge Univ. Press, 1990), 10.

rather than an occasional interruption in our world. As we have seen, in the Apocrypha Satan is personalized as the Black One.

Both Christians and non-Christians (pagans and Muslims) recognized the efficacy of supernatural powers. In medieval Europe, distinctions were made between natural magic (hidden powers at work in nature) and demonic magic (evil powers aimed at harming someone). It was not so much that pagans upheld magic and Christians opposed it; both opposed magic, but for different reasons. Non-Christians opposed magic because it was secret and evil and therefore antisocial; Christians opposed magic because they inherited the traditional belief of popular Judaism that it was demonic and the work of demons influencing human beings.[55]

In the sixteenth century, the church taught that the efficacy of beneficial magic over against occult magic depended on whether it relies on divine action, which supplicates God, or on demonic engagement, which tries to manipulate and coerce God. If the former, then it is not magic, but a gift from the divine, particularly in the case of healing; if the latter, then it is a gift of the devil and evil.[56] It is unlikely, however, that the general populace held to such a refined distinction. The line between sorcery and magic, on the one hand, and healing and miracle, on the other, was blurred in the veneration of the black madonnas. "When comparing popular with learned notions, we find in the history of magic a crossing point where the exploitation of natural forces and the invocation of demonic powers intersect."[57]

It is within this religious and cultural context that the phenomenon of the blackening of one of the Three Magi in Christian art began. Although there were precedents in twelfth-century art, in which servants to the Magi were sometimes painted black, this convention really emerged between 1340 and 1375. The Queen of Sheba is thought to be the biblical and popular source in Christian piety linking royal character to blackness for the populace. Believed to be queen of the land of Sheba (Saba), thought to be located either in northeastern Africa or immediately across the Red Sea at the bottom of the Arabian Peninsula, she was first depicted as black in European art in 1181 by Nicholas of Verdun in his Klosterneuburg altarpiece.

55. Ibid., 37.
56. Ibid., 14.
57. Ibid., 16.

The Magi in popular devotion had weighty allegorical and symbolic roles in Western iconography. Earlier, in the fifth century Pope Leo the Great (c. 400–61; pope 440–61) had passionately preached in a sermon:

> Let us, beloved sons, acknowledge in the Magi who worshipped Christ the first fruits of our vocation and our faith. . . . The truth which the Jews in their blindness refused to accept has shed its light over all nations.[58]

Through such writers as John of Hildesheim (*Historia Trium Regum*, 1364–75), and Saint John Mandeville (*Travels*, 1360), Europe began to believe that one of the Three Magi, Gaspar, was a black African. Mandeville wrote: "In this land of Ethiopia is the city of Saba, of which one of the three kings that offered to our Lord was king."[59]

The original theological interpretation of the Magi came from Hrabanus Maurus (776–856), a German theologian and abbot of the Benedictine monastery at Fulda, who later was also archbishop of Mainz. Maurus said the Magi were surrogates of the three known parts of the world: Asia, where Christ was born, Europe, where the Christian faith grew and was strongest, and Africa, where the faith was the youngest.[60] Their ancestors were the three siblings of Noah named in Gen. 9:18–27: Shem, Japheth, and Ham. Hence, the Magi represented primarily a theological view and secondarily a cultural view of blackness. But the Dutch scholar Henri Baudet observed that with the rise of these two conventions—the blackening of one of the kings and the representation of the generations of humankind as progeny of Noah—Shem was seen to represent Asia, Japheth Europe, and Ham Africa. With this "canonization" of African cultures as the youngest, a rudimentary patronizing attitude was implanted that finds its expression in modern Europeans referring to the Third World as "younger nations," whose populations are mostly people of color.[61]

In Germany the Magi took on a particular popularity. In 1164, in Cologne, the Magi were first given names, later popularized as Melchoir, Gaspar, and Balthasar. A twelfth-century apocryphal writing attributed

58. Quoted from one of Leo's collections of Epiphany sermons. Devisse, *Image of the Black in Western Art*, 2/i:133–134.

59. Kaplan, *The Rise of the Black Magus in Western Art*, 19.

60. Hans-Joachim Kunst, *The African in European Art* (Bad Godesberg, Germany: Internationes, 1967), 12.

61. Baudet, *Paradise on Earth*, 17.

to the Venerable Bede says Balthasar was dark-skinned, bearded, and dressed in a red tunic when he presented his gift of myrrh.[62] Possibly one of the oldest examples of a black wise man, dating from 1360, is found in the *Adoration of the Magi* mural of the Emmaus Monastery in Prague.[63]

Certainly by the fifteenth century the convention of painting one of the Magi black had taken hold in other parts of Germany: the altarpiece (c. 1400) in the chapter house at Sankt Florian and at a church (c. 1410) in the Rhineland, as well as in other parts of Europe.[64] A black Magus is seen in the works of such German painters as Friedrich Herlin the Elder (c. 1425–?) and Albrecht Dürer (1471–1528), the Flemish painter Rogier van der Weyden (c. 1400–1464), the German/Flemish painter Hans Memling (1430–94), and even the Italian Andrea Mantegna (1431–1506).[65]

62. Devisse, *Image of the Black in Western Art*, 2/i: 135.
63. Devisse and Mollat, *Image of the Black in Western Art*, 2/ii: 27.
64. Ibid., 37. For a survey of the black Magi outside of Germany, see 142–43.
65. This convention declined in subsequent centuries, although Rubens (1577–1640) followed this convention in his *Adoration*. It was renewed in the nineteenth century by such painters as Carminade (*Adoration of the Magi*) and Pietro Gagliardi and in the twentieth century by Karl Schmidt-Rottluff (1884–1976).

5 | Christendom and Black Slavery

*T*he first auction of African slaves in Portugal happened at the same time the Catholic hierarchy was meeting at the Council of Florence in 1441. In 1488, some forty-seven years after the first public slave auction in Catholic Portugal, Pope Innocent VIII (1432–92; pope 1484–92) gave black slaves as presents to his cardinals and the nobility after King Ferdinand of Spain had given him a gift of one hundred blacks.[1] In 1439, two years prior to the first slave auction, Pope Eugenius IV sent a legation to the heads of the Eastern Orthodox churches, which included a letter to the mythical Prester John in Ethiopia, inviting them to come to Florence.[2]

The first official shipment of Africans to the New World in 1510 was escorted by Catholic priests. They arrived to work the gold mines on the eastern part of the island of Hispaniola, near present-day Santo Domingo. Eight years later, Charles V issued a royal license to two

1. Marie Genoiono Caravaglios, *The American Catholic Church and the Negro Problem in the XVIII–XIX Centuries*, ed. Ernest L. Unterkoefler (Charleston, S.C.: n.p., 1974), 98–101.

2. The intent of the council was to reestablish unity between the West and the East, but the Ethiopians refused to sign the bull *Cantate domino*, issued in February 1442. The occasion of pope Eugenius presenting the bull to the Ethiopians is commemorated in the massive bronze doors (1445) guarding the entrance to Saint Peter's, Rome.

Flemish merchants granting them a monopoly in the slave trade to the island. The annual limit was set at four thousand slaves.[3]

Meanwhile, Castilian kings laid claim to Africa, which provoked a dispute with Portugal. Spain's ambitions were to dominate the seas as a superpower and to get a foothold in the profitable African slave trade. Until the pope settled the dispute in his 1455 bull *Romanus pontifex*, Spain had brought its slaves from Portugal and baptized them as did other Catholic European countries, including Sicily, Naples, Genoa, Venice, and France. Sicily even had a slave-breeding industry using African slaves. Hence, as I noted elsewhere, the early slave trade was a rudimentary model for what came to be a global market.

Christendom and African Enslavement

What were the social and cultural conditions that allowed this assurance of rewards in heaven and riches on earth via the slave trade in black Africa by Catholic countries? What was Christendom's view of blackness and African cultures as they indulged in this trade war—a trade war that included not only Catholic states such as Portugal, Spain, and France, but also Protestant states such as England and Holland? While Portugal began the occidental slave trade industry in Europe, the Americas, and the Caribbean, there also was an oriental slave trade (pre-Islamic and Islamic Arabs, Asian countries, and Russia) and an African slave trade (within Africa).[4]

The church had two minds about slavery. Pope Martin V (1368–1431) condemned the industry in 1425, continuing the tradition of his predecessors in a bull threatening excommunication to all Christian slave traders. It had little effect, however. Furthermore, the church and European Christians condemned the enslavement of people from Christian countries, but such rules of the game were suspended when it came to enslaving either "infidels" or "pagans" from black Africa and other non-Christian cultures. By tradition and canon law, slaves of a Jew or a heretic received automatic freedom upon submission to Christian bap-

3. Debs Heinl and Nancy Gordon Heinl, *Written in Blood: The Story of the Haitian People 1492–1971* (Boston: Houghton Mifflin, 1978), 13–14.
4. Patrick Manning, *Slavery and African Life: Occidental, Oriental, and African Slave Trades* (Cambridge, England: Cambridge Univ. Press, 1990), 28–32, 127–30.

tism, which had been sanctioned by the Third Lateran Council (1179) and the Code de Tortosa (1272).[5]

Pope Nicholas V (1397–1455; pope 1447–55), considered one of the least corrupt of the Renaissance popes, accommodated both the marketplace and the yearnings of the Christian soul. His 1454 bull *Dum diversas* authorized and sanctioned the invasion of Africa by the Portuguese, permitting them "to invade, search out, capture, conquer, and subjugate all Saracens and pagans whatsoever and other enemies of Christ wherever they exist . . . in those and adjoining regions and in the further and more remote areas."[6] In his 1455 *Romanus pontifex*, which settled the territorial dispute between the two maritime powers, Spain (Castile) and Portugal, the pope gave sweeping support to Portugal's claims to all African territories occupied before and after June 18, 1452, and its monopoly on the African slave trade.[7]

Furthermore, the morality of Christendom was often at odds with the teachings of the Christian church, even in the Middle Ages. Agobard (c. 769–840), archbishop of Lyons, for example, rebuked clergy who refused to baptize pagan slaves owned by Jews because the priests feared that the slaves would interpret baptism as emancipation from their bondage. Thomas Aquinas, relying on the Greek doctrine of the natural dominion of some over others by virtue of natural law, called the slave/master bond simply a metaphor reflecting the body/soul relationship in nature. This allowed for a theological reconciliation with the existence of slavery without calling it a sin. Yet at the same time Aquinas supported Pope Gregory the Great's condemnation of slavery as contrary to nature.

Medieval church canon law, on the one hand, said slavery was contrary to the *jus naturale*, since liberty belongs to the natural law. On the other hand, it observed that slavery was a part of the *jus civile* (civil law) and therefore could be supported by Christians, inasmuch as it was sin rather than nature that made some people free and others slaves. Sin disoriented the natural order.

5. David Brion Davis, *The Problem of Slavery in Western Culture* (Ithaca, N.Y.: Cornell Univ. Press, 1966), 98.

6. See an abbreviated text in Frances Gardiner Davenport, ed., *European Treaties Bearing on the History of the United States and Its Dependencies*, 4 vols. (Washington, D.C.: Carnegie Institution, 1917), 1:12; also Caravaglios, *The American Catholic Church and the Negro Problem*, 221.

7. See text in Davenport, *European Treaties*, 23–25; also Caravaglios, *The American Catholic Church and the Negro Problem*, 45.

Thus, the church legitimized slavery in three ways: (1) Its hierarchy, parishes, and monasteries were permitted to own slaves, ownership that was justified as a benefit to the ministry of the church. (2) Slaves could not be ordained; only free men could be ordained. (3) Bishops, abbots, and monks were forbidden to emancipate slaves owned by a church or an order unless they made up the loss from their own goods, for it was argued that sin necessitated the church to overlook practices in civil law that were not explicitly prohibited by natural law.[8] "The canonists clearly look upon the institution of slavery in such a sense authorized and sanctioned by God that any revolt against it was sinful."[9]

Others say that the slave trade came about through a corruption of the original intention of the Portuguese in Africa, which was to find gold and spice markets. But the domestic labor market and the labor-intensive sugar and coffee plantations in the New World colonies needed a steady and reliable pool of cheap labor. Portugal's task was made easier through Arab and African allies who were the brokers for the slavers. This system thrived not only because of the superior weapons and military prowess of the Europeans and the Arab traders, but also because Africans relied on the African traditions of a lord/vassal means of production and of victors in war taking tribute from the defeated. As one Africanist noted:

> The [African] rulers rented land for the construction of the trading posts, which were fortified mainly against attack by other Europeans rather than by African landlords. In fact, the white slavers and their landlords were dependent on each other, and usually cooperated to their mutual benefit. . . . These subjects took the goods inland and returned eventually with slaves or other produce.[10]

Furthermore, vested interests both in the colonies and in the motherland backed by powerful political interests and an embryonic supply-demand ethic protected this odious trade for some four centuries. These

    8. R. W. Carlyle and A. J. Carlyle, *A History of Medieval Political Theory in the West*, vol. 2: *The Political Theory of the Roman Lawyers and the Canonists, from the Tenth Century to the Thirteenth Century* (New York: Barnes and Noble, 1909), 34–41, 117–35; also Davis, *The Problem of Slavery in Western Culture*, 95–96.
    9. Carlyle and Carlyle, *Political Theory of the Roman Lawyers*, 122.
    10. L. S. Stavrianos, *Global Rift: The Third World Comes of Age* (New York: William Morrow, 1981), 108.

interests were not simply those of the slave traders and the slaveowners, but also a whole cornucopia of industries dependent on this practice comparable to the military-industrial complex that sprang up in many developed countries after World War II: insurance, shipbuilding, banking, suppliers, grocers, property agents, textiles, ironmongers, and other related cottage industries.

Still another view holds that the politics of the times was a major contributing factor. After Constantinople's occupation by the Turks in the fifteenth century, the Western side of the Mediterranean was effectively cut off from the supply of slaves coming from the eastern Mediterranean. The ensuing Ottoman Empire blockaded all trade routes going to the East.[11] The humiliation of an ancient see of the church under the domination of "infidels" affected the piety and spirituality as well as the exploration instincts of Christian Europe.

Winthrop Jordan says the physical feature of Africans that most fascinated Europeans and white Americans and aroused their curiosity was blackness.[12] In order to conceptually explain the origins of this blackness—the exact opposite to their own experience and history— whites searched biblical and theological sources for empirical reasons.

The intriguing question is what led Portugal and Spain, two strongly Catholic states (and later other Christian European countries), to inaugurate economically and to justify theologically the enslavement of black Africans. Was it simply a question of trade and an expansion of markets needed to stimulate and satisfy domestic consumer demands, particularly among the privileged classes? Was it a matter of state-supported missions aimed at saving pagan souls for the church and then for Christ, in that order? After all, as we have seen, only a short time had passed after Portugal had invaded Africa before Catholic missionaries were also sent to sub-Saharan Africa in the fifteenth century, although Christianity did not seem to take root there until the nineteenth century.

Nor was the importation of human slaves (Lat.: *sclava* = Slav: captive) as servants unique to Portugal and Spain. Even in the thirteenth century, Genoa and Venice imported slaves from Turkey and Mongolia. Other European nations bought Slav and Greek slaves. This slave trade continued into the seventeenth century. Eric Wolf notes that in the fifteenth

11. Eric Wolf, *Europe and the People without History* (Berkeley: Univ. of California Press, 1982), 204.
12. Winthrop D. Jordan, *White over Black: American Attitudes toward the Negro, 1550–1812* (New York: W. W. Norton, 1968), 4.

century in the Iberian peninsula—Portugal and Spain—there was a
mutual enslavement of Muslims by Christians and Christians by Muslims. Scotland and England shared the custom of enslaving coal miners
and salt mine workers, a practice that lasted well into the eighteenth
century, as well as the institution of indentured servants.[13] The new
element was the contractual treatment of human beings as legal property
based on a racial mythology.

Portugal's economic situation and political relationship with Spain
spurred it to seek new labor markets. Started as a border fief of Spanish
León in northwest Spain, where tolls were collected at a "land port" in
the city of Cale on the Douro River, Portugal's name dates from the
sixth century (Portucale). The saga of modern Portugal began with the
liberation of Lisbon from the Moors in 1147. In 1385 the Portuguese
defeated the last garrison of Spain's Castilian troops. Afterwards, Portugal
was dominated by religious military orders, a military aristocracy with
many privileges, and a large clerical order.

It was primarily an agrarian country. After the fourteenth-century
Black Plague depopulated Portugal's villages and rural areas, the survivors
rushed to the cities. This led to a shortage of farm workers, who paid
the nobility and aristocracy rents and fees. Faced with reduced income,
the nobility searched for labor resources beyond Portugal to work its
lands. Also after the 1385 war with Castile, the merchant class, which
thrived on trade, grew economically stronger and restless. They were
in search of new markets, particularly the merchants in Lisbon, where
(appropriately) the first slave auction was held. Of the estimated 150,000
slaves imported to Portugal between 1444 and 1500, most worked the
lands of the nobility and the islands of Madeira and the Azores.[14]

Blocked by Spain from access to the rest of Europe and from the
thriving Mediterranean trade routes by Italy and the Arabs, the Portuguese decided to search for new routes and markets to the East that
would bypass Spain and break the hold of Muslim middlemen in the
spice market. In 1444 they established the first foothold in Africa at
Cape Verde and returned to Portugal with gold, spices hitherto unknown,
pepper, ivory, leather, and blacks. In 1448 they built a fortress on Arguin
just off the Mauritanian coast, one of several fortresses/warehouses where
slaves were kept before transport to European markets. These "slave

13. Wolf, *Europe and the People without History*, 201–2.
14. Ibid., 110–11.

castles" line entire coasts of West Africa. In 1482 the Portuguese found gold in what is now modern Ghana, where they built the important coastal slave fortress at Elmina and named the territory the Gold Coast; five years later they sailed around the tip of Africa, which they named the Cape of Good Hope—present-day Cape Town, South Africa— thereby achieving their goal of finding a new route to the East and Asia.

The allure of gold and spices was the primary motivation for the first sea voyages, but rumors among captured Muslim prisoners in the 1415 war at Ceuta emboldened the Portuguese to make deals with Arab and African slave traders to sell or trade Africans to meet the labor shortage in Portugal.[15] They kept a monopoly in the African slave trade until the British and the Dutch broke through in the seventeenth century. As Portugal became a European naval superpower in the sixteenth century and founded colonies and markets in the New World, the new industry of slavery also enriched many of its families and individuals.

What about Portugal's competitor, Spain, which also wanted to expand its sphere of power and influence? By 1462, two decades after the first slave auction in Lisbon, the Portuguese had expanded slave markets to the Spanish seaports of Seville, Cádiz, Valencia, and Barcelona. Because of the political situation, whereby part of Spain was under the Germans and most of the rest under the Moors, two Spanish royal houses—the house of Castile and the house of Aragon—emerged as dominant. In 1469 the two houses created an uneasy union dominated by the Castilians. In 1492 Ferdinand V (1452–1516), king of Castile and León (1474–1504) and later king of Aragon (as Ferdinand II: 1479–1516), and Queen Isabella financed Columbus to find new markets and routes to the legendary riches of Asia. In 1479, because of increased Atlantic trade rivalry between Portugal and Spain, a treaty was drawn up by the pope, the first such bilateral trade treaty, which defined their spheres of influence. It was concluded in June 1494 at Tordesillas.

The Spanish were unsuccessful in breaking Portugal's monopoly, so they established a franchising system using a form of contract called asientos to authorize foreign shipping firms to supply slaves on behalf of Portugal in its New World colonies. In 1518, however, the king used asientos to bypass Portugal by contracting the Flemish to import slaves directly from Africa. In fact, these licenses became so profitable that

15. Stavrianos, *Global Rift,* 107.

the owner subleased them without his ships ever traveling to West Africa to secure slaves. (In the eighteenth century, ironically, England won the main asiento and thus became the official provider of slaves to the Spanish colonies.)

The doctrine of *limpieza de sangre* (purity of blood), a racial mythology derived from a religiously based doctrine about purity, arose in Spain during the Moorish occupation. Its aim was to exclude Moors and other non-Christians, such as Jews, from Spanish society. Initially based on nobility and Christian ancestry, it had a moral afterplay in that Spaniards regarded others with impure blood to be morally deficient. Spanish Moors who had converted to Christianity were called *Mozariba*; those who had not converted but spoke Spanish were called *Moriscos*. Iberian-born blacks who knew Spanish and Spanish customs (usually footmen and house servants), were called *ladinos*; African-born blacks who converted to the Catholic faith but spoke little or defective Spanish were called *bozales*, the manual laborers.[16] The broken Spanish of the *bozales* was sometimes caricatured by the Spaniards as *disfraces negros* ("dislocated Spanish") both in public and in literary works, where it was often spoken by buffoons called *bembóns* ("lips"), which was a pejorative name for blacks.[17]

The doctrine of purity of blood was transported to Spain's New World territories, where it became an ethnic belief about the inferiority of the indigenous Indians and the Africans and a rationale against miscegenation. By the seventeenth century, interracial sex in Spain's overseas colonies had produced new mixed-blood racial groups: mulattoes, mestizos (European and Indian), and zambos (Indian and African). From

16. Leslie B. Rout, Jr., "History of the Black Peoples of Spanish America," in *World Encyclopedia of Black Peoples* (St. Clair Shores, Mich.: Scholarly Press, 1975), 1:232.

17. Lemuel A. Johnson, *The Devil, The Gargoyle, and The Buffoon: The Negro as Metaphor in Western Literature*, National Univ. Publications Series on Literary Criticism (Port Washington, N.Y.: Kennikat Press, 1971), 68.

Blacks did appear favorably in Spanish literature, such as in works by Garcia de Resende (c. 1476–1536), Cervantes (1547–1616), and Diego de Enciso. For example, Cervantes' *El Coloso Extremeno* portrays a black servant and eunuch, Luis, who likes music and the arts. Juan Latino (died 1573), the adopted Christian name of an Ethiopian slave brought to Spain in 1528, who was a Christian convert, became so proficient in Latin and Greek that in 1557 he graduated with high honors from the University of Grenada, where he also was appointed to teach. This former slave's writings became a part of Spanish mainstream literature. See Carter G. Woodson, "Attitudes of the Iberian Peninsula (in Literature)," in *Blacks in Hispanic Literature: Critical Essays*, ed. Miriam DeCosta (Port Washington, N.Y.: Kennikat Press, 1977), 25.

the viewpoint of the doctrine of *limpieza de sangre*, such mixed blood was a sign of moral inferiority and intellectual deficiency; hence they and their offspring were forbidden to enter the Catholic priesthood and to matriculate at Spanish universities. A baptismal caste system comparable to the Creole system in Louisiana and other French colonies was created and used pejoratively and even in church records: *tercerones* (two-thirds white, one-third black); *cuarterones* (three-quarters white, one-quarter black); *quinterones* (seven-eighths white, one-eighth black). At the same time, all mixed-blood people were identified as *castas* and mulattoes; blacks were called *negros*, *ladinos*, *bozales* (Muslim slaves), and *wolofes* (slaves from Senegal).[18]

At this time, Spain and most Europeans distinguished between civilized heathen cultures and uncivilized heathen-savage cultures. The former included advanced non-Christian heathen cultures, such as the Greeks and the Romans. An exception was made for "uncivilized" cultures that were also savage, such as China and India. Those cultures that were uncivilized and savage usually were the New World Indians and Africa, the latter's position based largely on the myth of Noah's progeny Ham, Shem, and Japheth and their descendants, which later became popular in the Renaissance. As one student of the period observes, blackness stood for the alien dark underworld that opposed the Christian world of light:

> In the end a black was really received as an equal in God only to the degree that, dressed as a European dressed, speaking a dead or living European language, married according to the laws of the Church or being a cleric of the Church, he had lost all contact with his native culture. Such steps could not be expected of the slave to whom were denied both the costume and the written language and conferred equality, even if, at the outset, the Faith had been granted him. In the last analysis, what the Western Christian looked for in the African convert was a kind of mirror image of himself—a blackened Christian.[19]

While European art revealed several currents of thought and views toward blacks and blackness at work as Europeans encountered increasingly this black presence in their midst and in foreign wars, in Spain

18. Ibid.
19. Jean Devisse and Michel Mollat, *The Image of the Black in Western Art*, vol. 2/ii: *From the Early Christian Era to the "Age of Discovery,"* trans. William Granger Ryan (New York: William Morrow, 1979), 256.

and Portugal blackness and those stricken with its color continued to
be viewed as images of primal evil, sin, and forces at war with the Christ
and the Christian faith. The negative character of blackness was not
consistently extended to the dark skin color of Arab Muslims. The
Europeans distinguished between them and black Africans by calling
the dark-skinned Arabs "white Moors." A possible impetus behind such
a distinction might be that because so much of medieval Europe's
intellectual life derived from Arab intellectual thought (including classical
philosophy, astrology, astronomy, mathematics and decimals, medicine,
and even the concept of perspective that later revolutionized Western
art), Europeans decided that a distinction showing a skin-color alliance
with Arabs was necessary. Black Africans, on the other hand, through
their color, were more readily identified with the Hamitic myth, which
guaranteed the "natural" servitude and slavery of Africans for the benefit
of other peoples of the earth. Little of the ancient cultures of sub-Saharan
Africa was known in medieval European cultures; what knowledge there
was came from travelers' reports and religious tradition.

Nations aspiring to be medieval superpowers were not to be put off
by the papal decree awarding Africa to Portugal or by Portugal's monopoly of the slave trade, particularly the restless, avaricious merchant
classes in sixteenth-century England and Holland. The most enterprising
possibility was to break the Portuguese monopoly, which England eventually did. Hence, the African slave trade was an early prototype of a
global market economy created by the Spanish, English, Dutch, French,
and the Arabs as major players.

The unsuccessful attempt by the Spanish king Philip II to invade
England and the defeat of his Spanish Armada in 1588 broke Spain's
control of the Atlantic and North America. In 1500 Portugal ceased
being an Atlantic superpower when Spain defeated and annexed it. It
ceased being a power in the slave trade in 1642 when the Dutch occupied
the Portuguese fortress at Axim. Holland, wanting to expand its imperial
ambitions and sphere of influence, set up the East Indies Company in
1602 to get a foothold in the Asian spice trade, also a Portuguese
monopoly. But it was the commercial Dutch West India Company,
created in 1621 to break Portugal's monopoly of the slave trade and to
further Holland's intention to exploit Spain's weariness during the Thirty
Years' War (1618–1648), that began the global market in the African
slave trade. A local truce between Holland and Spain expired in 1621.

The Dutch successfully attacked Spanish settlements in Vera Cruz and San Juan in Mexico and Portuguese settlements in Africa and in Brazil. They occupied Bahia and northeastern Brazil, where they remained for some thirty years.

Sixteenth-century England was flushed with unbridled prosperity and accompanying confidence in spite of the constant threat of war. King Henry VIII, having wrestled the British church from the domain of the pope, needed to bring some class to the small island kingdom, which had continuing economic and political problems. Grand state and country houses began to replace fortress-like castles. Hans Holbein the Younger, a German-born artist who had an abiding influence on English portrait art, took up residence in Henry's court. Other famous European artists soon journeyed to England and enhanced its standing culturally among the other nations: Hans Eworth from Belgium, Lucas de Heere from Ghent. After 1555, black Africans began to be a fixture in England.[20]

Elizabeth I (1558–1603; queen 1559–1603), the product of Henry's second marriage, continued the prosperity. This "Iron Lady" also established peace and unity within the realm. Gheeraerts the Younger's portrait of Elizabeth at Hatfield House displays all the power, confidence, and flamboyance of this woman but also of the age. Bedecked with pearls and other jewels, Elizabeth holds a rainbow in her right hand symbolizing peace after all the storms of the kingdom; the inscription *non sine sole* links her to the sun, the source of the rainbow.

Blacks are thought to have lived in England since the thirteenth century, but documents say the first "certain black slaves, whereof some were tall and strong men," from the Guinean coast arrived in England on the ships of a John Lok in 1555.[21] London merchants forced Lok to return the Africans because they feared his venture would interfere with their profitable trade in gold and ivory with African tribes. But slavery also had a moral basis: "[Negroes] were a people of beastly living, without God, law, religion, or commonwealth."[22] In 1601, because of the increasing black population in England, Elizabeth banned all "blackamoores" from the nation, but failed to dislodge them altogether.[23]

20. Jordan, *White over Black*, 6.
21. James Walvin, *Black and White: The Negro and English Society, 1555–1945* (London: Allen Lane/Penguin Press, 1973), 1.
22. Louis Ruchames, ed., *Racial Thought in America*, vol. 1: *From the Puritans to Abraham Lincoln: A Documentary History* (Amherst: Univ. of Massachusetts Press, 1969), 16.
23. James Walvin, *The Black Presence: A Documentary History of the Negro in England, 1555–1860* (New York: Schocken Books, 1972), 13.

Elizabeth at first disdained the slave trade, but after learning of the profits to be made through the slaver Captain John Hawkins (1532–95), she changed her position. Indeed, she gave him one of her ships for his second voyage and became a partner in the enterprise. Several of her courtiers, such as William Cecil, the Earl of Pembroke, and Lord Clinton, the lord admiral, viewed slaving as a good investment and supported Hawkins' ventures. The religious and cultural beliefs toward blacks in Elizabeth's England were succinctly declared by Shakespeare in his *Love's Labour's Lost*: "Black is the badge of hell."[24] Elizabethans also were greatly influenced by ideas in George Best's accounts of his travels. In 1577 Best wrote that blackness was a curse derived from the biblical story of Noah in Genesis. One of Noah's white sons, Ham, disobeyed his father's instruction to reverence and fear God and not to engage in "carnal copulation" with their wives while in the ark. As punishment for his disobedience, God willed that

> a sonne should bee born whose name was Chus, who not onely it selfe, but all his posteritie after him should bee so blacke and loathsome, that it might remain a spectacle of disobedience to all the worlds. And of this black and cursed Chus came all these blacke Moores which are in Africa.[25]

Even Sir Walter Raleigh is said to have believed that the indigenous people of Guinea had "their eyes in their shoulders, and their mouths in the middle of their breasts."[26] Such views persisted in England and throughout Europe. Even in seventeenth-century England, King James I (1603–1625) in his Letters Patent to the companies of London and Plymouth that invaded the territories of the American Indians reflected a partnership between civility and the Christian faith:

> [A plan of colonization] which may, by the Providence of Almighty God, hereafter tend to the Glory of His divine Majesty, in propagating of Christian Religion to such people, as yet live in darkness and miserable ignorance of the true knowledge and worship of God, and may in time

24. Act 4, sc. 3, line 254.
25. Quoted in Jordan, *White over Black*, 41.
26. Cited in George M. Fredrickson, *White Supremacy: A Comparative Study in American and South African History* (New York: Oxford Univ. Press, 1981), 11.

bring the Infidels and Savages living in these parts, to human civility and to a settled and quiet Government.[27]

In 1530 the British broke through the Portuguese blockade, and some thirty years later they entered the slave trade via the sea captain John Hawkins. In 1562 Hawkins with three ships stole to the coasts of Guinea, secured a number of slaves partly through raids and partly through purchases from African chiefs. He sailed to the Spanish island of Hispaniola, where he sold them. Altogether Hawkins made about four trips back and forth across the Atlantic, setting the pace for what came to be called the Middle Passage: from England to Africa with products; from Africa to the New World with human slaves; from the New World to England with such products as sugar, tobacco, cotton, and rum. Judging from his portrait, he made a great deal of money and respectability before dying near Puerto Rico in 1595.

The most radical transformation of the traditional Christian view of blackness from a symbol and metaphor for evil and sin happened for a short-lived period in the late fifteenth and early sixteenth centuries. Christian art began to paint blacks as a part of the salvation drama. In a painting of the *Crucifixion* (1480–90) by the Frenchman Simon Marmion (1420–89), one of the elegantly clad soldiers guarding the dying Christ on the cross and looking at the Blessed Virgin is black. De Flandes includes a black among those watching Christ raising Lazarus in *Raising of Lazarus* (c. 1496). In *The Supper at Emmaus* (1506), the Venetian artist Marco Marziale (flourished 1492–1507) places a turbaned black servant standing next to Christ and fully aware of the revelation of Jesus as the Christ at Emmaus along with the disciples in the room. Likewise, the Italian Ambrosius Benson (died 1550) paints a well-dressed black among the spellbound spectators in *Descent from the Cross* (1530) and a black nun in the *Multiplication of the Loaves* (c. 1496–1504). This period of transformation of the black was brief, but as one art historian observes: "[The period] is one, which, by the multiplicity of the provenances, the variety of themes, a common spiritual intent, and a shared breadth of view, shows that some Europeans were giving much thought to the human condition when confronted with the diversity of peoples and, in particular, the image of the African."[28]

27. Ibid., 12.
28. Devisse and Mollat, *Image of the Black in Western Art*, 2/ii: 237.

Shades of Blackness and the
Protestant Reformation

Although much popular medieval piety during the Reformation (especially in Germany) focused on such black figures as Saint Maurice
and Prester John, none of the leaders of the Protestant Reformation
seemed to have taken a pejorative view of blackness as the color of a
people or of Africans. This question, however, has not yet been studied
by historians. There was obviously an awareness of black people in the
general public of northern and eastern Europe. Albrecht Dürer's (1471–
1528) drawings of Africans were known. His *Adoration* with a black
king was completed in 1507, but this convention was already apparent
in other German paintings and altarpieces by the mid-fifteenth century,
such as the works of Hans Memling. The statues of Saint Maurice in
Germany were unmistakably Negroid, as we have seen. Still, in spite
of the well-known slave trade in southern Europe—some 140,000 to
170,000 black slaves had been bought by Europeans, mostly around the
Mediterranean, in the Iberian Peninsula, and in southern Europe—
except for popular antiblack views in Anglican England, strong negative
views of Africans and blackness were not evident in the churches and
theologians in most of northern Europe.

This may have been because African slavery was not a firm social
institution in northern Europe, home of the Protestant Reformation.
Or perhaps the slaves were ill-suited for the agricultural and mercantile
economies of northern Europe, although countries such as England and
Holland, which became Protestant, did engage in and prospered greatly
from the slave trade at the time. There is no evidence, for example, of
slavery in rural Saxony in Germany, whose coat of arms included Maurice's insignia, and where Martin Luther (1483–1546) spent his entire
life. Dynamic commercial Geneva in French-speaking Switzerland,
whose mercantile economy depended largely on textiles, where John
Calvin (1509–64) reigned, and vibrant Zürich, the university town in
German-speaking Switzerland, where Ulrich Zwingli (1484–1531) dominated, were also absent of black slaves as domestic servants.

Bohemia, where John Huss (c. 1372–1415) lived and taught, was
familiar with the sight of African slaves because of blacks in the royal
court. Earlier, Frederick II (1212–50) as Holy Roman Emperor brought
black Muslims into Germany in 1230 and retained black African cour-
tesans as musicians and servants as visible political symbols to the rest

of Europe of his sovereignty over Egypt and Africa. Charles IV, king of Bohemia (1346–78), installed Maurice's coat of arms to legitimize his title as Holy Roman Emperor.

Martin Luther does address blackness briefly in his German translation of the Old Testament. Following the Vulgate tradition, he renders the German text of Song of Songs 1:5 as: "I am black, but quite lovely" (. . . *aber gar lieblich*). But he did not follow medieval theology in identifying evil with blackness or with the Ethiopians. In his commentary on the Song of Songs, he says the text ought to read "I am very dark . . . like the tents of Kedar. But nevertheless, I am comely . . . like the tents of Solomon." Kedar refers to the Arabs as something cheap and ugly, said Luther, whereas the tents of Solomon signify regality and beauty.[29] Commenting on the woman's description of herself as "black but comely," Luther remarks:

> Although I am in a state founded by God and adorned with the Word of God, yet I seem to be most wretched in appearance, there is no success. . . . Do not be offended by this appearance. Turn your attention not to my blackness but to the kiss which God offers me [Song of Songs 1:2], and then you will see that I am comely and lovable. For although outwardly I suffer all manner of vexation, yet I am desirable on account of the Word and faith.[30]

The church is also undesirable in its current appearance—"lacerated and wretchedly afflicted and exposed to the taunts of all men." But like the black woman, so too is the church's salvation anchored in the Word of God and God's faith.[31]

Luther's lectures on Genesis also display no particular negative view of blackness or Africans. He accepts the ancient view that Africa meant Libya and Cush meant Ethiopia, located somewhere in the "interior lands of the South." And he believed that Ham and his descendants populated the entire southern area of the known world (Africa), which he calls "the most excellent part of the world."[32] Nor does he interpret Ham's curse as the divine reason for blacks being enslaved. The curse

29. *Luther's Works*, ed. Jaroslav Pelikan, 55 vols. (St. Louis: Concordia, 1960–72), 15:201.
30. Ibid., 15:200.
31. Ibid., 15:200–201.
32. *Luther's Works*, 2:195.

in Genesis 9 is God's sui generis way of revealing divine freedom to exceed human expectations and to baffle humankind:

> Ham is cursed by his father, but he takes possession of the largest part of the world and establishes extensive kingdoms. On the other hand, Shem and Japheth are blessed, but if you compare them with Ham, and their descendants are beggars. How then can this prophecy be true? This prophesy and all others, whether they are promises or threats, are beyond the group of reason and understandable solely by faith. For God delays both the punishments and the rewards.[33]

Indeed, Luther said Ham's curse demonstrates the irony of divine goodness embedded even in God's wrath: the son of Ham was Canaan, who was cursed to be a slave to his brothers. But the brothers' descendants, who had Noah's blessing, themselves became servants of the Canaanites. "Since the Egyptians are the descendants of Ham, with what pitiful servitude Israel is oppressed in that country!"[34]

The Swiss reformer John Calvin in prosperous commercial Geneva failed even to connect the curse on Canaan with Africans at all. He observes that although Canaan was cursed to be "a servant of servants" to his brothers forever in Gen. 9:25, obviously this prophecy was delayed and even may have been a harmless joke, "since the Canaanites [at the time this was written] were outstanding in power, riches, and resources. Where then is their slavery?" Calvin replies that God's judgment is not always fulfilled immediately nor is it always visible to the human eye.[35]

In summary, it cannot be claimed that the church had a convincing and clear picture of its belief about blacks and blackness during the Middle Ages, its various texts to the contrary. The church was not entirely against the slave trade, especially since its lands and clergy benefited from the trade. The two major sea powers, Portugal and Spain, were both encouraged and supported through papal bulls and international treaties to pursue African slaves in order to convert them to the Christian faith.

33. Jaroslav Pelikan, ed., *Luther's Works*, vol. 2: *Lectures on Genesis, Chapters 6–14* (St. Louis: Concordia, 1960), 175–76.
34. Ibid., 176.
35. *Calvin: Commentaries*, trans. and ed. Joseph Haroutunian and Louise Pettibone Smith (Philadelphia: Westminster, 1958), 276.

A mind-set and an atmosphere, fortified by church theology and doctrines about infidels and the experience and dislike of the Moors—many of whom were dark-skinned—allowed what one writer described as "the certain expectation of heaven, and of profit here below, [which] made many a captain eager to venture."[36] In some ways similar to the racialist mind-set created in Nazi Germany to allow for the disenfranchising of gypsies, Jews, and the Slavic people in the East, so Europe in the Middle Ages dealt with blacks. This mind-set embraced Protestant as well as Catholic countries. Slavery as an institution was not new nor has it been totally abolished in some parts of the modern world. What was different about the African slave trade was its religious underpinnings and its declaring a person because of blackness to be sold as private property.

Although *race* is a modern concept, there is little doubt that such ethnocentric doctrines as Spain's *limpieza de sangre* were racial just as claims about Aryan blood in modern Germany were racial. This racialism was generated by the ecclesiastical and the political view of the Islamic Moors, and quickly became institutionalized in the New World colonies. The baptismal caste system is a good example of this, one that again demonstrates a lasting partnership between Christianity's beliefs about blackness and cultural practices and views. Such beliefs and practices also remind us that ideas about inclusiveness within the Christian churches are recent and have not been in the seedbed of the Christian tradition nor of Western Christendom.

36. Henry Marsh, *Slavery and Race: The Story of Slavery and Its Legacy for Today* (Newton Abbot, England: David & Charles, 1974), 83.

6 | Blackness in Europe and America

*N*ationalism, sea-power ambitions, and the search for new markets drove many European states to establish beachheads in the Caribbean and the Americas. England staked a tentative claim by occupying Barbados in 1605 (although it did not settle Barbados as a colony until twenty years later) and a permanent claim in 1622 with the founding of Saint Kitts, its first colony and a small tadpole island. By 1671, St. Kitts and other Leeward Islands received some seven thousand African slaves.[1] Within twenty years England imported black slaves regularly to work the sugar and cotton plantations in its Caribbean empire and to replace the dying indigenous Indian labor force.

In 1607 England followed the same strategy when it established its first colony in North America at Jamestown, Virginia; twelve years later, the first shipload of blacks arrived in the new colony. With the eventual settling of Barbados in 1627, England's colonial empire was on its way. By 1643 some 6,000 black slaves had been brought to that tiny pear-shaped island and by 1673 their numbers had increased to 33,200.[2]

1. Philip D. Curtin, *The Atlantic Slave Trade: A Census* (Madison, Wis.: Univ. of Wisconsin Press, 1969), 82.
2. Ibid., 59.

If "visual images are a part of a culture's structure and not simply expressions of its religious beliefs, historical myths, moral codes, aesthetic preferences, internal social system, and relationship with outsiders,"[3] then the art of sixteenth- and seventeenth-century Europe as cultural signatures of the time reveal important clues about European and British religious beliefs about blacks and blackness. This is so, even if only among intellectuals, the affluent, and artisans. The artworks reveal a legacy from Greco-Roman cultures and Christian influence that can be called a peculiar cultural metaphysics about blackness and Africa beneath a veneer of Christian civilized living.

Earlier European art depicted blacks at both ends of the spectrum of social class. In portraits of the aristocrats such as Charles Seymour Riley's *Sixth Duke of Sommerset* and Sir Anthony Van Dyck's (1599–1641) majestic portrait of *Henrietta of Lorraine*, blacks are depicted with some dignity. In caricatures about the poor, such as Cooper's *The Sailors Fleet Wedding Entertainment Figure*, a turbaned black (possibly representing a Turk), makes a lustful grab for a nearby prostitute. In a panel of Hans Grien's *Birth of the Virgin* (sixteenth century), a black woman servant with a basket on her head (along with a white woman servant holding a chicken) attends the Virgin at childbirth. William Hogarth (1697–1764) depicted blacks in some twenty pictures and engravings, more than any other English artist of his day.[4]

European Colonialism and Blackness

In 1634 the Dutch colonized Aruba, Curaçao, and Bonaire to establish military bases for attacking Spanish America. By 1640 the Dutch had captured Guiana and had founded a colony in the Americas that they called New Netherland, whose main settlement they named New Amsterdam (later changed to New York by the British). One scribe of the period said the Dutch victory over Spain was crucial for the later successes of England and France in the Caribbean. "Dutch victories strained the

---

3. Hugh Honour, *The Image of the Black in Western Art*, vol. 4/i: *From the American Revolution to World War I: Slaves and Liberators* (Cambridge, Mass.: Harvard Univ. Press, 1989), 14.

4. For an outstanding study of blacks in English eighteenth-century art, see David Dabydeen, *Hogarth's Blacks: Images of Blacks in Eighteenth Century English Art* (Athens: Univ. of Georgia Press, 1987).

overtaxed resources of Spain almost to a breaking point, and provided a naval screen behind which the English, the French, the Scots, and the Danes, without much danger of Spanish interference, could build up their colonies in a long string down the Atlantic coast from Newfoundland to Barbados."[5]

Precisely when the Dutch began importing slaves to their Caribbean island colonies is not known, although by 1625 they were supplying the Leeward Islands with knowledge about sugar plantations and slaves to work the plantations, which they colonized between 1630 and 1640. Well-informed estimates range from 20,000 slaves in the Dutch Antilles to 1.2 million in Bahia during the entire period of slavery until it was ended in those respective places in the late nineteenth century.[6]

Something of the belief about blackness in Calvinistic Dutch society is revealed in works of its great painters. Many Dutch artists painted blacks. Rembrandt (1606–69), for example, decided not to follow the convention of a black Magus in his painting of the Holy Family (modeled on the modest home of a Dutch carpenter), but nonetheless painted blacks to exude sovereignty and dignity in their own right, such as his *Negro with a Bow and Arrows.* Jan Steen (1626–79) in 1645 painted a scene of a marriage contract in the Netherlands in which the future bridegroom is black with obvious Negroid features and the bride is a European. An Indian looks at the scene as a spectator.

At the same time, European paintings reveal cultural changes in views toward blacks as European states acquired colonies in the New World and African slaves were imported. British painters and American artists working in London, for example, began to include blacks either as servants, as in John Singleton Copley's (1737–1815) *Watson and the Shark* (1778) and John Trumbull's (1750–1831) *George Washington* (1780), or heroic figures, as in Copley's *The Death of Major Peirson* (1782–84). One writer comments on the view of blacks in eighteenth-century English art:

> The vast majority of eighteenth century English images of blacks are, however, of anonymous men and a few women in domestic service. . . .
> Whether the blacks dressed in smart livery in English portrait groups

5. Quoted in Franklin W. Knight, *The Caribbean: The Genesis of a Fragmented Nationalism* (New York: Oxford Univ. Press, 1978), 37.
6. Curtin, *The Atlantic Slave Trade,* 89.

were technically slaves or free servants is indeterminate and was probably of little concern to their painters. These figures, associated by their activities with the West and only by their color with Africa, tended to be regarded less as members of a nation or geographically defined group than as representatives of a race differentiated physically, culturally, and socially from the other people among whom they lived and worked, whether in America or Europe.[7]

The Enlightenment: Blackness and Natural Inferiority

Eighteenth-century Europeans had a romance with the tropics. They fantasized about the inhabitants of the tropics living in an imagined simple "natural state" amid the lush foliage and vegetation of Africa, the Caribbean, and the South Pacific. They conjectured that this, rather than North America, was the real New World. The romance was a convergence of imagined exotic fantasies, a longing for a simple quality of life and government, and the legacy of primal mystery about blackness in European and Christian thought. It was also a romance that supported European claims of cultural hegemony, especially when those claims combined with high-sounding Christian concern for the "noble savage" in Africa and the Caribbean.

This claim of cultural hegemony allowed for a paternalism toward blacks, such as we find in some poets like William Blake (1757–1827), who defend the superiority of whites over blackness:

> My mother bore me in the southern wild,
> And I am black, but O! my soul is white;
> White as an angel is the English child,
> But I am black, as if bereav'd of light.[8]

Little empirical data supported such a convergence; much of it relied on travelers' journals and books that upheld rather flamboyant European

7. Honour, *Image of the Black in Western Art*, 4/i:30–31.
8. William Blake, *Songs of Innocence and of Experience.* Quoted in Philip D. Curtin, *The Image of Africa: British Ideas and Action, 1780–1850* (Madison: Univ. of Wisconsin, 1964), 50.

ethnocentric claims of cultural superiority. As a European traveler to West Africa reported:

> If the soil be vastly rich, situated in a warm climate, and naturally watered, the productions of the earth will be almost spontaneous; this will make the inhabitants lazy. Laziness is the greatest of all obstacles to labor and industry. Manufactures will never flourish there. . . . It is in climates less favored by nature, and where the soil produces to those only who labor, and in proportion to the industry of every one, where we may expect to find great multitudes.[9]

An eighteenth-century British physician who once practiced medicine in the Caribbean wrote:

> There is, in the inhabitants of hot climates, unless present sickness has an absolute control over the body, a promptitude and bias to pleasure, and an alienation from serious thought and deep reflection. The brilliancy of the skies, and the levity of the atmosphere, conspire to influence the nerves against philosophy and her frigid tenets, and forbids their practice among the children of the sun.[10]

Concurring, the distinguished French naturalist Comte George Leclerc Buffon (1707–88) argued that blacks were a lesser degeneration of the normative Greco-European archetype. Another Frenchman wrote that black intellect was inferior even to that of elephants, with an inclination toward perversity and depravity.[11]

The question of climate was widespread in Europe as it began its various colonial empires. Charles-Louis Montesquieu (1689–1755), whose social thought on government and political liberty greatly influenced many early American patriots, held that there is a correlation between climate and intelligence. In his *The Spirit of the Laws* (1748), while he personally deplored the slave trade and the enslavement of other human beings, he supported a good friend, the French economist

9. James Denham Stuart, "An Inquiry into the Principles of Political Economy" (1770). Cited in Curtin, *The Image of Africa*, 62.
10. Benjamin Mosely, *A Treatise on Tropical Diseases; and on the Climate of the West Indies* (London, 1787), 48. Cited in Curtin, *The Image of Africa*, 65.
11. David Brion Davis, *The Problem of Slavery in Western Culture* (Ithaca, N.Y.: Cornell Univ. Press, 1966), 457, 461.

Jean Melon, who defended slavery on the basis of expediency, the economic needs of Europe, and the natural inferiority of black people.[12]

Montesquieu believed that hot climates produce more sensuous people who are mostly concerned with bodily pleasures and sloth; cold climates produce people with greater interest in matters of the intellect. Because tropical primitive societies are loosely organized, their inhabitants have unlimited freedom and little exploitation since there is no money to create inequality. Natural rights and duties and natural law exist, however, which had to be respected by all, whether in primitive or more developed societies. Montesquieu allows for private slavery—servants to satisfy the pleasures of masters—and political slavery—prisoners captured in wars of self-defense and enslaved to maintain the conquest:

> Slavery, properly so called, is the establishment of a right which gives to one man such a power over another as renders him absolute master of his life and fortune. The state of slavery is in its own nature bad. It is neither useful to the master nor to the slave.[13]

At the same time, while contending that all races are born equal, Montesquieu also thinks that slavery is more appropriate in some countries, especially Africa and Asia, whose lack of a temperate climate inclined them to be the natural home for all kinds of bondage:

> But as all men are born equal, slavery must be accounted unnatural, though in some countries, it is founded on natural reason; and a wide difference ought to be made between such countries, and those in which every natural reason rejects it, as in Europe, where it has been so happily abolished.[14]

Presumably, Montesquieu's line of reasoning about climate also would support slavery in Africa, if not in Europe; hence some interpret the following text from him as ironic and satirical, others as implicitly racially imperialistic:[15]

12. Ibid., 404–5.
13. Charles-Louis Montesquieu, *The Spirit of the Laws*, bk. 15, chap. 1, trans. Anne M. Cohler, et al. (Cambridge, England: Cambridge Univ. Press, 1989), 246.
14. Ibid., bk. 15, chap. 7, 251.
15. Robert Anstey, *The Atlantic Slave Trade and British Abolition 1760–1810* (London: Macmillan, 1975), 104; Robert Shackleton, *Montesquieu: A Critical Biography* (Oxford, England: Oxford Univ. Press, 1961), 260–61.

It is hardly to be believed that God, who is a wise Being, should place a soul, especially a good soul, in such a black ugly body. . . . It is impossible for us to suppose these creatures to be men, because, allowing them to be men, a suspicion would follow that we ourselves are not Christians.[16]

In eighteenth- and nineteenth-century European social thought, a debate raged between two theories about race: the biological theory of *monogenesis* (at creation a single humankind was created in the image of God) and the geological theory of *polygenesis* (as a rock originates from different fragments held together by calcareous cement, so also at creation different racial types were established sui generis). Monogenists claimed that skin color distinguished different races in a hierarchial chain of being with the Europeans at the top and blacks at the bottom as a degeneration of original being. They believed, however, that even degenerate races could progress upward toward improvement over the centuries. One Frenchman theorized that all races were latent variants in the original union of the egg and sperm given to Adam and Eve, who were white. The black variants, driven off to Africa by the "normal" part of humanity, bred their own kind and color. It was not impossible, however, that one day they could change back into their original European race.[17]

Polygenists also assumed that Europeans were naturally superior and blacks naturally inferior, but they did not believe that blacks could progress intellectually or culturally. Blacks were a race separate from the offspring of Adam and Eve and inferior by nature. Polygenesis particularly appealed to Americans. A Swiss naturalist, Louis Agassiz (1807–73), who migrated to the United States in the nineteenth century, was a great influence in propagating the polygenesis view of blacks.

Agassiz had contact with blacks for the first time when he saw the servants in a Philadelphia hotel where he was staying. The experience was a "shaking of the foundations" (Tillich). In a letter to his mother, he wrote:

I can scarcely express to you the painful impression that I received. . . . Nevertheless, I experienced pity at the sight of this degraded and degenerate race, and their lot inspired compassion in me in thinking that

16. Montesquieu, *Spirit of the Laws*, bk. 15, chap. 5, 250.
17. Curtin, *The Image of Africa*, 40.

they are really men. Nonetheless, it is impossible for me to repress the feeling that they are not of the same blood as us. In seeing their black faces with their thick lips and grimacing teeth, the wool on their head, . . . I could not take my eyes off their face in order to tell them to stay far away. . . .[18]

Agassiz believed that while all humans are bound by a common structure, races are created separate from each other. He ranked the races on the basis of their "character." He felt that social equality was impractical because of the character of blacks, which he described as "indolent, playful, sensuous, imitative, subservient, good-natured. . . . Therefore I hold that they are incapable of living on a footing of social equality with whites, in one and the same community, without being an element of social disorder."[19] It is "mock-philosophy" to think that all races are equal with the same abilities and natural dispositions. A hierarchy exists:

This compact continent of Africa exhibits a population which has been in constant intercourse with the white race, which has enjoyed the benefit of the example of the Egyptian civilization, of the Arab civilization . . . and nevertheless there has never been a regulated society of black men developed on that continent. Does not this indicate in this race a peculiar apathy, a peculiar indifference to the advantages afforded by civilized society?[20]

J. C. Pritchard, a nineteenth-century ethnologist, perhaps represented the mind of many Americans (with the exception of the abolitionists) when he confirmed the theory that a hierarchy and typology existed among Negroes:

Tribes having what is termed the Negro character in the most striking degree are the least civilized. The Pepels, Nisagos, Ibos, who are in the greatest degree remarkable for deformed countenances, projecting jaws, flat foreheads . . . are the most savage and morally degraded of the natives.[21]

18. Stephen Jay Gould, "American Polygeny and Craniometry before Darwin," in *The Modern Condition II* (Needham Heights, Mass.: Ginn Press, 1993), 41.

19. Ibid., 43.

20. Ibid., 42.

21. J. C. Pritchard, *Researches into the Natural History of Mankind*, 2 vols. (London, 1939), 1:97. Quoted in Paul Johnson, *The Birth of the Modern: World Society 1815–1830* (New York: HarperCollins, 1991), 243.

American Colonialism and Blackness

In 1619, as is well known, African slaves first officially disembarked in the British American colonies—one year before the Pilgrims landed at Plymouth Rock. The secretary and recorder of Virginia, John Rolfe, noted that twenty African "Negers" (sometimes spelled "Negars") were delivered to Jamestown, Virginia, by a Dutch slaver, who had taken them from a captured Spanish ship.[22] What is less familiar is whether "Negers" referred entirely to a party of African blacks, who in fact may have been Christian indentured servants rather than chattel slaves, or to Indians. Although Rolfe wrote English names, at least eleven had Spanish or Spanish-origin names, which he may have Anglicized: a woman called Angelo, several named Antonio, Isabella, Juan, Guillen, Francisca, Eduardo, and Margarita. The Spanish-sounding names suggest that these were baptismal names.[23]

Furthermore, both Dutch and English borrowed *neger* (Lat.: *niger*; *negri*; Eng.: *negro*) from Spanish and Portuguese. The Spanish used *neger* and *negro* to mean "dark," "darkly colored," or "brown" in contrast to *blanco* or *loco*, meaning "white." It was used for Indians and Africans.[24] Thus, it is possible that the "twenty negers" may have included Indian slaves from South America, Indians from the Caribbean, black African slaves, and slaves of half-African, half-Indian origins. Both Spanish and Portuguese explorers, including Columbus, took brown- and dark-skinned Indian slaves back to Europe from the New World. The Dutch in the sixteenth and seventeenth centuries preferred *Moor* (meaning a blue-black color similar to the color of coal: "he is black as a Moor")[25] and *Moriaan* for black-skinned and dark nonwhite people. They called Muslims Turks rather than Moors.[26] Hence, like the Spanish, the Dutch

22. "About the last of August, there came to Virginia a Dutchman of Warre that sold us twenty Negars." Helen Tunnicliff Catterall, ed., *Judicial Cases concerning American Slavery and the Negro*, 5 vols. (Washington, D.C.: Carnegie Institution, 1926), 1:55; A. Leon Higginbotham, Jr., *In the Matter of Color: Race and the American Legal Process: the Colonial Period* (New York: Oxford Univ. Press, 1978), 20.

23. *Judicial Cases*, 1:56.

24. Jack D. Forbes, *Black Africans and Native Americans: Color, Race and Caste in the Evolution of Red-Black Peoples* (Oxford, England: Basil Blackwell, 1988), 75.

25. J. Verdam, *Middlenederlandsch Woordenbock* (The Hague: Nijhoff, 1912).

26. A 1639 Dutch-French-Spanish dictionary gave the following synonyms for the Spanish *negro*: "French: noir, sombre, obscur, offusque, brun; Dutch: swart, doneker, bruin." Ibid., 79.

referred to all slaves as *negro* and *neger* without restricting this sobriquet to black Africans.

According to the anthropologist Melville Herskovits, the greater number of African slaves brought to the United States came from the Senegambia region from the Senegal River in the north that goes around the great bend of West Africa to the Guinea coast to the Bight of Benin. This region also included coastal areas of modern Ghana, what is now the Republic of Benin, and, although the term *Guinea* itself was somewhat imprecise in the sixteenth century, what is now Sierra Leone, Ivory Coast, Liberia, Guinea-Bissau, Nigeria and Togo.[27]

Slaves arrived in New England in 1638 at the Massachusetts Bay Colony.[28] Other evidence, however, suggests that slaves may have been in the colony as early as 1624 as the property of a Samuel Maverick (c. 1602–76), who owned slaves before the 1629 Massachusetts Bay settlement.[29] In 1641 Massachusetts Bay passed the first colonial statute (Body of Liberties) that furthered the cultural ambiguity of blackness by both prohibiting and permitting slavery. On the one hand, "there shall be never an bond slaverie, villenage, or captivitie amongst us,"[30] but on the other hand, (1) "unless it be lawful captives taken in juste warres, and (2) such strangers as willfully sell themselves or (3) are sold to us," thus permitting slavery.[31] We know that in spite of this statute and the Puritan religion of the colonists, many Massachusetts Bay residents did participate in and profit from the slave trade. Some clerics, such as John Eliot (1604–90), opposed the slave trade to the Boston General Council, but on the whole failed to rally a significant public following:

27. Melville J. Herskovits, "The Ancestry of the American Negro," *The New World Negro: Selected Papers in Afro-American Studies*, ed. Francis S. Herskovits (Bloomington: Indiana Univ. Press, 1966), 116.

28. John Winthrop, *The History of New England, 1630–1649*, vol. 1, ed. James K. Hosmer (New York: Scribner's, 1908), 260.

29. Lorenzo Johnston Greene, *The Negro in Colonial New England 1620–1776* (New York: Columbia Univ. Press, 1942), 17.

30. According to Higginbotham, *villenage* was the feudal labor system of bondage in ancient England in which the worker was bonded to the manor like a serf. He or she was the personal property of the lord of the manor and could not own property, hence was comparable to a slave. The lord's property rights extended to the direct descendants of male villeins. The villein did have some legal and social status. The system was in decline by the end of Elizabeth I's reign. Higginbotham, *In the Matter of Color*, 323.

31. *Colonial Laws of Massachusetts Rep. from 1660 Supp. to 1672* (Boston, 1889), 91. Cited in George H. Moore, *Notes on the History of Slavery in Massachusetts* (1866; reprint, New York: Negro Universities Press, 1968), 10–30 *passim*.

This usage of them is worse than death. It seemeth to me that to sell them away as slaves is to hinder the enlargement of His kingdom. . . . To steel them away from all means of grace when Christ hath provided means of grace for them is the way for us to be active in destroying their souls, when we are highly obliged to seek their conversion and salvation.[32]

No widespread opposition to slavery existed in the Massachusetts Bay Colony, even though by 1688 only a few hundred blacks lived there. In fact, one of the earliest experiments to breed future black slaves occurred in Massachusetts in 1664.[33] By the eighteenth century, blacks made up only 3 percent of New England's population.[34] When the first federal census was taken in 1790, blacks made up only 16,800 out of a general population of 1,099,000 in New England, unlike the South, where blacks almost outnumbered whites in some colonies. Apparently the institution of indentured servitude met most of the needs of Massachusetts patricians and farmers. In addition, some Indians were enslaved after their defeat by the white colonists in the Pequot War in 1637. Why, then, were slaves tolerated and maintained in Puritan New England and particularly in Massachusetts with its Body of Liberties statutes?

Winthrop Jordan proposes that Massachusetts justified slavery as punishment for criminals, and captives in war. "Slavery as punishment probably derived from analogy with captivity, since presumably a king or magistrates could mercifully spare and enslave a man whose crime had forfeited his right to life."[35] There is some support for this position; in wars between England or other European states and non-Christian nations, prisoners were frequently taken and made slaves. The legal status of such slaves in British law was not clear.

32. John Eliot, "A Protest," in John Winsor, *The Memorial History of Boston*, vol. 1 (Boston, 1880), 322. Quoted in Higginbotham, *In the Matter of Color*, 65.

33. Daniel P. Mannix and Malcolm Cowley, *Black Cargoes: A History of the Atlantic Slave Trade 1518–1865* (New York: Viking Press, 1962), 56.

34. The first census of races in New England in 1715 showed 158,000 whites and 4,150 blacks. In 1776, blacks made up 1.8 percent of the general population in Massachusetts; in 1774 6.3 percent in Rhode Island and 3.2 percent in Connecticut; and in 1771 .04 percent of Vermont's population. See Greene, *The Negro in Colonial New England*, 73–74.

35. Winthrop D. Jordan, *White over Black: American Attitudes toward the Negro, 1550–1812* (New York: W. W. Norton, 1968), 69.

Although a sixteenth-century judicial decision (Cartwright [1549]) prohibited an Englishman from keeping a slave brought from Russia— "England was too pure an aire for slaves to breath in"—the first court case dealing with a black slave was *Butts v. Penny* (1677). The court distinguished between slaves who were white (most likely the situation in the *Cartwright* decision, although this decision was not referred to) and those who were black. Because blacks were "usually bought and sold among merchants, as merchandise, and also being infidels, there might be a Property in them," the court ruled that the plaintiff could recover the costs and value of personal property—in this case, a slave— wrongfully sold or used by someone else.[36] The court did not mention the slave's color, but it did stress that slaves were non-Christian, "Subjects of an Infidel Prince."[37]

At the same time, the 1727 letter of the bishop of London, who had ecclesiastical oversight in the colonies, claimed that the sacrament of baptism was not a license for granting liberty to black slaves. To gain some theological and legal clarity about the authority of the bishop's letter, George Berkeley (1685–1753), bishop of Cloyne in Ireland, came to America after he received a 1729 legal opinion from the attorney-general and the solicitor-general in England: "[A] slave, by coming from the West Indies, either with or without his master, to Great Britain or Ireland, doth not become free . . . and baptism doth not bestow freedom on him, nor make any alteration in his temporal conditions in these kingdoms. We are also of the opinion, the master may legally compel him to return to the plantation."[38] Berkeley reported later to the Society for the Propagation of the Gospel (SPG) in England that the colonists displayed "an irrational contempt of the blacks, as creatures of another species, who had no right to be instructed or admitted to the sacraments. . . ."[39]

But Massachusetts and the rest of New England supported slavery for more utilitarian reasons: (1) a shortage of labor in New England rum distilleries, and (2) profits from such important consumer products as sugar, rum, and molasses. Sugar and molasses from the West Indies

36. Higginbotham, *In the Matter of Color*, 321.
37. Ibid., 322.
38. Ibid., 327.
39. Lester B. Scherer, *Slavery and the Churches in Early America 1619–1819* (Grand Rapids, Mich.: Eerdmans, 1975), 91.

were distilled into rum in New England, thereby making the rum distillery business the largest industry in that region prior to the Revolutionary War.[40] By 1700 Boston was the chief port and Massachusetts along with Rhode Island (Newport) were the major colonies for supplying slaves to the whole of New England. A commodities market—lumber, produce, fish, horses, dairy products emerged also as the result of trading in slaves.[41]

Religious leadership in the North and the South found no moral offense or contradiction between slavery, the Bible, and the Christian faith. A survey of some 275 well-known Christian ministers from all churches who supported black slavery as a responsible moral action included Episcopal bishops as well as leading Baptist, Congregational, Presbyterian, and Jewish clerics. They represented a strong cross-section of the leaders and the elite of colonial society.[42] These were the movers and shakers of thought and moral norms. Most had graduated from universities, many of them north of the Mason-Dixon Line. The largest number graduated from Yale (19) and South Carolina College (14). After seminaries as institutions for professional ministerial formation came into vogue, many of these proslavery clerics took up additional education at such places as Princeton Theological Seminary (Presbyterian) in New Jersey, Andover (Congregationalist) in Massachusetts, and General (Episcopal) in New York City. Their sermons and writings reflected society's and the churches' general acceptance of slavery:

> Professionalization of the clergy, religious revivals, benevolent reforms, the missionary impulse, the rise of denominationalism, the infiltration of clergymen into educational institutions, and dozens of other currents in American religions paralleled and sometimes foreshadowed the course of proslavery history from the American Revolution to the Civil War.[43]

A survey of white clergy supporting slavery in their writings, speeches, and sermons between 1790 and 1865 reveals that most had been born into comfortable, affluent families in Europe, New England, the East,

40. Greene, *The Negro in Colonial New England*, 25–26.
41. Ibid., 22–24.
42. Larry E. Tise, *Proslavery: A History of the Defense of Slavery in America, 1701–1840* (Athens: Univ. of Georgia Press, 1987), 135, 363–66.
43. Ibid., xvii–xviii.

or the South. Such evidence refutes claims that proslavery views were primarily a proclivity in the South (see Table 1, below).

Table 1: Birthplaces of Proslavery Clerics According to Birthdate[44]

Region	1669–1800	1801–1815	1816–1839
Europe	15	16	13
New England	21	14	6
N.Y., N.J., Penn.	17	6	10
Middle West	0	0	5
Border States	1	7	3
Upper South	15	20	23
Lower South	12	23	29

Puritan slaveowners also had the dilemma of whether they should allow their slaves to be baptized. In accordance with their doctrine that no Christian ought to hold another Christian in bondage, they risked losing their property and investment, not to mention cheap labor, if their slaves were baptized. In Massachusetts baptism conferred church membership, which in turn conferred political privileges, such as automatic membership in the Company of Massachusetts Bay. Yet not to baptize slaves meant impeding the spread of the Christian faith to these "heathen." The Puritans felt a religious and patriotic duty to follow the 1660 instruction of King Charles II: namely, to spread the Protestant faith among the natives and slaves in order to compete with the Catholic Church. As he noted:

> Slaves may be best invited to the Christian faith and be made capable of being baptized thereunto, it being to the honor of our Crowne and of the Protestant Religion that all persons in any of our Dominions should be taught the knowledge of God and be made acquainted with the mysteries of Salvation.[45]

44. Ibid., 131.
45. *Calendar of State Papers: Colonial, 1574–1660*, 492–93. Cited in Greene, *The Negro in Colonial New England*, 263.

To protect their property rights, including slaves, some colonial leg-
islatures passed ordinances that prohibited baptism of slaves to preclude
this rite being cited as a reason for emancipation. The 1669 Fundamental
Constitution of South Carolina, whose authors included John Locke
(1632–1704), one of founders of British Empiricism and of the Enlightenment, said that whites in Carolina "shall have absolute power and
authority over Negro slaves, [regardless] of what opinion or Religion
soever."[46] In 1706 New York passed a law regulating this quandary of
slaveowners:

> In order therefore to put an end to all such Doubts and Scruples as have
> or hereafter at any time may arise about the same. Be it Enacted by the
> Governor Council and Assembly and it is hereby Enacted by the authority
> of the same, That the Baptizing of any Negro, Indian or Mulatto Slave
> shall not be any Cause or reason for the setting them free or any of
> them at Liberty.[47]

Some prominent Puritan clergy, for example Cotton Mather (1663–
1728), constructed a theological synthesis to resolve this dilemma. Mather urged owners to allow their black slaves as rational children of God
to be baptized and instructed in the Christian faith. Slaves are spiritual
"neighbors," even though they remain slaves. That means that slaves
and slaveowners are neighbors and brothers, since God has made all
humanity of one blood. We should love our neighbors, and therefore
slaves should be treated fairly, instructed in the Christian faith, and
baptized for the sake of their own salvation.[48] Slaves offered white
Christians an evangelistic

> opportunity to try, whether you may not be the happy instruments, of
> converting, the blackest instances of blindness and baseness, into ad-
> mirable candidates of eternal blessedness. . . . Suppose these Wretched
> *Negroes* to be the Offspring of *Cham* (which yet is not so very

46. *Statutes at Large of South Carolina*, vol. 1, 55. Cited in Higginbotham, *In the Matter of Color*, 163.
47. *Colonial Laws of New York*, chap. 160, 597–98 (21 October 1706). Cited in Higginbotham, *In the Matter of Color*, 127.
48. Cotton Mather, *Rules for the Society of Negroes (1693)*, reprint (New York: George H. Moore, 1888); Cotton Mather, *The Negro Christianized* (Boston: B. Green, 1706), in *Racial Thought in America*, ed. Louis Ruchames, vol. 1: *From the Puritans to Abraham Lincoln: A Documentary History* (Amherst: Univ. of Massachusetts Press, 1969), 61–65.

certain), . . . Let us make a trial, whether they that have been Scorched
and Blacken'd by the Sun of Africa, may not come to have their Minds
Healed by the more Benign Beams of the Sun of Righteousness.[49]

In his proposed catechism for instructing slaves in the Christian faith,
however, Mather reminded the slaves that conversion to the Christian
faith did not assure emancipation from their bondage or duties as slaves:
"I must love God, and Pray to Him, and Keep the Lord's Day. I must
Love all Men, and never Quarrel, nor be unchast, nor steal, nor tell a
ly, *nor be discontent with my condition*" (emphasis added).[50]

Among the leading wealthy slave merchants were many of New
England's first families: the Waldos, Fanueils (donors of the famous
Fanueil Hall, "cradle of liberty," in Boston), the Cabots, the Royalls of
Massachusetts, the Gardners, the Ellerys (a signer of the Declaration of
Independence), and the DeWolfs and Browns (patrons of Brown University) of Rhode Island, just to mention a few. Likewise, new industries
in New England, such as the news media, grew commercially from the
slave trade: the first lasting newspaper, the *Boston News Letter*, first
published in April 1704, carried advertisements for the sale of slaves.
Such advertising became an important source of income for subsequent
newspapers in eighteenth-century New England.[51]

Blacks appeared in paintings of patrician colonial America. In Edward
Savage's painting of George Washington's family, *The Washington Family*
(1796), a small black servant boy can be seen. Soon blacks began to be
depicted as noble and regal figures, such as Raphaelle Peale's *Portrait
of Absalom Jones* (1810) and Philip Tilyard's *Portrait of Citizen Jonathan
Granville* (1824). Black portrait painters also emerged: Joshua Johnston (1765–1830), Robert Douglass (1809–87), and Robert
Duncanson (1817–72).

What discreet visual art did not display about blackness was the
association of blackness with sex. This concurrent theme ran through
seventeenth- and eighteenth-century Europe and was carried over into
the American colonies. The historian David Davis claims that this
·association was a big obstacle to the black being accepted as equal by
Europeans.[52] To the contrary, I think that for most Europeans, carnality

49. Cotton Mather, *The Negro Christianized* (Boston: B. Green, 1706), 2–3.
50. Greene, *The Negro in Colonial New England*, 39.
51. Ibid., 33.
52. Davis, *The Problem of Slavery in Western Culture*, 446, 468.

with regard to blacks was what the nineteenth century called an "elixir of repression" whose origins can be traced to Greco-Roman times, early Christian theological influences, monasticism, and Christian ascetics. Erotic ideas about blacks provided Europeans a convenient way of venting their negative societal view of blacks, while at the same time allowing them a discreet indulgence in exceeding existing taboos about engaging black flesh. A seventeenth-century slave trader, Richard Jobson, felt no public restraint in commenting on "the enormous size of the virile member among the Negroes as an infallible proof, that they are sprung from *Canaan* [sic] for uncovering his father's nakedness, and had (according to the Schoolmen) a curse laid upon that part."[53] Another contemporary spoke of the sensuousness of young black women, whose "very large breasts . . . stand strutting out so hard and firm, as no leaping, jumping, or stirring, will cause them to shake any more, than the brawn of their arms."[54]

Anxiety about the erotic prowess of blacks also plagued the American settlers in the colonies. A major instrument of inhibition was laws permitting castration of black males both as a punishment and as a control mechanism. This practice apparently was an American specialty reserved for black slaves and occasionally for Indian slaves. British law had no provision for such a practice, and in fact British colonial authorities were staggered by its enforcement.[55] Statutory law in Antigua, Bermuda, North and South Carolina, and New Jersey permitted it. Pennsylvania was the single colony legalizing castration for whites as an alternative to capital punishment, but it was never used.[56]

Castration was considered a means of subduing "spirited" black males who were suspected of violating white women. The purpose was to control their sexual prowess, not dissimilar to what was done to bulls and stallions. Furthermore, castration was linked to carnal curiosity about

53. Astley, *New General Collection*, II, 268. Cited in Davis, *The Problem of Slavery in Western Culture*, 452.

54. Richard Ligon, *A True & Exact History of the Island of Barbados* (London, 1673), 12. Quoted in Davis, *The Problem of Slavery in Western Culture*, 449.

55. In the American colonies, by the eighteenth century the colonists failed to be threatened by Indians as potential lascivious virile competitors compared to blacks. One traveler said Indians had "constitutions untainted by lewdness." Another European claimed that the Indian male's organ was smaller than that of the European male. Only North Carolina and Virginia penalized Indians for illicit sexual relations with Christian white women. See Jordan, *White over Black*, 162.

56. Ibid., 155.

the black male's phallus, a legacy from ancient Greek and Roman society.
Sixteenth-century European illustrations and seventeenth-century diaries
and writings of Englishmen traveling in West Africa abound with no-
tations about the "extraordinary greatness of the Negroes' 'member.' "[57]
Eighteenth-century European science was fascinated with the claim that
black penises were larger and wider than those of European males, which
was a fairly commonly held belief in the general population at the time.[58]

Emerging pseudoscientific theories about race during the eighteenth
century also linked sexual prowess to color. Johann Friedrich Blumenbach
(1752–1840), the German founder of comparative anatomy and one of
the founders of cultural anthropology, was interested not only in comparing the skulls of different ethnic groups in order to rank their intelligence and beauty using the ancient Greeks as the norm, but also in
comparing the sexual organs of blacks. He devised one of the earliest
grids for ranking races: Caucasian (European, white), Mongolian (Chinese, yellow), Malayan (Asian, brown), Ethiopian (African, black), and
American (Indian, red). Relying on that ranking, Blumenbach remarked:

> It is generally said that the penis on the Negro is very large. And this
> assertion is so far borne out by the remarkable genitor apparatus of an
> Ethiopian, which I have in my anatomical collection. Whether this pre-
> rogative be constant and peculiar to the nation I do not know. It is said
> that women when eager for venery prefer the embraces of Negroes to
> those of other men. On the other hand, that Ethiopian and Mulatto
> women are particularly sought out by Europeans.[59]

It was a common practice for bidders at slave auctions to examine
the genitals of black men and women to see whether they merited the
bidder's investment, particularly if the future slaveowner was interested
in breeding slaves. On many Southern plantations, it was not uncommon
for black boys in their pubertal years or with fully matured organs to
serve dinner parties in only a shirt too short to cover their members.[60]

One of the earliest religious debates in colonial America about the
natural subserviency of blacks took place in June 1700 between Samuel

57. Ibid., 158.
58. Ibid.
59. *The Anthropological Treatises of Johann Friedrich Blumenbach* (London, 1865),
249. Quoted in Jordan, *White over Black*, 158 n.
60. Jordan, *White over Black*, 161.

Sewall (1652–1730), a magistrate, and Joseph Saffin, a fellow jurist. In an article, "The Selling of Joseph," Sewall refutes the claim that blacks are inferior because they are descendants of Ham. That slaves continue to aspire to the liberty they are denied shows not only that they have reason—a crucial natural attribute—but also are engaged in forced labor: "These *Ethiopians*, as black as they are; seeing they are the Sons and Daughters of the First *Adam*, the Brethren and Sisters of the Last Adam, and the Offspring of God; they ought to be treated with a Respect agreeable." Hence, it was wrong, said Sewall, for Christians to buy other Christians as slaves.[61]

Joseph Saffin, like most Puritans, believed that the Bible was a blueprint for scientific thought, so he appealed to it for arguments defending the enslavement of blacks. It was indeed wrong for Christians to buy other Christians as slaves; however, "any lawful captives of other heathen nations may be made bond men." Even though all persons are sons and daughters of Adam and creatures of God, nonetheless, even Christians are not bound to love and respect everyone alike, including slaves. "I may love my servant well, but my son better. Therefore, these expressions . . . seem to be misapplied . . . that we ought to tender pagan Negroes with all love, kindness, and equal respect as to the best of men." Even God has created according to rank: "some to be High and Honorable, some to be Low and Despicable; some to be Monarchs, Kings, . . . others to be Subjects, and to be commanded; servants of sundry sorts and degrees, bound to obey; yea, some to be born slaves, and so to remain during their lives."[62]

Many clergy, including Cotton Mather, also argued that Christian teachings made slaves more obedient and dutiful toward their owners and tasks. In the antebellum South, many white churches published special sermons, catechisms, and instructions emphasizing those biblical texts that supported this argument. In 1734 an Anglican cleric in Georgia, Stephen Hales, preaching at a service attended by the trustees of the colony, said that Christians were obliged and inspired to be generous and loving toward all of mankind: "[The Christian religion] binds the obligations to duty more strongly upon us; for the Gospel institution most strictly enjoins servants to be obedient to them that are their

61. Samuel Sewall, "The Selling of Joseph," in *Racial Thought in America*, 1:48–51.
62. Joseph Saffin, "A Brief and Candid Answer to a Late Printed Sheet, Entitled 'The Selling of Joseph,' " in *Racial Thought in America*, 1:56–58.

masters, according to the flesh, with fear and trembling, in singleness of heart."[63]

Robert Walsh (1784–1859), a noted Maryland Federalist, defended slavery against British criticism that the claims of liberty in the Declaration of Independence were spurious because the document excluded Indians and Negroes. America's concept of liberty was weakened because of slavery, which should have been eradicated by the founding fathers; however, with regard to reason in slaves:

> Their color is a perpetual memento of their servile origin, and a double disgust is thus created. We will not, and ought not, expose ourselves to lose our identity as it were; to be slain in our blood, and disparaged in our relations of being towards the stock of our forefathers in Europe. This may be called prejudice; but it is one which no reasoning can overcome, and which we cannot wish to see extinguished.[64]

American colonies both South and North steadily connected Christian doctrine with beliefs about blackness and blacks. For example, Maryland had a statute that provided "rights, liberties, immunities, privileges, and free customs" to all Christian inhabitants of that colony "as any natural born subject of England."[65] A Virginia statute allowed slaves to be baptized Christian, provided that "the conferring of baptisme doth not alter the condition of the person as to his bondage or freedom." In 1670 Virginia modified this clause by creating what I call layered slavery for "privileged" and "underprivileged" slaves. The law exempted from lifelong slavery those Africans who were baptized Christians when they first entered the colony. It called them servants instead of slaves. Non-Christian slaves imported by shipping would remain slaves the rest of their lives—the underprivileged layer; those imported by land—usually Indians—had limited servitude,—the privileged layer. Black children remained slaves for thirty years; black adults had to remain slaves only twelve years.[66]

In New York the legal system also enfranchised a religious view about black slaves and the church: "No Christian shall be kept in Bondslavery,

63. Ibid., 20.
64. Ibid., 49.
65. Jordan, *White over Black*, 74.
66. Higginbotham, *In the Matter of Color*, 37.

villenage or Captivity, Except Such who shall be Judged thereunto by Authority, or such as willing have sold, or shall sell themselves."[67] As we have seen, in 1706 the governor, Common Council, and General Assembly passed a statute saying that the baptizing of any slaves would not be reason for their emancipation.[68]

All of this, therefore, would dispute the claim of some scholars that in spite of Christians practicing and defending slavery, mainstream traditional Christian belief disagreed with the institution of slavery.[69] Indeed, as Winthrop Jordan points out, the British settlers in New England more often used the term *Christian* as a synonym for *English* to distinguish them from black Christians, (a distinction made all the more crucial after 1641, when a black woman joined a church in Dorchester, Massachusetts).[70]

> From the very first, then, vis-à-vis the Negro the concept embedded in the term *Christian* seems to have conveyed much of the idea and feeling of *we* as against *they*; to be Christian was to be civilized rather than barbarous, English rather than African, white rather than black. The term *Christian* itself had great elasticity. By the end of the seventeenth century it defined a species of slavery which had altogether lost any connection with explicit religious difference. . . .
>
> Virtually every quality in the Negro invited pejorative feelings. What may have been his two most striking characteristics, his heathenism and his appearance, were probably prerequisite to his complete debasement. His heathenism alone could never have led to permanent enslavement since conversion easily wiped out that failing. . . . Other qualities—the utter strangeness of his language, gestures, eating habits, [color], and so on—certainly must have contributed to the colonists' sense that he was very different, perhaps disturbingly so. In Africa these qualities had for Englishmen added up to *savagery*. . . .[71]

67. Ibid., 126.
68. Ibid., 127.
69. Such as Davis in *The Problem of Slavery in Western Culture*, 451–53.
70. Jordan, *White over Black*, 93.
71. Ibid., 94, 97.

7 | Ham's Children in America

Blacks on Blackness

The biblical story of Ham (older spellings: Cham or Chem) has been used historically to explain the origin and natural subordination of black cultures and peoples and the negativity of blackness. The myth reemerged in Christian Europe in the fourteenth-century as the African slave trade began. It also was a part of the Islamic tradition and the Jewish tradition about blacks. In all three faiths, Africa and its descendants were understood as the progeny of Ham who bear Noah's curse on Canaan: "A slave of slaves shall he be to his brothers" (Gen. 9:25).

For example, in the Midrash (Heb.: *darash* = to search, seek, examine, investigate; c. fourth to ninth centuries C.E.), which are rabbinic writings and commentaries about biblical texts, blackness is seen as punishment for Ham because he "unmanned" (castrated) Noah, thereby preventing Noah from producing more offspring. This linking of blackness with a curse and with carnality is made clear in Noah's rebuke of Ham in the Midrash:

> Since you have disabled me from doing ugly things in the blackness of night, Canaan's children shall be born black and ugly. Moreover, because you twisted your head around to see my nakedness, your grandchildren's hair shall be twisted into kinks, and their eyes red; again, because your lips jested at misfortune, they shall swell;

and because you neglected my nakedness, they shall go naked, and their male members shall be shamefully elongated. Men of this race shall be called Negroes; their forefather Canaan commanded them to love theft and fornication, to be banded together in hatred of their masters and never to tell the truth.[1]

Little evidence exists, however, that the extracanonical Jewish traditions had much influence on the medieval interpretation of Ham within Christendom. Jewish legends did put dogs, black ravens, and blacks under the same curse because, according to tradition, they violated a taboo against cohabitation with their counterparts while in Noah's ark. Under this curse, Ham and his descendants along with the Egyptians were condemned to be "men of dark-hued skin."[2]

Hamite originally was a European term for a group of African languages: Berber, Cushite, Northeast African (Somali, Afar, Beja, Galla), ancient Egyptian, and Hausa (now in modern Nigeria). This reflected European ideology that some African peoples—mostly in North Africa—of dark or mixed hues but not as dark as the sub-Saharan peoples, descended from a Caucasian (from the Caucasus mountains in the former Soviet Union near Georgia) branch of the Hamitic peoples in Egypt and North Africa. This myth and ideology had strong support in religious circles of the South. Noah's other sons, Japheth and Shem, were the progenitors of whites and brown peoples (American Indians, Asians, and Jews) respectively. As one nineteenth-century southern cleric wrote: "Subservient of the [Hamitic] race to Japheth will continue with time,

1. See B. Sanhedrin 72a-b, 108b; B. Pesahem 113b; Tanhuma Buber Gen. 49–50; Tanhuma Noah 13, 15; Gen. Rab. 341; in Robert Graves and Raphael Patai, *Hebrew Myths: The Book of Genesis* (Garden City, N.Y.: Doubleday, 1964), 121; also Louis Ginzberg, *The Legends of the Jews*, trans. Henrietta Szold, 7 vols. (Philadelphia: The Jewish Publication Society of America, 1968), 1:168–69.
The Ethiopian Jewish scholar Epraim Issac disputes the accuracy of both interpretations about all blacks being cursed in the Midrash. He maintains, for example, that the translation with regard to Ham's hair speaks of it being singed, not kinky, and his genitals as have a stretched foreskin (prepuce) because he did not cover his father's nakedness, rather than being cursed with elongated genitals. What he does *not* dispute is the negative view of the black descendants of Ham and Canaan in the Midrash. See Ephraim Issac, "Genesis, Judaism, and 'the Sons of Ham,'" *Slavery and Abolition* 1 (1980): 3–17.
2. Ginzberg, *Legends of the Jews*, 1:166. "Naked the descendants of Ham, the Egyptians, and Ethiopians, were led away captive and into exile by the King of Assyria, while the descendants of Shem, the Assyrians, even when the angel of the Lord burnt them in the camp, were not exposed, their garments remained upon their corpses unsinged." Ibid., 169–70.

but the *mode of that subserviency will not always be confined to personal bondage.*"³

James Sloan, a Mississippi Presbyterian cleric, held that the sons of Ham—Cush, Mizraim, Put, Canaan, and their black descendants—are intended by God to be subordinate to whites on all fronts: "Anatomy, physiology, history and theology . . . sustain one another."⁴ The plight of Ham's children in colonial America allowed the settlers to extend the doctrine of Manifest Destiny, particularly in the South. A Tennessee Methodist cleric, Samuel Baldwin, summarized quite well the nature of this Manifest Destiny with regard to the slaves:

> Japheth alone received [Christianity, which Shem rejected] as the messenger of light, and then sunk again to slumber through ages dark with dismal dreams. . . . [Providence] lifted the veil and showed him America, the birthright of Shem, and bade him inherit and enter, possess and improve. He gave him the ancient commission to coerce the race of Ham to bear its part of tribute by tilling the soil and subduing the earth.⁵

We must also be mindful of eighteenth- and nineteenth-century efforts to isolate Egypt from the rest of Africa, especially after Napoleon's invasion of Egypt and the subsequent creation of Egyptology. The argument, later joined by white American anthropologists and Egyptologists, is a familiar one: whether Egypt's origins are African (meaning black) or Mediterranean (meaning nonblack, that is, more European). These efforts, founded on the Platonic idea of a "pure race," each with its own geographical area and unique physical traits, were aimed at constructing what Martin Bernal, among others, calls a "fabrication of ancient Greece":

> [*Progress*] as a dominant paradigm damaged Egypt for two reasons. The country's great antiquity put it *behind* later civilizations; while its long and stable history, which had been a source of admiration, now became reason to despise it as static and sterile. In the long run we can see that

3. Thomas Virgil Peterson, *Ham and Japheth: The Mythic World of Whites in the Antebellum South*, ATLA Monograph Series (Metuchen, N.J.: Scarecrow Press and The American Theological Library Association, 1978), 97.
4. Ibid., 73.
5. Samuel Davies Baldwin, *Dominion; or, The Unity and Trinity of the Human Race* (Nashville: E. Stevenson and F. A. Owen, 1857), 118–19. Cited in Peterson, *Ham and Japheth*, 98.

Egypt was also harmed by the rise of racism and the need to disparage every African culture; during the 18th century, however, the ambiguity of Egypt's "racial" position allowed its supporters to claim that it was essentially and originally "white." Greece, by contrast, benefited from racism, immediately and in every way; and it was rapidly seen as the "childhood" of the "dynamic" "European race."[6]

Spurred on by the pioneering *Description de l'Egypte* (1809–28) in the new field of Egyptology, many Americans and Europeans supported the argument that Africans consisted of two branches: the Hamitic or Caucasoid Egyptians in the north and Negroid blacks in the south. Egyptians were said to be highly intelligent dark-skinned Caucasians, whose culture declined through intermarriage and interbreeding between the Hamitic Egyptians and the Negroid blacks.[7] As one scholar notes:

> The rulers of Kush were portrayed as "Caucasoid" ("Hamitic") when Kush was being described as a source of civilizing influences for the rest of sub-Saharan Africa, but these same rulers were characterized as blacks when the region's achievements were considered in relation to those of ancient Egypt.[8]

In the nineteenth century in the midst of the prevailing myths about Ham and black cultures, *Hamite* was assigned a rather positive meaning by Egyptologists. According to this theory, prehistoric colonists in northeastern Africa were Hamites, who were of the same racial stock as Ethiopians. They were tall, light-skinned, and biologically and intellectually superior to the Negroid types in sub-Saharan Africa. Because of their superior intelligence, the Hamitic peoples were able to defeat black Africans. The Hamitic peoples included the ancient Egyptians and descendants, Copts, pre-Islamic Berbers, Libyans, and peoples in parts of Ethiopia and Somalia. Descendants of Shem were Arabs, Akkadians (ancient Babylon), Phoenicians, Jews, Moabites, Ammonites, Aramaeans,

6. Martin Bernal, *Black Athena: The Afroasiatic Roots of Classical Civilization*, 2 vols. (New Brunswick, N.J.: Rutgers Univ. Press, 1987), 1:189.

7. See J. C. Nott and George R. Gliddon, *Types of Mankind or Ethnological Researches* (Philadelphia: Lippincott, 1855). Cited in St. Clair Drake, *Black Folk Here and There: An Essay in History and Anthropology*, vol. 1 (Los Angeles: Center for Afro-American Studies, Univ. of California, Los Angeles, 1987), 132.

8. Bruce G. Trigger, "Nubian, Negro, Black, Nilotic?", in *Africa in Antiquity: The Arts of Ancient Nubia and the Sudan*, 2 vols (New York: Brooklyn Museum, 1978), 1:28.

and peoples in parts of Ethiopia.[9] The ethnocentric intention of this classification was revealed by G. Elliot Smith, one of the participants in the first modern archaeological survey of Nubia: "the smallest infusion of Negro blood immediately manifests itself in a dulling of initiative and a 'drag' on the further development of the arts of civilization."[10]

The Hamitic origins of blacks were also cited in characterizing blacks' intelligence. Samuel G. Morton (1799–1851), an American physician and a founder of paleontology, studied human skulls for clues to racial and intelligence differences. He published two influential volumes, *Crania Americana* and *Crania Aegyptiaca*. Morton used the Ham myth to claim that the noblest race, the Caucasians, came from Shem, the first son of Noah and hence a descendant from Seth, the third son of Adam. The Mongolian races came from Japheth, Noah's third son, and the African races and Ethiopia from Ham, the second son.

In Morton's racial classification—(1) Caucasians, (2) Mongolians, (3) Malays, (4) Americans, (5) Ethiopians—the Caucasian family of races (Europeans, Arabs, Libyans, and the Nilotic races) is distinguished by high intellectual attainment. The Mongolians, who include the Mongol-Tartars, Turks, Chinese, and the Indochinese, are known to be intellectually ingenious. The Americans, meaning the American Indians, have an intellectual aversion to civilization, are slow to learn, revengeful, and prone to war. The Ethiopians, an overall category for Negroes, the Hottentots, and blacks in Oceania and Australia, are joyous, indolent, but intellectually diverse.[11]

Blackness as a primordial sign of evil and inferiority was the topic of many a Christian sermon. For example, many Episcopal clergy in the South were ambivalent about or disagreed with the claim that it was their Christian duty to instruct slaves. Frederick Dalcho, M.D. (1770–1836), assistant minister at Saint Michael's Church in Charleston, South Carolina (whose memorial plaque hangs in the church's interior), published a tract, *Practical Considerations, Founded on the Scriptures, Relative to the Slave Population of South Carolina*, to argue biblical support

9. George Aaron Barton, *Semitic and Hamitic Origins: Social and Religious* (Philadelphia: Univ. of Pennsylvania Press, 1934), 1.

10. Quoted in Trigger, "Nubian, Negro, Black, Nilotic?", in *Africa in Antiquity*, 1:28.

11. Samuel G. Morton, "Crania Americana." Cited in *Racial Thought in America*, ed. Louis Ruchames, vol. 1: *From the Puritans to Abraham Lincoln: A Documentary History*, (Amherst: Univ. of Massachusetts Press, 1969), 441–48.

of slavery and the natural inferiority of blacks. In a Fourth of July sermon at his parish, he said that the holiday was only for whites:

> The Declaration of the *Fourth of July* belongs exclusively to the white population of the United States. The American Revolution was a *family quarrel among whites.* In this the Negroes had no concern, their condition remained, and must remain, unchanged. They have no more to do with the celebration of that day, than with the landing of the Pilgrims on the Rock of Plymouth.[12]

In 1863 the presiding bishop of the Episcopal church, John H. Hopkins (1792–1868), also bishop of Vermont, published a controversial pamphlet, *Bible View of Slavery.* He too raised critical questions about whether the Declaration of Independence included black slaves:

> Where, then, I ask, did the authors of the Declaration of Independence find their warrant for such a statement ["all men are created equal" and "endowed with certain unalienable rights"]? . . . To estimate aright the vast diversity among the races of mankind, we may begin with our own, the highly privileged anglo-Saxon, which now stands at the head, although our ancestors were heathen barbarians only two thousand years ago. From this we may go down the descending scale through the Turks . . . the Abyssians, the Africans, and how is it possible to image that God has made them all *equal!* . . . The facts rather establish the very contrary. . . .[13]

At the same time Richard Allen and the Annual Negro Convention were urging blacks to observe the Fourth of July as a day of fasting and prayer to liberate them from their condition.[14]

12. Quoted in Stiles B. Lines, "Slaves and Churchmen: The Work of the Episcopal Church among Southern Negroes, 1800–1860" Ph.D. diss., Columbia Univ., 1960, 171. By contrast, Frederick Douglass wrote in an article, "What Is Your Fourth of July to Me?": "What to the American slave is your Fourth of July? I answer, a day that reveals to him more than all other days of the year, the gross injustice and cruelty to which he is the constant victim. To him your celebration is a sham; your boasted liberty an unholy license; your national greatness, swelling vanity; . . . your prayers and hymns, your sermons and thanksgivings, with all your religious parade and solemnity, are to him mere bombast, fraud, deception, impiety, and hypocrisy—a thin veil to cover up crimes which would disgrace a nation of savages." Quoted in *The Black Americans: A History in Their Own Words 1619–1983,* ed. Milton Meltzer (New York: HarperTrophy, 1987), 65.
13. John Henry Hopkins, *Bible View of Slavery* (New York: Papers from the Society for the Diffusion of Political Knowledge, 1863), 8.
14. Charles H. Wesley, *Richard Allen: Apostle of Freedom* (Washington, D.C.: Associated Publishers, 1935), 243.

Some blacks themselves believed the primordial foundations of their own racial and cultural identity in Ham. For example, James W. C. Pennington (1807–70), the Congregationalist minister, former slave active in the abolitionist movement, president of the Union Missionary Society, and one of the early advocates of such protest tactics as boycotting products produced by slaves, said that blacks were descendants of Ham via an amalgamation of Cush (Ethiopia) and Misraim (Egypt). He rejected, however, the belief that their servitude was the result of Canaan's curse:[15]

> The Carthaginians were Africans. But African does not mean the same as Ethiopian. Ethiopian is a name derived from the complexion of the inhabitants, while Africa is a name given to a tract of country inhabited by people of different complexions.[16]

Like other blacks, such as Episcopalian Alexander Crummell (1819–98) and Presbyterian Edward Wilmot Blyden (1832–1912), Pennington called Africa's cultures pagan. Their salvation and cultural liberation, he said, depended on black Americans of the diaspora returning to Africa as God's agents for bringing about European and American concepts of civilization.[17] He traced their "heathenism" to their polytheism. It is not that they have no knowledge of God; rather they wish to have knowledge of several gods and claim that all truth claims are equal. "When a man has virtually or in fact lost the knowledge of the only wise God, *he is a heathen. . . .* Our ancestors had sublime systems of religion; but the basis of it was false."[18]

Blyden said American blacks had a duty to take the "arts of industry and peace" learned in America to Africa in order to remove the "appalling cloud of ignorance and superstition which overspreads [Africa]":

> "God shall enlarge Jaspheth, and he shall dwell in the tents of Shem" was the blessing upon the European and Asiatic races. Wonderfully have

15. James W. C. Pennington, *A Text Book of the Origin and History, &c. &c. of the Colored People* (Hartford, Conn.: L. Skinner, 1841; reprint, Detroit: Negro History Press, n.d.), 7–13.

16. Ibid., 27.

17. For a good summary of this belief among black intellectuals, see Gayraud S. Wilmore, *Black Religion and Black Radicalism* (Garden City, N.Y.: Doubleday, 1972), 163–67.

18. Pennington, *Text Book of the Origin and History . . . of the Colored Peoples*, 34.

these predictions been fulfilled. . . . The promise to Ethiopia, or Ham,
is like that of Shem, of a spiritual kind. It refers not to physical strength
. . . but to the possession of spiritual qualities to the element of the soul
heavenward. . . . "Ethiopia shall stretch forth her hands unto God."[19]

Some of the embryonic Protestant sects, nevertheless, abandoned the
mythic curse of the Ham legend. The Methodists, for example, in the
eighteenth century explicitly acknowledged black slavery to be contrary
to the word of God. The founder of Methodism, John Wesley, visited
the colony of Georgia in October 1735. In 1774, after returning to
England, he published his *Thoughts upon Slavery*. Although he attacked
the slave trade, the traders, and the arguments of the plantation owners
defending the economic necessity of slavery, Wesley gave no theological
arguments against the institution. Instead he appealed to piety as the
foundation for a divinely intended natural egalitarianism among humankind:

> O thou God of love . . . thou who art the Father of the spirits of all
> flesh, and who art rich in mercy unto all; thou who hast mingled of one
> blood all the nations upon earth; have compassion upon these outcasts
> of men; who are trodden down to dung upon the earth! Arise, and help
> these that have no helper, whose blood is spilt upon the ground like
> water![20]

Although Wesley forbade Methodists to have slaves, both clergy and
bishops did own slaves. Yet at their 1780 Methodist Annual Conference,
they approved the following questions for their discipline:

> Question 16: Ought not this Conference to require those traveling
> preachers who hold slaves to give promises to set them free?
> Answer: Yes.

> Question 17: Does this Conference acknowledge that slavery is contrary
> to the laws of God, man, and nature, and hurtful to society, contrary to
> the dictates of conscience and pure religion, and doing that which we

19. Edward Wilmot Blyden, "The Call of Providence to the Descendants of Africa
in America," in *Negro Social and Political Thought, 1850–1920*, ed. Howard Brotz (New
York: Basic Books, 1966), 114, 121.
20. John Wesley, *Thoughts upon Slavery* (London, 1774), 12.

would not others should do to us and ours? Do we pass our disapprobation on all our friends who keep slaves and advise their freedom?
Answer: Yes.[21]

By the time of the abolitionist movement in the 1830s, however, strong convictions about the wrongfulness of the enslavement of Africans and blacks had dwindled. At their 1836 General Conference the Methodists passed by a large majority a resolution that opposed the abolition movement and disclaimed "any right, wish, or intention to interfere in the civil and political relation between master and slave as it exists in the slave-holding states of this union."[22]

African Traditions and African-American Identity

The question of identity has always been an ambiguous and ambivalent question for blacks and others. The issue has moved from simple ethnic identity to political to nationalist ideologies, varying from "Negro" to "colored" to "Afro-American" to "black" to "African American." The substance of American blacks' identity and concept of blackness is complicated because there is no straight line between that culture and Africa, as in the Caribbean and Brazil. But the cultural identity of blacks in terms of color has always depended on others. As far as I know, little work has been done on what blacks themselves thought of their identity.

Furthermore, the relationship between American blacks and Africa has been complex and tortuous, complicated by blacks internalizing religious and popular cultural views about the color black and Africa. But the identity question cannot be separated from Africa. Although the *black* as a source of identity was cited by a black as early as 1793, it never engaged blacks as a badge of racial and political identity until recent years.[23] And with the exception of such nineteenth-century black

21. *Minutes of the Annual Conference of the Methodist Episcopal Church 1773–1828*, vol. 1 (New York: T. Mason & G. Lane—Mulberry Street, 1840), 12. Cited in W. D. Weatherford, *American Churches and the Negro* (Boston: Christopher Publishing House, 1957), 85–86.

22. H. Shelton Smith. *In His Image, But . . . : Racism in Southern Religion, 1780–1910* (Durham, N.C.: Duke Univ. Press, 1972), 101.

23. Absalom Jones, *A Narrative of the Black People* (Philadelphia: Printed for the authors by William Woodward, 1794). In this publication, he alternates between "black" and "people of color" for identifying this people.

clerics and intellectuals as Alexander Crummell, Edward Blyden, and
Martin Delany (1812–1883); political nationalists such as David Walker
(1785–1830); and twentieth-century figures like W. E. B. Du Bois (1868–
1963) and Marcus Garvey (1887–1940), African American interest with
and engagement in Africa until the 1970s was largely characterized by
embarrassment, indifference, denial, negativity, condescension, and ambivalence. Even after African colonies began to win their independence
in the 1950s, 70 percent of American blacks could not name an African
country or territory, over against 55 percent of whites.[24]

The earliest record of color identity of blacks in Christian circles was
apparently 1623 when a slave was baptized in Virginia—a "William,"
son of Antonio and Isabelle, two of the original twenty slaves called
"negers," who had been brought to that colony in 1619. He was baptized
an Anglican.[25] His father, who took the name Anthony Johnson, had
been manumitted in 1621, probably under English statutes that recognized Spanish subjects baptized under Spanish law, even if enslaved.
Such persons had the privileges of a free person in England and its
colonies.[26] The slave Phillis Wheatley (c. 1753–84), first published black
American poet, who lived in Boston, was so persuaded by the teachings
and preaching of the evangelical Anglican George Whitefield that she
composed a poem to him to commemorate his death in 1770 and
deliberately mentions Africans as a people to be converted to Christ:

> Take him, ye *Africans*, he longs for you
> *Impartial Saviour* is his title due,
> Washed in the fountain of redeeming blood,
> You shall be sons and kings, and priests to God.[27]

Most American slaves were born in America, and therefore had for
some generations been exposed to Christian churches. Most historians
maintain that the import of Africans to the United States leveled off

24. Alfred O. Hero, Jr., "American Negroes and U.S. Foreign Policy: 1937–1967,"
Journal of Conflict Resolution 13 (June 1969): 223–35.
25. Helen Tunnicliff Catterall, ed., *Judicial Cases Concerning American Slavery and
the Negro*, 4 vols. (Washington, D.C.: Carnegie Institution, 1926), 1:55.
26. J. W. Schulte Nordholt, *The People That Walk in Darkness*, trans. M. S. van
Wijngaarden (London: Burke Publishing, 1960), 20. Nordholt identifies the son as
"Anthony" (Sp.: Antonio), which he may have confused with the father's name.
27. Phillis Wheatley, *The Poems* (London 1773; reprint Philadelphia: R. R. and C.
C. Wright, 1909), 16.

after 1760. Some even think that from 1710 onward, the majority of slaves in American colonies were born second- and even third-generation.[28] Evidence shows, however, that the peak periods in importing slaves directly from Africa or indirectly from the Caribbean did not cease either after 1710 or 1760. Additional peak periods occurred well into the nineteenth century (for example, 1780–1810 and 1830–50).[29] As a consequence, Africa and its traditions as a point of reference and identity did not die out as early as many mainstream historians have told us, even with an increase in second- and third-generation native-born African Americans.[30] Hence, as these home-grown slaves and free-men began to define their identity in the United States, Africa cannot be overlooked.

At the same time, the conversion of black slaves to Christianity was informed and nourished by ongoing conversations with their African traditions, many of which were retained or adapted to the new harsh, strange, alien conditions. That is, in spite of the large number of second- and third-generation African Americans in early America, many African traditions survived in their religious identity. These traditions afforded blacks a *negation of the negating*—the negating of plantation Christianity, brutal labor-intensive exploitation in colonial and antebellum economies, the negating of their community and their ancestors through practices and laws aimed at destroying their identity and self-worth. Many of these surviving traditions, such as dreams, visions, dance rituals, and a spirit-filled cosmology, acted as filters in the slaves' experiences to con-firm for many the worth of Christian claims.

28. Robert William Fogel and Stanley L. Engerman, *Time on the Cross: The Economics of American Slavery*, 2 vols. (Boston: Little, Brown, 1974), 1:24, 2:28–31. Cited in Mechal Sobel, *Trabelin' On: The Slave Journey to an Afro-Baptist Faith* (Westport, Conn.: Greenwood Press, 1979), 371–72, n. 1.

29. Austin, *African Muslims in Antebellum America*, 60. Revised figures on slave imports indicate that between 1769 and 1810, at least 596,000 slaves came directly from Africa. (See Fogel and Engerman, *Time on the Cross*, 2:28–31.) In light of these figures, even Philip Curtin extended his dates for the peak periods of slave arrivals directly from Africa, saying that most likely two nearly equal peak periods occurred. (See his personal note to Mechal Sobel in *Trabelin' On*, 372.)

30. For example, African imports leveled off earlier in northern colonies than in southern colonies. Between 1715 and 1767, 4,551 slaves were imported into New York and New Jersey; however, only 930 of them were born in Africa. In the two largest southern slave colonies—South Carolina and Virginia—in contrast, 86 percent of the former's slave population came directly from Africa and 83 percent of the latter's. Sobel, *Trabelin' On*, 23.

Furthermore, blacks' understanding of their group and individual identity as Africans or African descendants, even though they came from different tribes and ethnic groups and in spite of temporal and geographical discontinuity, provided a common affinity, shared rituals, a mutual pride, and fuel for spiritual survival in an otherwise hostile land with its strange songs of Christianity and plantation captivity. As one former slave characteristically described her spirituality at slave Christian worship:

> I'd jump up dar and den and holler and shout and sing and pat, and dey would all cotch de words and I'd sing it to some old shout song I'd heard 'em sing from Africa, and dey'd all take it up and keep at it, and keep a-addin' to it, and den it would be a spiritual.[31]

One of the earliest views by blacks about blackness in white Christian society appeared in an American magazine as a reprint from an English journal published in 1789. Drawing parallels to Shylock's lament in Shakespeare's *The Merchant of Venice*, except for substituting "Negro" for "Jew" and "white" for "Christian," the writer asks:

> Can it be contended, that a difference of color alone can constitute a difference of species?—if not, in what single circumstance are we different from the rest of mankind? What variety is there in our organization? What inferiority of art in the fashioning of our bodies? What imperfection in the faculties of our mind? . . . Are then the reason and the morality, for which Europeans so highly value themselves of a nature so variable and fluctuating, as to change with the complexion of those, to whom they are applied? Do the rights of nature cease to be such, when a negro is to enjoy them?—Or does patriotism, in the heart of an African, rankle into treason?[32]

When blacks created their first cultural and religious organizations in the eighteenth and nineteenth centuries, they consciously used the

31. Jeanette R. Murphy, "The Survival of African Music in America," *Popular Science Monthly* 55 (September 1899): 660–61. Cited in John W. Blassingame, *The Slave Community: Plantation Life in the Antebellum South*, rev. ed. (New York: Oxford Univ. Press, 1979), 33.

32. "A Letter on Slavery by a Negro," *American Museum*, vol. 6 (1789): 77–80. Cited in *Racial Thought in America*, 1:200–205.

term *African* in institutional names.[33] In November 1780, the first black social service organization was established by Newport Gardner and others for (1) mutual help at times of distress, (2) compilation of a registry for black vital statistics, and (3) job apprenticeships. It was named the African Union Society. Richard Allen and Absalom Jones (1746–1816) created a similar organization in Philadelphia in 1787, which they called the Free African Society. In 1796 the African Society was founded in Boston.[34]

Nor was it coincidental that, although the term *colored* still identified some black organizations (for example, the Colored Reading Society of Philadelphia for Mental Improvement [1828]; the Colored Female Free Produce Society of Pennsylvania [1831]; *The Colored American* newspaper [1837]), many black churches self-consciously carried the name *African* in their titles: African Baptist Church, Lunenburg (Mecklenburg), Virginia (1758); First African Baptist Church, Savannah, Georgia (1787); St. Thomas African Episcopal Church, founded by Absalom Jones and others in Philadelphia (1791); the African Meeting House (1806) in Boston; Bethel African Methodist Episcopal Church (1794), Philadelphia; the African Methodist Union Church (1807); the African Methodist Episcopal Church (AME), founded by Richard Allen and others in 1816; the African Methodist Episcopal Zion Church (AMEZ), founded by James Varick (1750–1827), Abraham Thompson, and William Miller in New York (1820).

Significantly, the incorporation papers (the Articles of Association) of the first black denomination, the AME, insisted that its leaders and trustees be of African descent. The Articles of Association specified: "It is hereby further provided and declared, that a majority of the trustees and official members, convened agreeably to notice, given at least one Sabbath day previously to such meeting, shall and may nominate and appoint one or more persons of the *African race*" (emphasis added).[35] Several years later the AMEZ specified in its Articles of Association that "none but Africans or their descendants shall be chosen as Trustees of the said African Methodist Episcopal Zion Church, and such other

33. James Holloway, ed., *Africanisms in American Culture*, (Bloomington: Indiana Univ. Press, 1990), xix; Sterling Stuckey, *Slave Culture: Nationalist Theory and the Foundations of Black America* (New York: Oxford Univ. Press, 1987), 200.

34. See the bylaws of the African Society in the collection of documents by Dorothy Porter, *Early Negro Writing 1760–1837* (Boston: Beacon Press, 1971), 9–12.

35. Ibid., 38.

church or churches as may or shall hereafter become the property of
this Corporation. . . ."[36]

As late as 1813—two hundred years after the first slaves had come
from Africa—blacks in the South continued to call upon their common
ancestry in Africa as a source of empowerment and resistance. In a
Hymn of Freedom usually sung at "praise houses" in the Sea Islands of
South Carolina, the slaves shouted:

> *Hail! all hail! ye Afric clan*
> *Hail! ye oppressed, ye Afric band,*
> *Who toil and sweat in slavery bound*
> *And when your health and strength are gone*
> *Are left to hunger and to mourn.*
> *Let independence be your aim,*
> *Ever mindful what 'tis worth.*
> *Pledge your bodies for the prize*
> *Pile them even to the skies!*[37]

This same hymn was sung as a source of empowerment by the unsuccessful Denmark Vesey uprising in Charleston, South Carolina, in the
early 1820s.

In 1834, even in the extravagant language of the famous "A Declaration of Sentiment" of the National Convention of Free People of Color,
Africa was praised as the ancestral land for black identity. This group,
organized by some blacks to oppose the programs and goals of the
American Colonization Society that called for expatriating and repatri-
ating blacks to Africa, included former slaves Bishop Richard Allen and
the Reverend James W. C. Pennington, who said he was proud of "his
unadulterated African blood." They met to resolve racial friction between
escaped black slaves in Cincinnati, Ohio, and whites in the job market
by purchasing land in upper Canada for blacks who wished expatriation
from discrimination and prejudice.

At the first convention in 1830, the delegates affirmed both their
African heritage and their American culture: "And it is only when we
look to our own native land, to the birthplace of our *fathers*, to the land

36. William J. Walls, *The African Methodist Episcopal Zion Church: Reality of the
Black Church* (Charlotte, N.C.: AME Zion Publishing House, 1974), 60–61.
37. Archie Epps, "A Negro Separatist Movement in the 19th Century," *The Harvard
Review* 4 (Summer-Fall 1966): 75.

for whose prosperity their blood and our sweat have been shed and cruelly extorted, that the Convention has cause to hang its name in shame."[38] The conventions attracted many prominent black clerics, such as Henry Highland Garnet, Martin Delany, and James Theodore Holly, as well as such nonclerics as Frederick Douglass. At the 1834 convention, "A Declaration of Sentiment" was released, which lauded the country of their ancestry as a continent

> enrolled in the history of fame; whose glittering monuments stand forth as beacons, disseminating light and knowledge to the uttermost parts of the earth, reduced to such degrading servitude as that under which we labor from the effect of *American slavery* and *American prejudice*. The separation of our fathers from the land of their birth, earthly ties and earthly affections, was not only sinful in its nature and tendency, but it led to a system of robbery, bribery and persecution, offensive to the laws of nature and of justice.[39]

Africa as a focus of self-identity came into disrepute during the black opposition to colonization schemes aimed at returning blacks to Africa in the early nineteenth century. As a political strategy, many black organizations removed *African* from their titles to refute white propaganda that blacks were not full Americans (for example, the Convention for the Improvement of Free People of Color). Such appeals generally did not get widespread support.

Even the AME Church debates in the 1870s about whether to retain *African* in its title ended with a reaffirmation of its African ancestry. The debate arose as a reaction to discussions about the proposed Fifteenth Amendment in 1867. In a letter to the AME *Christian Recorder*, a correspondent insisted that *African*, a reminder of blacks as slaves and as pagans, ought to be deleted from the church's name, and instead *American* be substituted so that the traditional name AME would still make sense.[40] Another reader replied that the Fifteenth Amendment did not "make black men white nor white men black. . . ." Since all other Americans boast of their ancestry, "is the African ashamed to

38. *Minutes of the Proceedings of the National Negro Conventions, 1830–1864*, ed. Howard Holman Bell (New York: Arno Press and The New York Times, 1969), 12.
39. Ibid., 28.
40. *The Christian Recorder*, 9 (August 20, 1870): 2.

boast of his?"[41] Benjamin Tucker Tanner (1835–1923), born a freeman
in Pittsburgh, elected an AME bishop (in 1888), father of the artist
Henry Ossawa Tanner, editor of the AME *Christian Recorder* (1868–
84), vigorously defended retaining *African* in the church's title because
it said something theologically about the humanity and dignity of Christian African Americans:

> What then is the intended force of the title African? Is it doctrinal or
> national: it is firstly "doctrinal" and secondarily "national." The doctrinal
> goal to which the AME Church aspired was the humanity of the Negro
> . . . it sought to become a church wherein the claim to humanity of this
> despised class would be practically recognized. The sublime truth; and
> means only that men of African descent are to be found there, and found
> as men, not slaves; as equals, not inferiors. The doctrine of the Negro's
> humanity is its primary significance.[42]

Early black poets pioneering an emerging black literature also established their identity based on Africa and the Christian faith, a reflection
of a particular doctrine of the *imago Dei* through their African heritage.
Phillis Wheatley, thought to have been born in Senegambia, was sold
as a young girl to the Wheatley family in Boston. No doubt she had
been traumatized by the voyage; her owners, particularly the wife,
Susannah Wheatley, were her patrons in the literary circles of Boston.
Impressed with the evangelical teachings and preaching of the Great
Awakening, Wheatley was baptized a Christian in 1771 at the Old South
Meeting House, Boston. Yet she also reflects about a land, even if in a
mood of nostalgia, that she no longer knew, a place she viewed as a
sanctuary of paganism and sin from which Christianity had liberated
blacks. In a poem dedicated to the Earl of Dartmouth, William Legge,
on the occasion of his royal appointment as secretary of state for North
America, she wrote about herself:

> I, young in life, by seeming cruel fate
> Was snatched from Afric's fancied happy seat;
> What pangs excruciating must molest,
> What sorrows labor in my parents' breast?

41. Ibid., 9 (August 27, 1870): 2.
42. Benjamin Tanner, *Apology for African Methodism* (1867). Quoted in Epps, "A
Negro Separatist Movement," 79.

Steeled was that soul and by no misery moved,
That from a father seized his babe beloved:
Such, such my case. And can I then but pray
Others may never feel tyrannic sway?[43]

After the British occupied Boston and some lodged at the Wheatley house, Phillis Wheatley wrote her "Reply" to some conversations she is thought to have had with British officers who had been to Africa:

Charmed with thy painting, how my bosom burns!
And pleasing Gambia on my soul returns, . . .
There as in Britain's favour'd isle, behold
The bending harvest ripens into gold;
Just are thy views of Afric's blissful plain,
On the warm limits of the land and main.[44]

Conversation between the formation of an identity and their African legacy by blacks was particularly evident in certain rituals, such as the famous ring shout. This was not simply a ritualized dance by the slaves, but an anamnesis (a re-presenting or re-memorying) of bonds with the ancestors.[45] The ring shout was not simply a religious memorial or a communal recollection of the ancestors as the absent ones; rather it was a re-presenting, a reliving, and a renewal of obligations to the ancestors so characteristic in most African cultures—a significant tradition still retained in many African and Afro-Caribbean indigenous Christian churches.[46]

43. Wheatley, *The Poems*, 51.
44. Ibid.
45. See the innovative discussion of the relationship between the ring shout and the ancestors in Stuckey, *Slave Culture*, 16.
46. For the role of ancestors in African traditional religion, African indigenous churches, and Afro-Caribbean cultures, see George C. Bond, "Ancestors and Protestants: Religious Coexistence in the Social Field of a Zambian Community," *American Ethnologist* (Fall 1987): 55–72; Robert E. Hood, *Must God Remain Greek? Afro Cultures and God-Talk* (Minneapolis: Fortress, 1990), 62–76, 217–44; Marthinus L. Daneel, "Shona Independent Churches and Ancestor Worship," in *African Initiatives in Religion*, ed. David Barrett (Nairobi: East African Publishing House, 1971), 160–70; Berthold A. Pauw, *Christianity and Xhosa Tradition* (Cape Town: Oxford Univ. Press, 1975); Russell Lynn Staples, "Christianity and the Cult of the Ancestors: Belief and Ritual Among the Bantu-Speaking Peoples of Southern Africa," Ph.D. diss., Princeton Theological Seminary, 1981, 146–56.

The exact African origins of the ring shout, which was not literally a shout but a choral syncopated foot-dance in worship, are uncertain. Similar ceremonies are known among the Bakongo tribes on the Gold Coast of West Africa and in Suriname in South America.[47] Singing accompanied by clapping hands, stamping feet, clicking heels, and tapping sticks and branches on the floor or ground maintained both the rhythm and the tempo as the people performed a shuffle dance in a counterclockwise circle and sang until reaching ecstasy or halted by the leader. Some think that many black spirituals originally were improvised songs sung during the ring shout, particularly those talking about parents and relatives.[48] This particular Africanism could still be found in some black churches, such as the African Church near Charleston, South Carolina, and churches in Tennessee and Louisiana as late as 1880.[49]

AME Bishop Daniel Alexander Payne (1811–93), born in South Carolina, where the ring shout was familiar, and educated as a Lutheran in that church's theological seminary in Gettysburg, Pennsylvania, where his family had migrated after the failed Denmark Vesey rebellion in South Carolina, complained in 1888 that black Christians still persisted in mixing what he alternatively called "ridiculous and heathenish" dances, "Fist and Heel Worshipers," and "Voodoo dance" with their Christian belief. At one church a congregant replied to Payne's complaint about the ring shout in worship: "The Spirit of God moves upon people in different ways. At camp-meeting there must be a ring here, a ring there, a ring over yonder, or sinners will not get converted."[50]

A second link to their African identity was dreams and visions as a mode of conversation and communion with the slaves' African traditions as they confronted the Christian faith of the Europeans and their descendants in the United States. In Afro cultures of the Americas and

47. For similarities and parallels between the North American and South American experiences, see Melville J. Herskovits and Frances S. Herskovits, *Rebel Destiny: Among the Negroes of Dutch Guiana* (New York & London: Whittlesey House, McGraw Hill, 1934).

48. Harold Courlander, *Negro Folk Music, U.S.A.* (New York: Columbia Univ. Press, 1963), 194; Stuckey, *Slave Culture*, 27–30.

49. Stuckey, *Slave Culture*, 52. I myself saw some remnants of a "holy dance" in Morris Brown AME Church, Charleston, South Carolina, on a field research trip in 1987.

50. Daniel Alexander Payne, *Recollections of Seventy Years* (Nashville: AME Sunday School Union, 1888; reprint, New York: Arno Press and The New York Times, 1968), 254.

Africa, dreams were (and continue to be) significant windows of revelation and communication between this world and the world of the
spirits, ancestors, and the divinities. In Jamaica, for example, it was
customary to send a candidate for baptism "into the bush" to have a
dream or vision in order to test his or her fitness for Christian baptism.[51]

For the slaves, dreams confirmed and affirmed. Their content was
considered authoritative and taken seriously.[52] For white Christian missionaries, dreams in the slave community were a puzzlement. Charles
C. Jones, a Presbyterian missionary, complained of "dreams, visions,
trances, voices all bearing a perfect or striking resemblance to some
form or type which has been handed down for generations."[53]

Jarena Lee (born 1783, Cape May, N.J.), for example, the widow of
a black (African?) preacher, Joseph Lee, and the first AME female
preacher, reported her visions. According to Lee, a vision directed her
in 1811 to marry Joseph Lee, a pastor of a black congregation in isolated
Snow Hill, Philadelphia. She initially resisted the thought of living in
such an isolated place. Having seen sheep in a vision, she heard a voice
tell her: "Joseph Lee must take care of these sheep or the wolf will come
and devour them." She awoke and joined him in Snow Hill.[54]

Writing about her conversion to the AME Church after being rejected
by the Episcopal church in Philadelphia, Lee testifies that she learned
in a vision that it was her duty to preach the gospel. She told Richard
Allen of the AME Church about this, but he rejected the idea because
he said it was against the gospel of Christ. "Although at this time, when

51. Leonard Tucker, "Glorious Liberty": The Story of a Hundred Years' Work of the
Jamaica Baptist Mission (London: Baptist Missionary Society, 1914), 8–9.

52. For commentaries on the role of dreams and visions in African American culture,
see A. P. Watson comp., God Struck Me Dead: Religious Conversion Experiences and
Autobiographies of Negro Ex-Slaves, (Nashville: Social Science Institute, Fisk University,
1945); reprint, ed. Clifton M. Johnson (Philadelphia: Pilgrim Press, 1969); Newbell
Niles Puckett, The Magic and Folk Beliefs of the Southern Negro (New York: Dover
Publications, 1969). For the role of dreams in traditional African culture and churches,
see Harold W. Turner, History of an African Independent Church: The Church of the Lord
(Aladura), 2 vols. (Oxford, England: Clarendon Press, 1967); E. Bolaji Idowu, African
Traditional Religion: A Definition (London: SCM Press, 1973).

53. Charles C. Jones, The Religious Instruction of the Negroes in the United States
(Savannah, Ga.: Thomas Purse, 1842); reprint (Freeport, N.Y.: Books for Libraries Press,
1971). Quoted in Sobel, Trabelin' On, 107.

54. Jarena Lee, The Life and Religious Experience of Jarena Lee, A Coloured Lady
. . . Written by Herself (Philadelphia: Author, 1836), in Sisters of the Spirit: Three Black
Women's Autobiographies of the Nineteenth Century, ed. William L. Andrews (Bloom-
ington: Indiana Univ. Press, 1986), 36.

my conviction was so great, yet I knew not that Jesus Christ was the
Son of God, the second person in the adorable trinity. I knew him not
in the pardon of my sins, yet I felt a consciousness that if I died without
pardon, that my lot must inevitably be damnation."[55]

Slave narratives tell how slaves frequently went into the woods alone
to prepare themselves for a vision. They told of being "struck" by God
in a dream or vision just before their conversion or their decision to
become Christians. One slave reported:

> I was killed dead by the power of God one evening about four
> o'clock. . . . Like a flash I saw my soul in the form of an angel, leap
> from my old body which was lying at the greedy jaws of hell. . . . Then
> there appeared before me a little man dressed up in white linen and
> with golden locks hanging over his shoulders and parted in the middle.[56]

Such narratives report that the slaves would fall ill or have sleepless
nights. Often they would first withdraw into the woods, where they had
a vision in which God and the devil appeared, often revealing the mythic
struggle between the order of evil, represented by a black devil, and the
order of Christian good, represented in the dream by God in white:

> When I was killed dead, I saw the devil and the fires of hell. . . . I left
> hell and came out pursued by the devil. God come to me as a little man.
> He came in my room and said, "Come on and go with me." He was
> dressed in dark but later He came dressed in white and said, "Come and
> I will show you paradise and the various kinds of mansions there." . . .
> The devil, his face as black as it could be and his eyes red as fire, told
> me to come and go with him. . . .[57]

Even the African belief in incarnation traveled across the Atlantic
with the slaves. One slave tells how during her pregnancy, her mother
appeared to her in a dream and asked her questions. After the mother
went away, the woman immediately connected this appearance with her
Christian faith: "I always take Dr. Jesus with me and put him in front."[58]

55. Lee, *The Life and Religious Experience of Jarena Lee*, in *Afro-American Religious History: A Documentary Witness*, ed. Milton C. Sernett, (Durham: Duke Univ. Press, 1985), 165.
56. Watson, *God Struck Me Dead*, 30.
57. Ibid., 39.
58. Ibid., 45.

Other blacks who cite a communion between visions and their identity were Sojourner Truth (c. 1797–1883), whose vision of God directed her to transform herself and her role by first changing her name from Isabella to Sojourner and "to travel up and down the land, showing people their sins and being a sign unto them"; and Nat Turner (1800–37), who linked a vision of the Holy Spirit to his rebellion as a legitimate moral agent against whites in Virginia. On 12 May 1828, according to his confessions, this same Holy Spirit directed him to take the yoke of Christ and "fight against the serpent, for the time was fast approaching when the first should be last, and the last should be first."[59] After another dream showed him a sign—the eclipse of the sun—he prepared to fight and slay whites.[60] After Denmark Vesey's failed rebellion, South Carolina's legislature forbade blacks to assemble for worship, pointedly noting that "churches could be centers of intrigue and that slaves could acquire what seemed to Carolinians the most erroneous *religious visions*" (emphasis added).[61]

Blackness and the Divine

Even before the advent of black churches, slaves and free blacks had rudimentary views of the relationship between their blackness and the divine. These views linked not only their African homeland, but also a view of positive divine attributes of God seldom associated with black slaves. Some of the earliest expressions of how blacks viewed this bond can be found among the writings of Benjamin Banneker (1731–1806), son of freed slaves in Maryland and assistant to the surveyor of Washington, D.C., Andrew Ellicott. In 1791 Banneker replied to an article by Thomas Jefferson about black intelligence. Jefferson had written in "Notes on Virginia" that "blacks, whether originally a distinct race, or made distinct by time and circumstances, are inferior to the whites in the endowment, both of body and mind." Because of "this unfortunate difference of color and of faculty," blacks should not be so readily liberated by whites. Banneker retorted: "Our universal Father hath given being to us all, hath made us not only of one flesh, but without partiality hath

59. *The Confessions of Nat Turner, Leader of the Late Insurrection in Southampton, Va.*, reprint (Miami: Mnemosyne Publishing, 1969), 5.
60. Ibid., 6.
61. Stuckey, *Slave Culture*, 52.

given us the same sensations and endowed us with the same faculties. . . . I am of the African race, and in that color which is natural to them of the deepest dye."[62]

In 1779 Connecticut blacks petitioned that state's General Assembly to abolish slavery, citing a theological grounding:

> We perceive by our own Reflection, that we are endowed with the same Faculties with our masters, and there is nothing that leads us to a Belief, or Suspicion, that we are any more obliged to serve them, than they us, and the more we Consider of this matter, the more we are Convinced of our Right (by the laws of Nature and by the whole Tenor of the Christian religion, so far as we have been taught) to be free; we have endeavored rightly to understand what is our Right, and what is our Duty, and can never be convinced that we are made to be Slaves.[63]

Likewise, in a sermon preached in thanksgiving for the end of the slave trade in 1801, Absalom Jones, cofounder with Richard Allen of the Free African Society and founder of St. Thomas African Episcopal Church, Philadelphia, underscored this bond:

> Our text (Ex. 3:7-8) mentions . . . that they were not forgotten by the God of their fathers, and the Father of the human race. Though, for wise reasons, he delayed to appear in their behalf for several hundred years, yet he was not indifferent to their sufferings. . . . The history of the world shows us that the deliverance of the children of Israel from their bondage, is not the only instance in which it has pleased God to appear in behalf of oppressed and distressed nations, as the deliverer of the innocent, and of those who call upon his name. . . . Yes, my brethren, the nations from which most of us have descended, and the country in which some of us were born, have been visited by the tender mercy of the Common Father of the human race. He has seen the affliction of our countrymen, with an eye of pity. . . . Dear land of our ancestors! Thou shalt no more be stained with the blood of thy children, shed by

62. Benjamin Banneker, "To Thomas Jefferson," in *Religious Thought in America*, 1:213–14. In 1791 Banneker, an astronomer, and Ellicott surveyed parcels of land in Maryland and Virginia for the layout of the future District of Columbia. They determined its boundaries by using the stars to find its latitude and longitude.

63. Herbert Aptheker, *A Documentary History of the Negro People in the United States* (New York: International Publishers, 1962), 11.

British and American hands, the ocean shall no more afford a refuge to their bodies, from impending slavery.[64]

In one of Phillis Wheatley's poems, "On Being Brought from Africa to America," although Africa is pictured as a sanctuary of paganism and sin from which Christianity had liberated blacks, she nonetheless insists that blacks even with their "diabolic" color are within God's redemption plan:

> 'Twas mercy brought me from my *Pagan* land,
> Taught my benighted soul to understand
> That there's a God, that there's a Saviour too;
> Once I redemption neither sought nor knew,
> Some view our sable race with scornful eye,
> "Their color is a diabolic die."
> Remember *Christians, Negroes*, black as *Cain*,
> May be refined and join th' angelic train.[65]

God as affirming instead of negating blacks was clearly at the heart of Richard Allen's theology. In his memoirs, Allen wrote about his reaction to the complaints and threats from the white Methodists about blacks using the name Methodist:

We told him we were dragged off of our knees at St. George's church, and treated worse than heathens; and we were determined to seek out for ourselves, the Lord being our helper. He told us we were not Methodists and left us. . . . [We told him] if you deny us your name, you cannot seal up the scriptures from us, and deny us a name in heaven. We believe heaven is free for all who worship in spirit and truth. . . . We believed if we put our trust in the Lord, he would stand by us.[66]

That this God is the supreme deity even under the guise of the doctrine of the Trinity and not a conveniently manufactured God devised

64. Absalom Jones, *A Thanksgiving Sermon, Preached on January 1, 1808, in St. Thomas's, or the African Episcopal Church: On Account of The Abolition of the Slave Trade,* in John M. Burgess, ed., *Black Gospel/White Church* (New York: Seabury Press, 1982), 3.
65. Wheatley, *The Poems,* 12.
66. Richard Allen, *The Life Experience and Gospel Labors of the Rt. Rev. Richard Allen* (Reprint, Nashville: Abingdon, 1960), 27.

to met the context of the Allenites alone is made clear in Allen's draft of "Acts of Faith" for the young AME Church:

> I believe that in the unity of the Godhead, there is a trinity of persons; that Thou are perfectly one and perfectly three; one essence and three persons. I believe, O blessed Jesus, that Thou art of one substance with the Father, the very and eternal God; that Thou didst truly suffer, and were crucified, dead and buried, to reconcile us to thy Father and to be a sacrifice for sin.[67]

David Walker, a member of a black Baptist congregation in Boston, further underscored God as deliverer of blacks. He remarked how whites had misused the mandate of the gospel given in Jesus Christ. The whites tried to convert the African heathens, but themselves were heathens in their enslavement and treatment of blacks. "Does [God] regard the heathens abroad, more than the heathens among the Americans? Surely the Americans must believe that God is partial, notwithstanding his Apostle Peter. . . ." Justice is a part of the godhead itself: "although you treat us and our children now, as you do your domestic beasts—yet the final result of all future events are known but to God Almighty alone, who rules in the armies of heaven and among the inhabitants of the earth . . . and the whole American people shall see and know it yet, to their satisfaction."[68]

Many maintained that blacks reflected the same image of God as whites. One of the early black newspapers, *The Colored American*, established in 1837 by Samuel A. Cornish, a black Presbyterian minister, thundered: "Prejudice against color is nothing short of hating God's image because he has dyed it a darker hue"; and in another issue stated, "If God hates one sin, more than all others, it is the hating of his image in his afflicted colored brethren of the United States."[69]

Hosea Easton, a nineteenth-century black preacher, also claimed the *imago Dei* as the theological basis for blacks being regarded as fellow human beings with whites:

67. Ibid., 42.
68. Art. 3 in David Walker, *Walker's Appeal in Four Articles; Together with a Preamble, to the Coloured Citizens of the World, But in Particular, and Very Expressly, to Those of the United States of America* (Boston: D. Walker, 1830).
69. *The Colored American*, 7 October 1837, and 22 December 1838. Cornish and John B. Russwurm were cofounders of *Freedom's Journal* in New York, the first black U.S. newspaper.

. . . one great truth is acknowledged by all Christendom, viz.—God hath made of one blood all nations of men for to dwell on the face of the earth. . . . No constitutional difference exists in the children of men, which can be said to be established by hereditary laws. The variety of color, in the human species, is the result of some laws which variegated the whole creation. The same species of flowers is variegated with innumerable colors, and yet the species is the same, possessing the same general qualities, undergoing no intrinsic change, from these accidental causes. So it is with the human species.[70]

Easton disputed claims that blacks are inferior in intellect. If any difference in intellect exists, he said, it is an affliction of all races as the result of the fall and not of color: "The mind has been subject to the influence of every species of evil."[71] It is not for want of intellect that Africa is in her present state. Rather it is because of warlike efforts against Africa and the deportation of its people into slavery. "Slavery partakes of all that is bad on earth and in hell."[72]

In summary, the Romulus and Remus of America are blacks and whites within their entangled history, slave/master culture, and carnal engagement. This does not mean that the American Indians' saga in the formation of America is not significant. But it must be admitted that the formation of American culture cannot be understood without Ham's children in the very formation and development of America's character.

Retention of classical and biblical themes and beliefs about blackness and blacks dating from Greco-Roman times and early Christian literature survived in colonial America and afterwards: carnality, inferiority, supposed lack of civilization, "natural" subordination to Europeans and white Americans. The question is why these beliefs have persisted.

The Christian tradition, whose primary role in the formation of the Western mind cannot be underestimated, is a major reason for this persistence. Within that formation, the biblical narrative about Ham and his brothers has been cited more often than any other legend to authenticate the "natural" subservience of blacks to other cultures. Even

70. Hosea Easton, *A Treatise on the Intellectual Character and Civil and Political Condition of the Colored People of the United States; and the Prejudice Exercised Towards Them: With a Sermon on the Duty of the Church to Them* (Boston: Issac Knapp, 1837), 5.
71. Ibid., 7.
72. Ibid., 38.

Jewish and Islamic traditions make use of this Old Testament story to explain the negativity and inferiority of black peoples. We come back to the initial question of whether blackness is a universal ontological variant of whiteness that has taken on religious, economic, social, and political character. The retention of the story of Ham to explain both the origins and subservient nature of blacks points to the deep-rootedness of a primal myth that is all the more powerful because it is rooted in religion with all its emotional impact. That the Hamitic story also links carnality to the curse of blackness only heightens the emotional impact of negative beliefs about blacks. As we saw, Europeans and Americans even tinkered with redefining the term *Hamite* to include the languages and cultures of Egypt and North Africa in order to exclude or reclassify downward the languages and cultures of sub-Saharan Africa.

Although the Hamite legend was also internalized by many black Americans, including some early founders of Pan-Africanism, blacks— free and slave—forged an identity and a status for themselves in American society particularly with regard to Africa. In establishing this identity, black Americans relied on a different interpretation of the biblical texts taught them by whites and on traditions retained from African culture, with which even third- and fourth-generation American-born blacks were conversant. This dialogue was important for blacks' survival and identity. The frequent reference to Africa in the formation of their cultural and religious institutions was conscious and deliberate.

This link between Africa and black American identity also moved blacks to go beyond the Hamitic curse to a more universal understanding of creation and race—a new departure in Christian theology of inclusiveness instigated by blacks supported and adapted by the later abolition movement. From one blood God created all men, many blacks believed as they began to reinterpret the "white" Bible and make it their own. As early as the eighteenth-century, some blacks insisted publicly that if reason was a divine gift that made a person human, then blacks had the same facility and therefore were equal to whites. They also linked the divine to engagement in social and political action, that is, freedom and emancipation. Blacks, whether moderate or militant, never surrendered this bond. It was a divine affirmation rather than a negation of blackness, possibly the first time such a claim was made in the Christian tradition, as that tradition was broadened beyond its European and colonial legacy in the West.

Epilogue

*W*hoever controls the images of a people or a culture is crucial to the domination and identity of that people or culture. The images of blacks have been largely shaped, controlled, and nourished by beliefs about blackness within the dominant cultures of Europe and America. In modern times the image of blacks in mainstream America has been greatly shaped by the media, crime statistics, urban riots, poor neighborhoods, drugs, inadequate education, and other negative social conditions. Such social factors validate many negative perceptions and beliefs about blacks, although some observers would like to absolve many blacks of any responsibility and cast blame solely on the social conditions created by mainstream society. These social factors, of course, have been injurious when, together with older myths about blacks, they have become the basis for racial prejudice and racial stereotypes.

Throughout American history blacks have undertaken efforts to reshape and control their image, beginning with early petitions about their status in colonial New England and continuing with former slaves such as Sojourner Truth and Frederick Douglass and twentieth-century blacks like W. E. B. Du Bois, Marcus Garvey and his Universal Negro Association, Martin Luther King, Jr., and the civil rights movement, and the Black Power movement. But mainstream instruments shaping public images and public discourse, while sometimes paying attention to such efforts by blacks, are not necessarily influenced by such efforts in the absence of a racial crisis.

Neither the images of blackness and blacks nor the control and shaping of those images by Europeans and Americans began simply with the fifteenth-century slave trade, as we have seen. Images of blackness and blacks have deep primal roots that were established in the very formation of Western culture from its Greco-Roman antecedents and its Christian underpinnings. In Western thought these images have shifted from the mysterious to the exotic to the sensuous to the negative to the inferior to the subordinate to the dangerous. A dialectic between evil and sin, eroticism and carnality, sanctity and magic has characterized beliefs and images of blackness in Christian thought. This same dynamic has also eroded the claims of racial inclusiveness in Christian thought as a theological foundation.

The concept of blackness as inferior initially was related to a cultural appraisal of strangeness from the vista of the Greeks, captured in the word *barbarian*. The Romans added ethnicity as a negative component of the inferiority of blackness. The Christian tradition provided the moral and metaphysical category of the inferiority of blackness via its doctrines of the struggle between darkness and light and its reinterpretation of the devil as a creature of evil and sin. Early Christian literature and Christian theologians identified the devil as the Black One or Dark One, so marked because of his falling from the light of God's grace. This allowed for a more lasting, deeply grained emotional legacy in the Western psyche than the mythical beliefs of Greek culture or the cultural beliefs of the Roman Empire based largely on war and myth.

Paralleling the view that blackness and blacks (meaning Africans and their descendants) conveyed both a theological and a natural inferiority, however, was the belief that blackness and blacks also meant the exotic and the sensual. This deep-seated belief was depicted in sculptures of the mythical satyrs—those bacchanalian rogues of ancient Greece. In Roman culture, the importation of African pygmies satisfied the erotic thirst and domestic needs of the affluent. The carnality of blackness was perpetuated in Jewish thought and Christian thought, particularly after Europe began to have regular contacts with Africans. It continued to have a strong appeal to whites as a reason for assaulting and lynching blacks, particularly black men suspected of having intimate relationships with white women.

The institutional Christian church in more recent times has taught that the doctrines of creation and Christology, on the one hand, and biblical motifs of love and reconciliation, on the other, have been traditional cornerstones of Christian claims to cultural and racial inclusiveness. Within a heterogeneous nation like the United States, these teachings have generated a civic-oriented spirituality and mainstream Christian ethics that functions as (1) chaplain supporting the political and ideological claims and social goals of inclusiveness of the state with its increasing culturally and racially diverse populations, and (2) guardian of a civil religion and morality of tolerance. The Christian faith and the modern Christian church have frequently based their own beliefs about racial and cultural inclusiveness on claims that racial inclusiveness has been a foundation of Christian faith from its very origins. As we have seen, with regard to race and blacks, this is an erroneous claim.

Hence, "theologically correct" revisionist thinking has evolved that acts like a filter through which selected biblical texts are read, heard, interpreted, and preached by mainstream churches, theologians, and the wider ecumenical network, such as the World Council of Churches and the National Council of Churches. This filter functions in many ways like the fourth-century Greco-Latin doctrine of the Trinity, which has been universalized by theologians in the East and West and interpreted as being present, albeit hidden, even in the Old and New Testaments.

■   ■   ■

Blackness and black complexions, however, have always carried baggage in Western civilization and the Christian tradition that counter this theologically correct interpretation. Even after Ethiopians came into Western consciousness through Greek poetry, writings, and chronicles, a mysterious and ambiguous veil hung over the identity of these dark-skinned people. Their origins as Africans were mythical. Africa's name and its boundaries historically and culturally retained the veil until the nineteenth century, when European powers drew up maps and geographical divisions of modern Africa. Prior to that time, no accurate map of this enormous continent existed. At one time the name Africa in the West meant only northern and northeastern territory west of Egypt. At another time it meant what we now call North Africa and Egypt. In fact, the Romans dug the *fossia regia* to demarcate their concept of Africa from the rest of the black-skinned peoples of that vast land mass.

Although Greek art represented Africans five centuries before Homer named the Ethiopians in the eighth century B.C.E., Ethiopians were already a respected and feared people in ancient Greece, albeit without a continent, at least one known to the Greeks and the Romans. Both Greeks and Romans distinguished between the dark complexions of Egyptians, Ethiopians, and Nubians. An early characteristic of blacks that emerged in classical Greek and Roman cultures, inherited by the Christian tradition and retained into modernity, has been blacks' legendary erotic and carnal powers. Sixth-century B.C.E. sculptures of the satyrs with exaggerated phalluses are unmistakably Negroid. Greeks believed that these ithyphallic mythical figures originated in Africa. Hence, although with the rise of a black aesthetic in both Greek and Roman thought blackness did not carry moral or prejudicial characteristics, nonetheless it did carry a social stigma as the color of a people's complexion.

■   ■   ■

While not identified as such, the African countries familiar to Christians in the Roman Empire were Egypt, which included Nubia, and Ethiopia. The Egyptians perceived of their land as black (*kemit*: from *kmt*), although, as was noted, there is some dispute among Egyptologists about whether this referred to the Egyptians' complexion or to their arable black soil. We know there was a strong Nubian presence and influence in Egypt. Nubians lived in Egypt since 3000 B.C.E. and were most likely a major antecedent in the establishment of kingship in Egypt, which was the infrastructure of Egyptian civilization and religion. In the sixth century B.C.E., the Nubians took over the Egyptian capital of Memphis and united Egypt and Nubia. Therefore, blackness was certainly one of the characteristics identifying people known in the Roman Empire as Egyptian.

In light of this, Matthew's Gospel suggests that Egypt as an African country was a unique link to Jesus Christ as the Messiah. This cannot be simply a rhetorical reference to the Egypt of the Old Testament, as mainstream New Testament scholars traditionally maintain. In the subsequent development of Christian faith and doctrine, Egypt and Ethiopia as harbingers of the Monophysites and North Africa as the center for the Donatists certainly implanted African countries in the Christian consciousness and history.

Early Christian literature and doctrine carried on the Greco-Roman legacy about blackness and Persian dualism about the cosmic struggle between the forces of light and the forces of darkness. This established a permanent negative moral characteristic of blackness. Christian thought transformed Satan from a member of the divine family in the Old Testament, who sometimes has the role of advocate for humankind before the heavenly judiciary, to the prince of evil leading the forces of darkness/blackness against the forces of light. Satan was personalized as the devil in Christian literature, such as the first-century *Epistle of Barnabas* and the second-century *Acts of Peter*, where the devil is described as "the Black One." Thus blackness (*melas*) acquired a moral significance, which was embedded in Christian spirituality.

The devil fell from the light of God's grace and thus took on the blackness of evil and sin. Blackness symbolized the way of death and eternal punishment, superstition, and transgression. The devil was totally deficient in goodness and the possibility of perfection, according to the doctrine of privation in the early church. Later in medieval Europe, this inferiority of being was transformed into inferiority of intellect and religion with regard to black Africans and slaves. At the same time, blackness signified chaos or the absence of order, and what Paul Tillich would call the threat of nonbeing both to the cosmic order and to the social order.

Jerome, a Latin-speaking theologian, was the first critic to take the negativity of blackness and the Black One a step further. He linked it to carnality and sensuousness, a knot already established in earlier Greek and Roman thought and art. Now the African, which meant the Ethiopian, was undeniably stigmatized because of his blackness. The Ethiopian for Jerome represents Satan as the roaring lion stalking and seducing Christians. "In the past we were Ethiopians, being made so by our sins and vices." How?, asked Jerome. "Because sin had made us black." This attribute of blackness has been retained in Western thought and nurtured in Christian thought through the legend of Ham in Genesis. The aesthetic, the carnality, and the negativity of blackness were confirmed at the fifth-century Council of Toledo, which proclaimed that the devil was a monster that had, among other features, cloven hooves and a large phallus.

■　■　■

The legacy of blackness as something negative assumed a peculiar destructiveness when it was identified as the mark of Antichrist, the declared enemy of Christ and tempter of Christians who comes in the last days. While this stigma distinguished the Moors, who occupied several European lands, blackness also represented a new translation of salvation. This became evident in the eleventh-century black Saint Maurice, the popular twelfth-century cults of black madonnas, the fourteenth-century convention in art of portraying one of the Magi with a black complexion, and the fifteenth-century legend of Prester John. It is difficult to determine how blackness as an aesthetic became a visible sign of divine grace in Western medieval art.

Contributing circumstances included: (1) political factors, at least in the case of Maurice, who was such a popular military saint that he was counted among the ranks of the saints George, Jacques, and Sebastian; (2) theological factors entwined with exotic curiosity about black complexions, as in the case of Prester John, who was elevated as the hoped-for savior of European Christians against the Turks and other Muslims; (3) mythical factors, such as the black madonnas, who combined the legacy of the Earth Mother of pre-Christian peoples that was brought into Christian piety and devotion and a suspected legacy of blackness as a mark of sorcery and magic with the traditional Marian devotion as *Theotokos*. Some claim that black madonnas have powers, particularly exotic ones disguised as miracles, different from those of white madonnas.

Blackness as a sign of the exotic and magic came to the forefront in Western Christian thinking with the Magi (from Persian: *magus* = an ancient Persian priestly caste), those visitors from the East bearing gifts, who were not only among the earliest witnesses to the Christ, but also some of the first converts. They were so awed and convinced that they chose not to return to their land to report to the king (Matt. 2:12). Hellenistic Judaism, the environment of early Christianity, stigmatized these magical arts as arts of darkness under the leadership of the prince of darkness and evil demons, Satan or Belial (Eph. 6:11-12). Thus, all these developments represent blackness as a positive channel for grace.

This development, however, did not permeate or influence either social or theological thinking when economic factors made possible by the slave trade and the ensuing burgeoning slave industry dominated. Although canon law and some popes forbade Christians from enslaving other Christians, no such instruction was vigorously adhered to with regard to Catholic sovereigns supporting the enslavement of black Africans and New World Indians. Inasmuch as liberty is a part of the natural law, the *jus naturale*, enslavement was forbidden. But it was determined that Christians could engage in African slavery because slavery belonged to the civil order, *jus civile*, as a mark of sin, which distorted the natural order. By means of this interpretation, the church satisfied both its own conscience by insisting that slaves be baptized before they were auctioned, and the requirements of the marketplace in Catholic countries, such as Portugal and Spain, and their colonies. Churches, priests, and the hierarchy were permitted to own slaves as an extension of their ministry. Indeed, as we saw, popes accepted slaves from Catholic sovereigns as gifts and handed them on to others as presents.

This revisionist thinking about the moral rightfulness of Christians engaging in the African slave trade was not peculiar to Catholic countries. Protestant countries such as England and Holland thought and acted similarly, using the Ham story and the mythical paganism of African traditional religion as religious legitimization and raw imperialist ambitions as an economic and military rationale. The Dutch waged war against Spain in Mexico and Portugal in Brazil, whose northeastern territory they occupied for some thirty years. In 1640 they established New Amsterdam in North America. England occupied Barbados in 1605, the Spanish colony of Jamaica in 1655, and Havana, Cuba, in 1762. Both Holland and England expanded the use of slaves in their conquests. British North American colonies had slaves almost from their beginning, first in Virginia and then in Massachusetts. Protestant countries also had a quasi-theological doctrine of "Manifest Destiny" that justified the enslavement of Africans as the divine will for bringing Western civilization and Christianity to the heathen, not to mention the economic needs of their New World plantations in the Caribbean and North America for a free labor force.

■   ■   ■

Even prior to the slave trade, blackness theologically represented cosmic chaos and disorder and culturally represented bestiality and paganism. Slavery only reinforced these beliefs. With the advent of the Enlightenment in the West, these traits were outranked by blackness as a sign of natural inferiority. The Enlightenment's philosophical premise that humanity is defined by natural reason, which therefore enables all persons to share a natural equality, did not extend to people with black complexions—although Haitians in the eighteenth century adopted this philosophical claim against their French overlords to launch their successful revolution. Much casuistry went on during the Enlightenment in Europe and in America in order to legitimize slavery in spite of the claim that all persons have inalienable natural rights and duties. As Montesquieu remarked: "It is impossible for us to suppose these [black] creatures to be men because, allowing them to be men, a suspicion would follow that we ourselves are not Christians" (see chap. 6, note 16 above). John Locke wrote that it was urgent that slaveowners retain absolute authority and power over their slaves regardless of natural rights and religion. This casuistry reminds us of George Orwell's pigs in *Animal Farm*: All animals are equal, but some are more equal than others.

The assumed natural inferiority of blacks played a strong role in American colonial thought and the legitimation of black bondage. Neither monogenists nor polygenists in their philosophical battles doubted the inferiority of blacks as a state of nature that could not be erased. New England Puritans and Virginia Anglicans were children of their times in this regard, including the author of the Declaration of Independence. Clergy in all churches North and South supported slavery for this same reason. Christian baptism might free blacks of the bondage of sin, but it did not absolve them of their bondage to whites.

It was blacks themselves in the American colonies, particularly free and freed blacks, who challenged these claims. They negated their own negation on rational and religious grounds. First, they reinterpreted the doctrine of creation. Second, they initiated an ongoing dialogue between the Bible and their African religious tradition. Third, they established a new interpretation of God as an affirming and engaged God in the affairs and conditions of the oppressed and the enslaved. Blacks and whites are, "of one flesh . . . [with] the same sensations and endowed . . . with the same [rational] facilities," wrote Benjamin Banneker in the late eighteenth century (see chap. 7, note 70 above).

This negating of their own negation also motivated biblically grounded political and social action among the blacks, such as the revolts led by Denmark Vesey in South Carolina and Nat Turner in Virginia. Hence, from their perspective their blackness as a people who walked in darkness was taken into the godhead. Their civil condition or the negativity of blackness no longer negated them or reconciled them to their condition of bondage. Nor did it reconcile them to the primal myths about blackness and black complexions or to the interpretation of Christian teachings handed on to them by the churches and their slavemasters. As Absalom Jones proclaimed: "[T]hey were not forgotten by the God of their fathers, and the Father of the human race. . . . [H]e was not indifferent to their sufferings" (see chap. 7, note 72 above).

Index